W9-BVB-561

IMPERIAL LEGEND

IMPERIAL LEGEND

The Mysterious Disappearance of Tsar Alexander I

ALEXIS S. TROUBETZKOY

Arcade Publishing • New York

FIRST EDITION

All illustrations in the photo insert are courtesy of N. K. Shilder, *Imperator
Alexandr pervy*, St. Petersburg: S. A. Suvorin, 1998, Volume IV, unless
otherwise noted.

Library of Congress Cataloging-in-Publication Data

Troubetzkoy, Alexis S., 1934–
   Imperial legend : the mysterious disappearance of Tsar Alexander I /
   Alexis S. Troubetzkoy.
     p. cm.
   Includes bibliographical references and index.
   ISBN 1-55970-608-2
     1. Alexander I, Emperor of Russia, 1777–1825—Death and burial.
     2. Alexander I, Emperor of Russia, 1777–1825—Legends.
     3. Russia—Kings and rulers—Biography. 4. Russia—History—
   Alexander I, 1801–1825. I. Title.

   DK192.T767 2002
   947'.072'092—dc21   2001045750

Published in the United States by Arcade Publishing, Inc., New York
Distributed by AOL Time Warner Book Group

Visit our Web site at www.arcadepub.com

10 9 8 7 6 5 4 3 2 1

Designed by API

EB

PRINTED IN THE UNITED STATES OF AMERICA

To my father,
who encouraged me all the way,
and to the memories of
Nicholas S. Arseniev (1888–1977),
who told the tantalizing tale, and
H.I.H. Grand Duchess Olga Alexandrovna (1882–1960),
who spun the mystery

CONTENTS

Author's Note

As a youngster, I was much taken by the apparently fathomless knowledge and prodigious memory of Professor Nicholas Arseniev (1888–1977), who seemed like an awesome Methuselah. Arseniev frequently summered with us at our wilderness retreat in the Laurentian Mountains, where he tutored me in Russian history.

After we had covered the Napoleonic Wars, the soft-spoken scholar casually moved on to the mysterious death of Tsar Alexander I — "probably no death at all," said he laconically — and the appearance some years later in Siberia of the enigmatic Feodor Kuzmich. Over the years rumor that Kuzmich *was* Alexander I grew into legend — a legend that, however incredible, has persisted for almost two centuries. In the lessons that followed, Arseniev went on to weave one thread after another of intriguing detail into an intricate tapestry of the Legend's manifold aspects.

Those fascinating sessions with Arseniev left a profound and indelible impression on my young mind. If as alleged, Kuzmich *was* the tsar, what could possibly have caused Alexander to engage in such extraordinary duplicity? In 1825, the year of Alexander's presumed death, he was at the height of his power: supreme ruler of the world's largest country, conqueror of the indomitable Napoleon, possessor of untold wealth, wined and dined by all of Europe, a man who broke female hearts at will. How could the beloved emperor, Autocrat of All Russia, simply throw everything over and disappear from the scene, to reemerge as a starets, a mystical wanderer in the vast Siberian steppes, living a simple life of monastic seclusion? For this teenager, the very notion seemed impossible, a fairy tale. Yet the mystery continued to obsess me through the years.

In 1958, Grand Duchess Olga, the sister of Tsar Nicholas II, confided in me that her family "had no doubt" about the veracity of the Legend. With this startling revelation, the shadow of the haunting story loomed even larger in my mind. Over the next several years I studied whatever sources I could find on the subject, but serious research gave way to the more immediate priorities of teaching. With the crumbling of the Soviet regime in 1989, new openness provided me fresh opportunities to pursue the Legend, and my interest in the dormant subject was rekindled. This work was long in developing, and over the years my views of the Legend passed through several phases. When Arseniev first told me the story, I pegged it as a wonderful fairy tale, no more. When later the grand duchess took me into her confidence, it became a mystery. Since then, I "have marched and countermarched" on the issue — the scores of pieces that make up the puzzle are, after all, circumstantial. When all is said and done, however, in answer to the question, Do I believe that Feodor Kuzmich and Alexander I were one and the same?, I can say that I most emphatically do. Before long, science may well provide us with the final answer. In fact, in writing this work, I hope that it will serve as a catalyst for a methodical, scientific investigation of this almost two-hundred-year-old mystery. Particularly with DNA's refinement, we have the required tools; let the graves be opened, the truth confirmed, and the mystery forever put to rest.

*   *   *

The transliteration of names from the Cyrillic into the Latin alphabet inevitably invites argument. Troubetzkoy, for example, might variously be found as Troubetzkoi, Trubetzkoy, Trubetzkoii,

Troubetskoi, and so on. The Library of Congress Slavic Transliteration System appears to be the one most favored by academics, although many universities use altered diacritical systems. In this work I have generally transliterated names according to the less complicated *New York Times* form (where, for example, Troubetzkoy becomes Trubetskoi). In rare instances, however, the commonly accepted English usage has been retained, e.g.: Tsar Nicholas instead of Tsar Nikolai, and Catherine the Great instead of Ekaterina the Great.

Most of the sources used in this work were written in pre-1918 Russia and are therefore dated according to the Julian calendar. For ease in reading the narrative, the original dating system has been retained in this book. In February 1918, Russia adopted the Gregorian calendar, the one favored by Western Europe and the Western Hemisphere. Therefore, post-1918 dates are reported according to this "New Style." Today, there exists a difference of thirteen days between the two calendars. In the nineteenth century the gap was twelve days. (In today's terms, therefore, Alexander's reported death occurred on December 1, not on November 19.)

Generous use has been made here of the work of others. For details, the reader is referred to the reference notes and the bibliography.

Acknowledgments

For their assistance and unfailing courtesy, I wish to thank the staffs of the Bodleian Library, Oxford and the State Archive of the Russian Federation, Moscow, as well as the personnel of the British Library, London, and the New York Public Library. I also owe much to the staffs of the University of Toronto and McGill University for their various courtesies. My gratitude to Sergei Mironenko, director of the State Archive of the Russian Federation, for generously sharing his insights on the Legend and for making available certain original documents. I thank Dr. B. Woelderink, director, and the staff of the Royal Collections of the House of Orange, The Hague, for assistance in archival research.

For professional advice on matters related to Alexander's illness and postmortem condition, I am grateful to Doctors J. D. McLean, director of the Center of Tropical Medicine, McGill University; David Chaisson, chief pathologist for the Province of Ontario; Leslie Lukash, chief medical examiner for Nassau County, New York; and Yasmine Ayroud, McGill University. And a thank-you to Father Siluan, abbot of Bogoroditsko-Alexeyevsk Monastery in Tomsk, for details on Feodor Kuzmich's remains. And to Dr. Eric Lohr of Harvard University: special thanks for the proofreading and constructive criticism of the initial draft. I owe much to my American publisher, Dick Seaver, and Arcade's editor

Darcy Falkenhagen, for their inspired editing of the manuscript. Thanks too to Bill Hanna, my agent, for his many kindnesses and to my Canadian publisher, Patrick Crean. To Justina Burgess, my deep appreciation for encouragement over the years as this work developed.

Without the inspirational tutelage way back when of Professor Nicholas Arseniev of St. Vladimir's Seminary, New York, this book would not have come to be written. Above all, I owe a special debt to my father, Serge G. Troubetzkoy, for his unwavering interest in the research and for his thoughtful criticism and encouragement throughout the process of writing.

Labelle, Quebec, 2001

AN ABRIDGED ROMANOV GENEALOGY

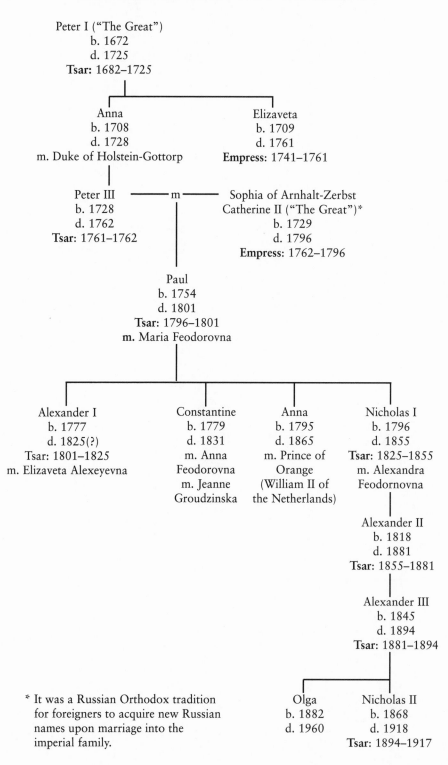

Peter I ("The Great")
b. 1672
d. 1725
Tsar: 1682–1725

Anna
b. 1708
d. 1728
m. Duke of Holstein-Gottorp

Elizaveta
b. 1709
d. 1761
Empress: 1741–1761

Peter III ——— m ——— Sophia of Arnhalt-Zerbst
b. 1728   Catherine II ("The Great")*
d. 1762   b. 1729
Tsar: 1761–1762   d. 1796
                          Empress: 1762–1796

Paul
b. 1754
d. 1801
Tsar: 1796–1801
m. Maria Feodorovna

Alexander I
b. 1777
d. 1825(?)
Tsar: 1801–1825
m. Elizaveta Alexeyevna

Constantine
b. 1779
d. 1831
m. Anna
Feodorovna
m. Jeanne
Groudzinska

Anna
b. 1795
d. 1865
m. Prince of
Orange
(William II of
the Netherlands)

Nicholas I
b. 1796
d. 1855
Tsar: 1825–1855
m. Alexandra
Feodornovna

Alexander II
b. 1818
d. 1881
Tsar: 1855–1881

Alexander III
b. 1845
d. 1894
Tsar: 1881–1894

* It was a Russian Orthodox tradition
for foreigners to acquire new Russian
names upon marriage into the
imperial family.

Olga
b. 1882
d. 1960

Nicholas II
b. 1868
d. 1918
Tsar: 1894–1917

IMPERIAL LEGEND

1

Paris, 1814–
Tomsk, Siberia, 1864

PARIS: MARCH 31, 1814. It was a brilliant day. A cloudless sky stretched over the city, and the rays of early spring warmed the huge animated crowds that had gathered in the streets. Boulevards flowed with humanity and cafés buzzed with excited chatter. In the early hours that morning Marshal Marmont had signed the official document of capitulation: France had surrendered to the allied forces; Napoleon had been vanquished. Russian, Prussian, and Austrian armies were mustered on the city's eastern fringes and were about to enter in a grand victory parade.

By eleven o'clock, the first of the Russian cavalry came into view, a troop of massive Cossacks, mustaches flowing, wearing bright red tunics, chests covered with cartridges. They sat tall in shiny saddles, and from their black Persian lamb caps the gold of the double-headed imperial eagle flashed in the sun. Immediately after the Cossacks came the hussars and cuirassiers of the Prussian Royal Guard, followed by the hussars and dragoons of the Russian Imperial Guard — thousands of men in order of rank. Then, at last, came the three conquering heroes: on one side, the king of Prussia; on the other, Prince Schwarzenberg, representing the emperor of Austria. At the center rode Alexander I, Tsar of All Russia, mounted on a dark Arab mare — ironically, a gift from Napoleon. The sovereigns were accompanied by a retinue of a thousand generals, and in their wake a multinational force passed by — Prussians, Austrians, Croats, Hungarians, and among the Russians, Tartars, Circassians, and others from the empire's multitudinous minorities.

Alexander was wearing the dark-green-and-red tunic of his beloved Semeonovsky Regiment. White kid trousers clung tightly to his muscular legs and polished black boots came to the knee. The massive epaulettes and collar gleamed with gold, and the dark blue sash of the Order of St. Andrew conspicuously crossed his chest. Even as a boy, Alexander had been strikingly handsome, but now, at thirty-six, with his aquiline nose and delicate features, he looked like the reincarnation of some god out of classical antiquity. The rays of the spring sun lit Alexander's face, a smile of contentment seemingly carved on it, while his deep blue eyes flashed proudly. Cries echoed in the streets. *"Vive Alexandre! Vive les russes! Vive les alliés!"* (Long live Alexander I! Long live the Russians! Long live the allies!) At one point he halted the procession and, waving his huge white plumed hat, answered the cheering throng in fluent French: "I have come to you not as an enemy but as a friend! I bring you peace." After nearly two decades of wars and bloodshed, the French were exhausted; they were pleased to see the last of Napoleon's adventurism and they were ready to welcome a restored Bourbon monarchy. The crowd continued to roar in approval; Alexander was at his pinnacle.

"After Bonaparte, Alexander is the greatest historical figure of the era," wrote Chateaubriand. By 1812, Napoleon had successfully conquered and annexed virtually all of Europe. Only Britain and Russia remained free of his grasp. And then he went for Russia and there suffered a resounding defeat. Now, two years later, the tsar paraded his troops through the streets of the French capital, down the Champs Elysées. "The Agamemnon of the people," they were calling him. The French offered to change the name of the Bridge of Austerlitz to Alexander Bridge. He declined, saying, "It is enough that it be known that the emperor of Russia has passed over it with his armies." Clearly, Paris was in the palm of his hand.

And who was this impressive conqueror, this Tsar Alexander I? At the time, he ruled the world's largest country, a vast expanse that covered nearly one-seventh of the earth's habitable surface. For over four centuries Russia had grown at a rate of almost twenty square miles a day. Within that territory lived some 44 million subjects, over whom he ruled as an absolute monarch. "God is master of the universe," wrote the eighteenth-century Russian historian Ivan Pososhkov. "The tsar is master of his country. In the domain assigned to him he can, like God, create what he wills." The emperor was the alpha and the omega of his nation's well-being.

Some 30,000 troops paraded in Paris that day. It took six hours for the massive assembly to complete its route, which was lined with cheering crowds. The days that followed were a glorious cornucopia of balls, receptions, honors, and state visits. Still, the tsar found time one afternoon to call on the aging widow of his childhood teacher and mentor, Frédéric La Harpe. The two had tea in her humble residence and, before leaving the house, Alexander showered her with gifts.

Nearly ten weeks after his triumphant entry into Paris, Alexander left France and traveled to England, where he was received almost as enthusiastically. "Your nation has every right to my esteem," he declared in fluent English. "I have always shown myself a faithful ally of Great Britain, and in peace I shall be her constant friend." All were enchanted by the handsome, charming monarch, so regal and straight in bearing. His manner was simplicity itself; particularly striking was his habit of inclining his head slightly toward the person with whom he was speaking, conveying an impression of warm sincerity. Actually, the emperor was simply deaf in one ear, the result of his being quartered in childhood close to where the cannons roared to celebrate feast days. The climactic event was the dazzling banquet by the city of London, offered at Guildhall, which, declared the Annual Register, was "a dinner as sumptuous as expense or skill could make it." Later, in a colorful and traditional ceremony, Oxford University conferred on the tsar a Doctorate of Civil Laws. Seven especially written odes were recited at that occasion: two in Greek, one in Latin, and the remainder in English.

The festivities and celebrations over, Alexander returned home, following a brief stopover in Holland. Napoleon had been exiled to Elba, and the tsar and other European statesmen now gathered in the glittering Congress of Vienna to define a lasting peace. Over the next seven years, these leaders met repeatedly, as they came to terms with one crisis or another that threatened continental harmony.

Alexander continued to reign over his vast country, and then, suddenly and quite unexpectedly, having contracted a mysterious illness, he died on November 19, 1825, in Taganrog, a backwater port on the Sea of Azov, in the empire's remote southernmost reaches. The sovereign was only forty-eight years old. He had always been active and vigorous, in the best of health; his death came as a complete shock to the nation. After an autopsy, the body was embalmed, then slowly transported, through hundreds of towns and villages, back to St. Petersburg for interment in the imperial crypt of the Fortress of St. Peter and St. Paul.

And herein lies the mystery. Did Alexander really die, as reported? Many believe he did not. But that is not totally surprising, considering the emperor's relative youth, his strong constitution, and the remote setting of his sudden and unexpected passing. The pages of history contain several accounts of imperial deaths that allegedly did not occur as reported — King Philip of Macedonia and Louis XVII are but two examples. The untimely and singular circumstances of Tsar Alexander's death are without doubt controversial, riddled with unresolved questions. Despite the presence of qualified physicians at his deathbed, why was the puzzling illness never properly diagnosed? And why did the tsar find himself in such a spot as Taganrog in the first place? Above all, if the death was staged, what led Alexander to resort to such an extreme measure? If he did shed the throne, where did he go and what happened to him? These and scores of other tantalizing questions combine to nurture one of the great mysteries of history, which has come to be known as the Imperial Legend.

*   *   *

TOMSK, SIBERIA: JANUARY 1864. The inverted bowl of winter pallor, stretching limitlessly across the frozen landscape, hangs heavy in Siberia in January. Communities of skeletal birches blend effortlessly into the white landscape, while heavy pines, burdened by winter's weight, sag in welcome contrast. Snow, ice, and silence ruthlessly blanket slumbering earth; sighs of spring are yet far off. But breaking the apparent monotony of frozen gray are the not infrequent days of brilliant sunshine and dazzling blue sky — nature's respite, a gift to a grateful world.

It was on such a day in 1864 that death hovered over the little wooden cabin in which a frail old man lay on his narrow cot. Shortly after New Year's, he had come down with a serious fever and taken to his bed. Since then, his condition had deteriorated alarmingly, and with every passing day his breathing grew more labored. To occasional visitors, it was obvious that the fragile figure on the sickbed was not long for this world. The years had been difficult for him. The recently developed stoop in his shoulders seemed to derive as much from the weight of untold spiritual burdens as from his advanced age, for he was in his mid-eighties. The ascetic mode of the old man's life did little to enhance his health. His was an existence of seclusion and spare diet, of material modesty, meditation, and prayer. Large calluses marked the man's knees, from the long hours he had spent on the hard wooden floor in prayer.

He called himself Feodor Kuzmich, but few people believed that was his true name. He never spoke of his past and revealed nothing of his background. He was, however, well-educated and refined in speech, as familiar with Russian history as he was with politics and government, and fluent in at least two languages. His bearing was military, and when meeting strangers he frequently paced the room, as if he were accustomed to giving orders. He was slightly deaf and sometimes bent down, the better to hear the other, which made his stoop appear more pronounced.

For over twenty years Kuzmich had wandered throughout Siberia, but in 1858 he finally settled on the outskirts of Tomsk, where one of the city's more prosperous merchants, a certain Simeon Khromov, constructed for him a small hut on his property — "a cell," it was called. From the beginning, Khromov was enchanted by this remarkable old man — by his piety, manner, and bearing — but above all he was fascinated by the aura of mystery that enveloped him. He was certainly a starets, one of the many genuine ascetic wanderers, penitents who moved about from place to place living off charity and offering support and comfort to those in need — not a spiritual wise man, not a hermit, but more of an untonsured monk. This particular starets was unlike scores of others who found refuge in the Siberian expanse — unfrocked priests, escaped prisoners, fundamentalists, messianic prophets, monks gone wild, or a host of others, insane or on the fringes of lunacy.

Within a fortnight of taking to bed that January, Kuzmich was refusing all food, sustaining himself on only milk and water. On the nineteenth it became clear that the end was near, and Father Raphael, the abbot of a neighboring monastery, was summoned to hear his confession and to administer the sacraments. In his memoirs, the monk recalls that, following the religious rite, Khromov's wife approached the sickbed and tearfully asked Kuzmich, "Father, tell us at least the name of your angel[†] so we might remember it in our prayers."

The dying man shook his head and quietly muttered, "This God knows."

An attending Khromov family friend pursued, "Then, Father, at least tell us the names of your parents, so that we might pray for them."

[†]In Russian Orthodox tradition, a person is named after a saint, and the feast day of the chosen patron or "angel" becomes more significant than one's birthday. Special prayers are said on the feast day. Perhaps Mrs. Khromov intended, after Kuzmich's death, to pray to his "angel" to intercede for his soul.

"This too is not for you to know." Kuzmich sighed. "The Holy Church prays for them." Even on his deathbed, Feodor Kuzmich refused to reveal his identity.[†]

Khromov became so concerned about the worsening condition of the starets that he moved into the man's tiny hut. The next few days passed in relative silence, and then, on the night of January 31, Kuzmich raised his head and announced in a firm, clear voice, "The end is near." At this point, Khromov recalled, "having prayed to God, I fell on my knees before the starets and said, 'Bless me, Father, in asking you one important question.'

"'Ask it,' replied Kuzmich, 'and God will bless you.'

"'Rumor has it,' I continued, 'that you, Father, are none other than Alexander the Blessed. Is that true?' At these words, the starets crossed himself and replied, 'A wondrous inquiry yours is, my friend . . . there is no secret which does not unlock.' And thus ended our conversation."

Kuzmich awoke briefly and motioned for a candle, which was given him. He held it in a trembling hand for a few fleeting moments and then let it fall. He inhaled one deep breath and then sighed in surrender — "his soul had departed."

On February 4, the starets, clad in a simple white shirt of unbleached linen, was interred in the cemetery of Tomsk's seventeenth-century Bogoroditsko-Alexeyevsk Monastery. Three ranking clergymen officiated at the service, and a large crowd of mourners was in attendance. The grave was unpretentious, eventually enclosed by a small white picket fence, at the four corners of which small cedars were planted. A simple wooden cross was erected at the head, bearing the inscription, "Here lies the body of the Great and Blessed starets Feodor Kuzmich." Soon thereafter, on the orders of Governor Mertsalov of Tomsk and for reasons unknown, the words "Great and Blessed" were painted

---

[†]The exchange that took place regarding names was also reported by Khromov and by his daughter, Anna. Neither, however, made mention of confession or the partaking of sacraments. Throughout his Siberian experience, the starets avoided going to confession, presumably to avoid having to divulge his true name.

over. But in time the weathered paint faded and they became legible again.

Just as those words defied obliteration, so the rumors that swirled about the life and death of the mysterious recluse refused to die. In the decades that followed, even to this day, the identity of this enigmatic person has remained a puzzle. Historians and commentators of every ilk record vignettes in which Kuzmich, by his words or actions, gave pointed or oblique hints of his past. Some of these anecdotes are on good authority, others are of questionable provenance. But over the years the rumors not only persisted but grew.

Was the "Great and Blessed" none other than Tsar Alexander I, called "the Blessed"? Is it possible that the Autocrat of All Russia did not really die in 1825 on the remote shores of the Sea of Azov? Could the sovereign have indeed suceeded in engineering his own disappearance by substituting another's body for interment in the imperial crypt in St. Petersburg?

The freshly covered grave in the cemetery of that remote Siberian monastery contained the remains of the starets. The man had been a wandering vagabond, penniless and dependent on the goodness of others. Once, he had been arrested and flogged. Sent into exile into the interior of the vast country, he had labored in a vodka distillery and in the gold fields. He had lived out his years in modest, if not primitive, circumstances. Was the humble starets Feodor Kuzmich in fact the beloved tsar? Had Alexander successfully shed the weight of the imperial crown he had felt pressing on him insufferably and realized his declared ambition "to resign my functions and retire from the world"? Could this possibly be the same person who, some fifty years earlier, had paraded his army down the Champs Elysées after defeating the mighty Napoleon?

For almost four decades, Kuzmich's grave remained unchanged, save for the steady growth of the four stately cedar trees. In 1902, State Secretary Galkin-Vraski, acting "on orders from on high," oversaw the erection of a modest chapel over the grave, and a white marble slab replaced the wooden cross. No documentation has come down to us regarding who commissioned the chapel.

There is reason to believe, however, that the order to have it built emanated from no less a personage than Tsar Nicholas II himself. In 1890–91, as the twenty-two-year-old heir to the throne, the tsarevich was sent on a tour of India and Japan. On July 5 and 6, 1891, during his return home through Siberia, Nicholas made a stop in Tomsk, where he visited Bogoroditsko-Alexeyevsk Monastery. Under the darkening sky of a midsummer night, he returned to the monastery and went directly to its cemetery, to the grave of Feodor Kuzmich. There he stood in silence, immersed in deep contemplation. The inscription the young man read on the marble slab before him was identical to that of the original wooden cross. The word "Blessed" stood out poignantly.

The image of a youthful, bareheaded Nicholas pondering the Siberian grave of an unknown starets conjures up an even more haunting scene. One sees, on March 13, 1826, the solemn funeral procession of Tsar Alexander slowly wending its way through the frigid, windswept streets of St. Petersburg — the muffled drums, the cadence of marching troops, the clatter of horses' hooves on the cobblestones, the quiet sobbing of the populace, and, walking behind the cortege, the deceased's brother, another Nicholas — the First — newly acceded to the throne. If Alexander's death was a fabrication, there is little possibility that the charade could have taken place without his successor's knowledge. One wonders what thoughts might have passed through the new tsar's mind as he followed the casket in which, perhaps, lay the earthly remains not of his brother but of some stranger. But for the peace of Russia, and above all for the preservation of the throne's legitimacy, there was no way that the terrible secret could be divulged. Nobody but the trusted few who were personally involved in the drama could ever know, not even the closest members of the family. The truth must be buried in the cathedral crypt of St. Peter and St. Paul Fortress. And on that March day, after the coffin had been lowered and the tomb sealed, Emperor Nicholas I no doubt took satisfaction in believing that the secret was indeed buried as well.

Who *was* this Feodor Kuzmich, and why had he gained such notoriety in the Siberian hinterland? Qualified historians of impeccable credentials have written about him. Grand Duke Nikolai Mikhailovich, for example, chairman of the Imperial Historical Society (granduncle to Nicholas II) and Prince Vladimir Bariatinsky, also of the historical society and an honorary member of Britain's Royal Society — both men examined firsthand official records of Kuzmich's presence in Siberia and researched his life. Numerous memoirs about this singular person by contemporary witnesses have also come down to us, as have a collection of stories and anecdotes from secondary sources. For well over a century and a half, the starets has been the subject of speculation and conjecture.

Even the great novelist Leo Tolstoy took an active interest in the Legend. Researching Kuzmich's life and Alexander's death, he intended to develop the Legend into a book, and labored on the subject off and on for over fifteen years. "Feodor Kuzmich captivates me more and more," reads his diary entry for October 15, 1905. By that time he was well into the subject, but then he abruptly stopped. "Not only shall I not complete it, but I am unable even to continue. Not ever — for I must now prepare myself for the ultimate transition." And then, in November 1910, he died.

Before his death, however, Tolstoy wrote to Grand Duke Nikolai Mikhailovich that "whatever was hidden behind the name of the hermit Feodor, the drama of that life is profoundly familial with deep and intimate connections to the national soul. So let historical evidence fail to connect Alexander with Kuzmich, the legend lives in all its beauty and sincerity."

In the grand duke's treatise *The Legend of the Death of Alexander I in Siberia in the Person of Feodor Kuzmich*, published in 1907, he analyzes for himself the evidence available at the time and then takes a firm stand against the Legend. "Let us hope," he concludes, "that someday somebody will solve this riddle and determine the true identity of Feodor Kuzmich." It should be noted, however, that before he was murdered in 1919 by a Bolshevik firing squad, the grand duke had reversed his position and had become a believer in the Legend.

.   .   .

As a young naval officer in 1958 I was briefly stationed in Hamilton, Ontario, not far from where Grand Duchess Olga Alexandrovna lived. She was the sister of Nicholas II, daughter of Alexander III. In early 1920, she and her commoner husband, Colonel Nikolai Kulikovsky, with their two infant sons, managed to escape the Russian revolution. Their journey took them out through the Black Sea, to Belgrade and to Denmark, whence they immigrated to Canada. The couple bought a farm in rural Ontario, and there, with their two sons, lived a life of exile. After the colonel's death, the grand duchess moved to what is now Mississauga, where she died in 1960.

I visited Her Imperial Highness on a number of occasions. She and I got along famously, and with the brashness of youth, I asked her scores of questions about Russian history and her own past. With candor and charm she replied patiently to all my inquiries. During our third or fourth meeting, I broached the subject of Feodor Kuzmich. Here she visibly blanched and then declared rather curtly, "In our family Feodor Kuzmich was not a subject for discussion." I was much taken aback by this frigid and uncharacteristic reaction. A pregnant silence followed, but then she took my hand into hers and, with a touch of a smile, said, "We really didn't discuss it. But I am old and not long for this world; you are young and apparently have understanding of these things. You should know that we have no doubt that Feodor Kuzmich *was* the emperor."

2

Conspiracy at
Mikhailovsky Castle

ST. PETERSBURG, MARCH 11, 1801. A STEADY MARCH WIND blew in from the Gulf of Finland, relentlessly whipping the darkened, ice-covered streets. The city appeared deserted save for the occasional illuminated window of some sleepless soul. Aside from the group of bundled figures resolutely approaching Mikhailovsky Castle, the city was dead. The heartless wind lashed the faces of the puffing men, penetrating the thickest greatcoats. Even for St. Petersburg, it was an unseasonably bitter night, in addition to being inordinately dark.

Earlier that evening, the men trudging the empty streets had gathered in the warmth of various homes to share dinner and draw strength from one another's company — and from the free-flowing brandy. It was an uncommon night in every respect, and certainly theirs was a fateful mission. Their goal: to overthrow the tsar, Paul I. If they were successful, a new and better dawn would break upon the Russian Empire. If they failed, each of them would lose all he held dear, including, in all probability, his life.

Near eleven o'clock on that night of March 11, the conspirators left their homes and gravitated to the quarters of General

Georgy Simeonovich Talyzen, commanding officer of the prestigious Semeonovsky Regiment. Here they held their final assembly, the last of many planning sessions. As the clock ticked closer to the appointed hour, tensions mounted. Some of the men became restless, while others began to have second thoughts and lose their nerve. Count Pyotr Alexeyevich von Pahlen, governor-general of St. Petersburg, called for everyone's attention and made an impassioned speech that concluded with the words, "Rappelez-vous, messieurs, que pour manger une omelette il faut commencer par casser les oeufs" (Remember, gentlemen, one cannot make an omelette without first breaking the eggs). Glasses were refilled and toasts raised to success. Shortly after midnight, the men gathered themselves into the night and set off for Mikhailovsky Castle and their fateful encounter with the hated emperor.

But the Autocrat of All Russia, Emperor Paul I, slept on, oblivious to the conspiracy developing outside and the mortal danger about to envelop him. Earlier that day, acting on the advice of his trusted adviser Count Pahlen, he had taken several precautions, including nailing shut the door between his bedroom and that of his mistress, Princess Gagarina. Now the only way into his chamber was through the well-guarded hallway door; he was protected. Shortly after midnight Paul climbed into bed, no doubt feeling as secure as his troubled mind permitted.

Paul had come to the throne some five years earlier — on the night of November 6, 1796, when his mother, Catherine II, finally expired in an agonizing death. Had the old empress seen her despised son ensconced on the throne, her death throes doubtless would have been all the more tormented. It was the last thing she wanted; more than once she had openly discussed the possibility of passing the throne on to her beloved grandson, Alexander, Paul's firstborn. Unfortunately, no official manifesto had been issued to that effect, and in the absence of such, Paul wasted little time in assuming his lawful place. Alexander, who was then only nineteen, would have to wait his turn — provided, of course, he survived the intrigues of the Russian court.

On that dark winter night, Alexander had not yet turned twenty-four. He was a tall, handsome young man who found favor with most everybody — except his father. The tsarevich came from a mixed and complicated lineage: on the one hand, a number who were intelligent and determined, and on the other, some who were unstable, even mentally deformed. The bitter and unpredictable Paul was the son of the formidable and enlightened Catherine, who was the wife of the sickly, quasi-retarded Peter III, grandson of the visionary, strong-willed Peter the Great. Alexander's inheritance of the diverse genes of these and others of his family was evident in the formation of this complex person. But of all the influences exerted on his development, none was stronger than that of his grandmother.

Not without reason was Catherine called "the Great," and in the pantheon of the world's notable female rulers, she deservedly ranks very high indeed. As a Pomeranian teenager of startling beauty and talent, Catherine had come to Russia by way of a marriage contract to the future tsar Peter III; as a mature woman of confidence and devastating ambition, she came to the Russian throne by way of a coup d'état.

Peter III's flash through the pages of Russian history is a web of contradictions. That he was mentally unbalanced is undisputed. That he "had absolutely no resemblance to an emperor," as one courtier put it, is undeniable. Yet, perhaps despite himself, during his brief reign, he managed to steer Russia on a fresh course. Many of the liberal reforms contemplated and wrought by Catherine and her successors found root in Peter's legacy. His is a peculiar, complex story.

In early childhood, young Peter, the Germanic Duke of Holstein-Gottorp, was named successor to the childless king of Sweden, Charles XII, his granduncle. Orphaned in infancy, the boy was brought up by a certain Adolf Brümmer, chief steward of the old duke's household, a coarse, ill-educated person with a barrack-room mentality. In 1741, the thirteen-year-old Peter was shipped off to Stockholm to commence training and a new life. The Lutheran

Church warmly embraced the child, as did the Swedish court. In 1741, however, the single-minded Elizaveta Petrovna, Peter's child-less aunt, came to the Russian throne and declared the thirteen-year-old grand duke to be *her* successor — he was, after all, not only her nephew but the grandson of Peter the Great.

She wanted the boy for herself. The connection between the Russian imperial family and the German courts had by now be-come something of a tradition. Peter's successors and their brothers all married Germans, right through Nicholas II; unquestionably German blood flowed thickly in Romanov veins. The great Rus-sian poet, Alexander Pushkin, delighted in poking fun at the Teu-tonism of the imperial family. One evening, at a party of friends, he called for a bottle of red wine, several glasses, and a decanter of water. He lined up the glasses in a row and filled the first one to the brim with wine. "This glass," he announced, "is our glorious Peter the Great; it is pure Russian blood in all its vigour. Observe the rich crimson glow!"

In the second glass, representing Peter's successor, he mixed wine and water in equal quantities. In the third, he poured one part wine and three parts water, and continued thus to mix each fresh glass in accordance with the same inverse progression. At the sev-enth glass, which represented the tsarevich, the future Alexander III, the proportion of wine had become so small (1/64) that the liquid was hardly tinged. Had Pushkin survived to carry out this demon-stration during the reign of Nicholas II, the contents of the glass rep-resenting the tsar's son, Tsarevich Alexey, would have been virtually clear — a proportion of 1 part Russian to 256 parts foreign.

The determined Elizaveta prevailed in her demands that the Swedes surrender Peter, and the youngster was whisked off to St. Petersburg. The painful process of transforming the confused lad from a Lutheran Swede to an Orthodox Russian had a crippling effect on the youngster, who already suffered from insta-bility. As one observer put it, "his mental capacities were lim-ited" — others, more severe, simply judged him retarded. Even in his late teens, he was incapable of falling asleep without the reas-

suring presence of his doll, a habit that, much to the bewilderment
of his bride, he carried into adulthood. As a thirty-three-year-old,
Peter was observed at Empress Elizaveta's funeral procession from
time to time purposely falling behind the hearse, only to skip rapidly forward as he watched with amusement the shadows of his
flapping coattails.

Peter was obstinate, neurotic, belligerent, and often quite
violent. Even as emperor he was unable to resist infantile satisfaction in silly or grotesque pranks. One story is told of how he personally captured a rat that had the misfortune of being seen
nibbling at the battlements of a paper castle that sat on the imperial desk. The captor convened a formal court of justice and the
unhappy rodent was brought before a council of solemn judges.
Three doubtless embarrassed courtiers had been detailed to assume the roles, and at the appropriate moment they delivered the
required verdict. Peter brought the bizarre charade to a close by
donning an executioner's mask and personally decapitating the
offending animal.

Physically, the boy was unattractive, and people commented,
sometimes openly, on how homely he was — some even going so
far as to describe him as "repugnant." His aunt, Elizaveta, once
noted that she had heard him called "a scarecrow." In any event,
from the moment of his arrival back in St. Petersburg, Peter resisted Russification, looking with equal scorn on the Orthodox
Church and the Russian court. To everyone's dismay, Peter took as
his role model Frederick the Great of Prussia, thus exacerbating the
burgeoning estrangement of the grand duke from the world about
him. He seemed to find security and solace in the company of
his rough-hewn Holstein troops, whom he delighted in drilling
and parading. At age sixteen he was married off to the charming
and highly intelligent fifteen-year-old Princess Sophia von Arnhalt-
Zerbst, the future Catherine the Great. (Foreign-born Russian
empresses went through the ritual of Orthodox baptism and in the
process acquired new names.) From the beginning Peter treated her
with boorish scorn. On one occasion he blatantly announced that

he had no use for her; he toyed with the idea of having her locked up in a convent. For the young Pomeranian princess, the initial years in her newly adopted country proved confusing, boring, and humiliating. The union brought neither party anything of the fulfillment and joy they had been led to expect. Peter's attention soon gravitated to some of the royal courtesans, particularly to Countess Elizaveta Vorontsova, who openly became his mistress. This limited and impulsive woman was given to drink, for which Peter himself quickly developed a lifelong predilection. While the grand duke cavorted with his homely, largely useless mistress, Catherine bided her time in the confines of her quarters. She took refuge in the works of Voltaire, Rousseau, and Montesquieu, and in the study of the Russian language and history. Through his outrageous behavior, the grand duke soon found himself virtually ostracized by St. Petersburg society. The disillusioned Empress Elizaveta came to lament her choice of heir — "my nephew is a monster!" she once exclaimed. That she contemplated setting Peter aside in favor of his son Paul was a poorly held secret. She died, however, before any legal arrangement for succession had been made. In all fairness, it must be noted that much of what we know about Peter comes to us through Catherine's own memoirs and those of her courtiers. In fact, it could legitimately be argued that the negative remarks about Peter that pervade these sources were inserted to justify the coup against him.

Peter's reign lasted all of 197 days.[†] During that brief period, however, certain decisive developments took place that proved critical to the country's evolution. The nobility, for example, was exempted from military service and awarded privileges of property ownership, including that of serfs. A significant segment of society was thereby freed from the monarch's rigid control, and from this change an intelligentsia flowered, whose influence eventually had a

---

[†] In the thirty-seven years between the deaths of Peter the Great and Peter III, six rulers governed Russia. Even within that sequence, the brief reign of Peter III was a record. Other brief rules in Russian history: Empress Irina, 54 days in 1598; Feodor Godunov (son of Boris), 57 days in 1605.

profound effect on the country's intellectual and political development. But as the nobles rose in stature, the serfs fell into even greater misery. A series of laws were promulgated that further removed certain rights and defined additional obligations; serfdom became more fully entrenched. The Secret Chancellery — a dread police force that operated through terror in search of subversives — was abolished in favor of legally defined structures; the law began to grow into a legitimate force. The sect of Old Believers was granted freedom from persecution and given lands in Siberia. For generations, these people had resisted the church reforms introduced in the mid-seventeenth century. The dawn of religious toleration thus came to be in Russia. It might rightly be said that many of Catherine's social and political reforms and those of her successors emanated from Peter's manifestos.

In foreign affairs, Peter abruptly reversed the traditional thrust of Russian policy. Through the better part of the eighteenth century, and particularly in the wars immediately preceding his accession, Prussia had been the implacable enemy. For Peter, however, Prussia and its king were much to be admired, if not faultless. To the dismay of his ministers and councillors, Peter abruptly allied his country with that Germanic state, forsook the hard-won gains made during the Seven Years' War, and lined himself up against his former allies. On another front, to appease his Holstein friends, he initiated preparations for a war against Denmark. The precipitous turn of Peter's foreign policy, and the impossible quirks of his irascible and unpredictable character, fueled blossoming opposition. Before long a group of prominent leaders of St. Petersburg society came together, motivated by their disdain of the tsar but also linked by a common bond: they were all admirers of Catherine, and more than one had shared her bed. Catherine's fondness for attractive young men was passionate, and her sexual appetites seemingly insatiable.

On the night of June 28, 1762, a palace coup occurred by which Peter was forced to sign an act of abdication. Eight-year-old Paul, the legitimate heir to the throne, was simply passed over in favor of his mother. The daring event was planned and launched with determined efficiency by Catherine's admiring friends; she herself carefully refrained from appearing to lead any opposition movement — at least initially. Eight days before the forced abdication, Peter, who was at his palace of Oranienbaum, some twenty-five miles from the capital, had received warning that a coup was in the making. Relying on the loyalty of his army — certainly that of his personal regiments — the threatened tsar order the erection of barricades to protect the center of government within the city. As he set out to return to the capital, Catherine declared herself openly by leading to the Winter Palace a detachment of troops faithful to her. The palace was quickly taken and the seat of Peter's government collapsed. The defeated tsar reluctantly agreed to retire to a monastery. After a few days languishing in the fortress of Ropsha, the unfortunate man "suffered another of his habitual hemorrhoidal attacks, together with violent colic." The court records went on to explain laconically, "To our great sadness we receive news that God's will had put an end to his life." In reality, his life had been extinguished by a combination of poison and human hands, probably those of Alexis Orlov, who together with his friends not long thereafter lined up to receive rewards from a grateful newly declared empress. Two months later, on the night of September 18, in Moscow, young Paul was hustled out of bed and carried, in the arms of his tutor, Count Panin, to the Uspensky Cathedral at the center of the Kremlin, where he witnessed the coronation of his mother, Catherine, as empress of Russia. The ambitious and unscrupulous woman had managed to wrest the throne from her young son. "Thou, my Lord and God," she intoned in prayer, "instruct me in the work Thou hast assigned to me. Send me understanding and guidance in this great service. Let the wisdom which dwells at Thy throne be with me." Such was the solemn oath; nothing about observing the fundamental laws and no promises to anyone or for anything.

Some eighteen years earlier, when the teenage Catherine had first arrived in Russia, her aunt the Empress Elizaveta had taken her in hand. The tsarina had but one interest in Peter's charming wife, and that was the service she might provide Russia by the delivery of a son for future succession. As noted, the relations between Peter and Catherine were anything but loving, and the conjugal bed for years continued pristine. However, after ten years, Catherine suddenly announced to a thunderstruck capital that she was with child. Whether the pregnancy resulted from a miraculous reversal of the impotence everyone assumed of Peter, or from a liaison with the wildly handsome Serge Saltykov, is a matter of historical conjecture. In any event, within minutes of Paul's birth the newly arrived infant was whisked away by the ecstatic empress, leaving Catherine abandoned and in frustrated isolation. Baby Paul was sequestered by Elizaveta, who initially smothered him in motherly attention and reared him as she judged best. Catherine herself had nothing to do with the infant's upbringing, and in fact did not lay eyes on the child until he was six! Even then, she was granted only a weekly visit; mother and son were strangers to one another, and they remained so for the balance of their lives.

During Catherine's thirty-four-year reign, from 1762 to 1796, Russia underwent profound changes. In a move to replenish the imperial treasury that had been emptied by her aunt, the new empress secularized church property — nearly a third of the country's land and serfs. The clergy thus lost what power it held and was reduced to a corps of minor, state-paid functionaries. The funds Catherine now had at her disposal enabled her to execute a variety of educational and cultural projects. The national school system was overhauled and expanded; universities, technical colleges, and libraries were established, as was the Academy of Science. Catherine was an avid collector of paintings, sculpture, jewelry, and other works of art, and her countless acquisitions eventually formed the basis of the Hermitage museum. Music, theater, and the arts blossomed, and Catherine's court was as brilliant as any in Europe. Together these measures led to the development of an intelligentsia, which within a few decades would be clamoring for further liberal reforms.

Even before her accession, Catherine had dreamed of emancipating the serfs. This vast segment of the population propelled the country's agricultural output, which accounted for ninety-five percent of the economy. Serfs were permanently attached to the land, and a nobleman's wealth was measured not in the acreage he possessed but in the number of "souls" he owned. Upon coming to the throne, however, the empress quickly realized that she required the support of the nobles and that they would never tolerate emancipation, which would mean the loss of their own means of support. However determined she was to implement the teachings of the French Enlightenment, Catherine's indebtedness to the nobility for bringing her to the throne prevented her from acting forcefully as she doubtless would have. Liberating the serfs would have to wait another day.[†]

In the area of local government, Catherine created new administrative systems that survived until the fall of the monarchy in 1917. The country's large administrative units established by Peter the Great were divided into smaller components, and greater autonomy was granted them. A hierarchy of provincial officials was established with precisely defined responsibilities. The justice system came under local authority, and certain of its officials came to office by election. Towns and cities received greater freedom in managing their affairs, really the beginning of self-government.

Under Catherine, two wars were fought with Turkey and one with Sweden; the Russian Empire expanded some 200,000 square miles, incorporating Lithuania, major sections of Poland and the Ukraine, and other formerly independent territories. Most important, the north shore of the Black Sea and the Crimea became Russian, and now a gateway was opened to the Bosphorus and westward, into the Mediterranean. By the time of her death, Catherine had so expanded her empire and strengthened the military that Russia had become one of modern Europe's superpowers.

[†]Alexander II liberated the serfs in 1861. Two and a half years later Abraham Lincoln signed the Emancipation Proclaimation that freed the American slaves.

The intelligence, vision, and energy of the Empress Catherine were all traits that her son Paul appeared to lack. After the first years of heartache, of being denied the comfort and joy of having her son at her side, Catherine all but forgot the child. As the infant grew, he developed from an attractive lad into a sickly, puny youth, tormented and, some say, resembling his putative father. He had the same clumsy movements, nervous tics, and staccato voice. The initial enthusiasm the newly crowned empress had for the duties of motherhood soon waned, and the youngster's daily care was entrusted to tutors, maids, and nannies. The boy was coddled, subjected to oppressive ministrations, and fed a peculiar folk diet. He grew up a fragile, whimpering child, often sick and frightened. By late adolescence, however, through the dedicated attention of the enlightened Count Panin, Paul had received a rounded education. Years later a French courtier wrote of Paul, "His conversation, and everything he said that I can recall, revealed not only an extremely penetrating and very educated mind, but also a subtle understanding of all nuances of our customs and all the subtleties of our language."

Catherine greatly admired physical beauty in males; she found none in Paul. He had bulging eyes and a wild expression; his nose was ugly, and his morose and distrustful bulldog features twitched uncontrollably. The peculiar circumstances of his early upbringing, the tenderness he never knew, and his own sense of unworthiness combined to make him distinctly unlovable. Catherine certainly displayed no affection for her dull and introverted child. In fact, she found him somewhat repulsive. "Why do children so often resemble their fathers," she asked, "when it would be better to resemble their mothers? This is not common sense: Mother Nature is often a blockhead!"

As the years passed, Catherine became increasingly aware of her maturing son — for all the wrong reasons. As long as he lived, no one else would rule the Russian Empire. She determined that Paul would grow up in her shadow, educated but submissive — a *possible* successor but not a rival. Russia at the time, it must be noted, had no law of primogeniture, and the throne passed on by the will of the monarch. Thus the succession became a series of palace revolutions — in one thirty-year period no fewer than seven rulers governed Russia. "Le trône russe n'est pas possessif; il est occupatif" (The Russian throne is not inherited; it is occupied), quipped Frederick the Great. Paul's father had left no will. Nevertheless, in the eyes of many citizens, his son's legitimacy to the throne was significantly more substantial than was Catherine's. At the time of Peter's murder, Paul was, as noted, still a young child, and the expectation by many was that Catherine would rule temporarily as regent. It soon became evident, however, that the ambitious empress's intentions were none other than to enjoy the autocratic throne of Russia until she died.

At nineteen, Paul was presented with a bride. Whatever else he might be or become, the grand duke remained the dynastic implement for succession.

After a couple of disappointing forays into Germanic courts, Catherine search ended with the selection of Princess Wilhelmina of Hesse-Darmstadt. The princess was brought to Russia, converted to Orthodoxy, given the name Natalia Alexeyevna, and married off to a delighted Paul. The joy Paul found in Natalia was unreciprocated; she wasn't in the least taken by her husband. "The grand duke," she discovered, "not only has a weak character; he has none at all!" Within months she found solace in the arms of Count Razumovsky, a man whom Paul considered his closest, perhaps only, friend. The dreams of personal happiness that Paul had expected from the marriage soon vanished, and he became more morose and suffered frequent bouts of depression, often punctuated by open weeping. Paul seemed worshipfully in love with Natalia, despite her open aversion to him, and when, three years into their marriage, she died in childbirth, he was inconsolable.

A second wife was selected for Paul, Princess Sophia Dorothea of Württemberg, who became the Grand Duchess Maria

Feodorovna. This time Catherine's choice of bride proved entirely satisfactory from everyone's viewpoint. The young couple was tremendously happy, and Maria became not only a dutiful wife but also something of the mother Paul had never had. The union proved prolific, producing a bevy of handsome children, the first of the ten being a boy. Catherine was ecstatic that an heir had been born, a joy that only grew when the second child arrived, also a boy — dynastic insurance. At their births, in 1777 and 1779, the empress took possession of the babies, naming them Alexander and Constantine, respectively. The infants were sequestered in her personal quarters, to be brought up according to her precepts. The unhappy parents had been dismissed, having been judged incapable of rearing the children responsibly. The youngsters saw a lot of their doting grandmother and virtually nothing of their parents. For Catherine, nothing was too good for the boys, upon whom she lavished boundless attention, time, and energy. No thought was given to the pain she had inflicted on her son and daughter-in-law by usurping their parental rights. Nor was she the least bit concerned about the humiliation inflicted by her announcement that the two were incapable of fulfilling their parental duties. Even more galling, the mother's love Paul had never known was clearly being lavished on his own young sons.

As a fully mature man and heir presumptive, Paul continued to suffer the same neglect at the hands of Catherine that had plagued his earlier years. The empress calculatingly denied him responsibility of any sort, fearful that someday he might seize the throne. By age twenty-one, the grand duke had taken only a few symbolic steps toward involvement in the workings of the government. Even years later, happily remarried and the father of a large family, Paul continued to be denied any form of responsibility or authority. Honors and appointments that he might reasonably have expected did not come his way. But his mother's favorites were showered with titles, orders, and money — individuals such as Stanislas Augustus, crowned by her king of Poland; Grigory

Orlov, who stood at her side for twelve years; and the great love of her life, Grigory Potemkin, who rose to become the most influential person in the realm. Paul was a grand duke without function or duty, isolated from the inner circle of government, with little to occupy his time. As a sop, he was given the empty title of grand admiral and awarded a small estate in Pavlovsk, a remote site far from the capital, situated in dense forests, with primitive roads frequently made impassable by the weather. In contrast, Grigory Alexandrovich Potemkin, Catherine's favorite at the time, was presented a grand and flourishing estate immediately adjacent to her own at Tsarskoye Selo.

Paul's bitterness and hatred of his mother continued to fester, but Catherine seemed quite oblivious, or unconcerned. She made little effort to soothe his injured pride; in fact, she seemed to take every occasion to exacerbate the situation. In 1774, for example, to commemorate her forty-fourth birthday, she presented the grand duke an inexpensive watch, but to Potemkin she gave 50,000 rubles, the precise amount Paul had earlier requested to pay off the debts of his extravagant young wife. On learning of the generous present, Paul was understandably furious.

As the years passed, Paul nonetheless found certain happiness and satisfaction in the next eight children born to the couple, one of whom was a third son, Nicholas — also a future tsar. To celebrate the birth of the couple's first daughter, the empress, in a burst of generosity, bestowed on Paul and Maria Feodorovna a large and prosperous estate, Gatchina, some twenty-five miles from the capital. With its 6,000 serfs, Gatchina soon grew into a mini-kingdom, which Paul ruled with an iron hand. The battalion of 2,400 troops provided by his mother to protect the property was developed into a rigidly drilled cadre of parade-square automatons. The outdated parade techniques of Frederick the Great were adopted as the quintessence of good military order. Antiquated Prussian-style uniforms and military regulations were extolled as gospel. The estate soon developed into a military camp, a vast drill ground. The cut of a tunic, the polish of boots, and the dress of the ranks became significant matters of state. Any deviation from Paul's orders was viewed as a direct challenge to his authority. Life in Gatchina was brutal for the troops. On the other hand, Paul's private fiefdom developed in many ways into a model estate. Churches were built, including three for the Lutheran Finns who resided there. Schools and hospitals were established, and universal medical care was provided the residents. The estate's sewers and gutters were among the first introduced in rural Russia. Theatricals and musicals were performed at the manor house, and its library eventually accumulated an impressive 45,000 volumes. A despot may have ruled Gatchina, but he did so with an enlightened hand.

Paul was an eclectic reader, taking a special interest in history and contemporary issues. The revolutionary events unfolding in France were of particular concern to him. The grand duke suffered from paranoia, and soon he became convinced that the disastrous developments in that unfortunate country were a direct threat to him and his personal power. Security at Gatchina had always been repressive, but now, through Paul's fresh initiatives to shield against real or imagined enemies, conditions on the manor developed as though it was under siege. Those serving Paul never knew when the axe might fall for any number of logic-defying reasons. On one occasion four officers were imprisoned because their braids appeared overly short — outward and visible signs of revolutionary spirit. It was said that officers appeared on parade with full wallets, for they never knew whether they might not be ordered into exile on the spot.

Gatchina provided Paul with diversion, as did the eight children who had not been removed from him by the empress. All the while, however, he continued to seethe with anger at his mother, and he took every occasion to complain about the humiliating treatment he had suffered at her hands. To one diplomat he confided that had he owned a pet, his mother would undoubtedly have had it drowned. To another, he angrily promised that when he came to the throne, he would personally flog each of his mother's councillors. The empress, however, paid no attention to these wild ramblings and continued to treat her son with the same mixture of disdain and neglect she had always shown him. When the time came for Alexander and Constantine to marry, Catherine concluded all the arrangements, without so much as a word with their father. The estrangement between Paul and Catherine grew nearly complete.

In 1784, the French ambassador to St. Petersburg, Comte de Ségur, gave this assessment of Paul:

> One was struck by the great vivacity and nobility of character. These, however, were only first impressions. Soon one noticed, above all when he spoke of his personal position and future, disquiet, a mistrust, an extreme susceptibility, in fact oddities which were to cause his faults, his injustices, and his misfortunes. In any rank of life he might have made himself and others happy; but for such a man the throne — above all, the Russian throne — could not fail to be a dangerous shoal on which he could climb without expecting to be speedily hurled down. The history of all dethroned and butchered tsars was his idée fixe, darkening his mind and unhinging his reason.

Five years later, the Comte de Ségur upon his return to Paris wrote further of the grand duke:

> He combined plenty of intelligence and information with the most unquiet and mistrustful humor and most unsteady character. Though often affable to the point of familiarity, he was more frequently haughty, despotic, and harsh. Never had one seen a man more thoughtless, more frightened, more capricious, in a word, less capable of rendering him and others happy. His reign proved it. It was not malignity that inspired so many injustices or led him to disgrace or exile so many people; it was a sickness of mind. He tormented all who approached him because

he unceasingly tormented himself. The throne always seemed to him surrounded by precipices. Fear upset his judgment. Imagined perils gave rise to real ones, for a monarch inspires the mistrust which he exhibits and the terror he feels.

Catherine's spies in Gatchina dutifully reported on all Paul's comings and goings; the close scrutiny, coupled with the actual treatment meted the grand duke, was in effect house arrest. Increasingly, Catherine pondered Paul's suitability to succeed her. "I see into what hands the empire will fall when I am gone," she exclaimed. Paul's behavior was so unpredictable, often bizarre, that even his loyal wife began to wonder if he was suitable for the throne. "There is no one who does not every day remark on the disorder of his faculties," she wrote.

Meanwhile, Paul's eldest son, Alexander, had flowered into manhood, a precocious, gifted, and startlingly handsome young man. He was tall and blond, with fine features, impeccable manners, and amazing charm. He was intelligent and he possessed the gift of putting others at ease. Few were the young ladies of St. Petersburg who did not fall madly in love with the young grand duke. Alexander was everyone's favorite, particularly his grandmother's, whom he adored and sought above all to satisfy.

But for Paul, Alexander was yet another threat, one rapidly developing into a dangerous rival for the throne. As time went on, Catherine became more and more convinced that her grandson was the perfect successor, and there is little doubt that she had actually decided on the matter. But she procrastinated; confidence in her own longevity kept her from actually issuing a formal manifesto to that effect.

Catherine's reign so far had been glittering. The empire had expanded remarkably and prosperity prevailed. Despite manifold court scandals, her people held the empress in the highest esteem. But the foibles and peculiarities of Paul were legendary, and people were afraid. In his memoirs, Prince Adam Czartoryski summarized the atmosphere that prevailed in Russia during the final years of Catherine's reign:

> Catherine, who, judged from a distance, possessed neither virtue or even decency, had won the veneration and even love of her entourage and subjects, above all in the capital. From her date of accession, the Muscovite Empire had gained in consideration abroad and in order at home far beyond that which prevailed under Anna and Elizaveta . . . the grand duke figured as a shadow in the picture . . . the terror he inspired fortified the general attachment to the rule of Catherine. Everyone desired the reigns of government to remain as long as possible in her strong hands. The universal fear of Paul increased the admiration for the power and the lofty abilities of his mother, who kept him on a leash, far from his rightful throne.

On September 2, 1796, a grand ball was held at the Winter Palace in honor of Gustavus, the seventeen-year-old king of Sweden. The young monarch had arrived in St. Petersburg to claim the hand of the fourteen-year-old Alexandra, Catherine's eldest granddaughter. The empress had labored hard to arrange this match, and she was delighted that at last the troublesome Swedes would be more closely brought under Russian influence. Since the days of Peter the Great, Russia and Sweden had vied with one another for supremacy of the Baltic region. Within the century, three wars had been fought between the two countries, the latest being in 1788–90, a brief six years before Gustavus's visit.

It was one of the most glittering occasions St. Petersburg had ever witnessed. The entire imperial family was in attendance, including Grand Duke Paul and Maria Feodorovna. After all, it was their daughter who was being betrothed, albeit without their consultation. The splendid uniforms, dazzling jewelry, and opulent gowns were awhirl in the magnificence of the imposing ballroom, richly sparkling in gold leaf. Liveried attendants passed refreshments, while the orchestra played the fashionable dances of the day. At seven o'clock, the empress had made her grand entrance into the hall, covered with diamonds and wearing the Swedish Order of St. Seraphim. All progressed swimmingly well and Catherine radiated dignity and unruffled majesty, despite her irritation with the young Swedish king, who had not yet deigned to present himself.

By eight o'clock the disturbing news reached the empress that Gustavus was refusing at the last moment to sign the marriage contract. All the details of the match had been negotiated and agreed upon, save one that had escaped everyone's notice until the very last moment: the question of religion. As head of the Orthodox Church, Catherine had all along stipulated that Alexandra retain the faith into which she had been born. Platon Zubov, her emissary in the negotiations, had carelessly neglected to raise the point with the Swedes, and now Gustavus, as ruler of a strictly Lutheran country, balked — he could not permit a queen of Sweden to worship in an Orthodox chapel, attended by Orthodox priests.

Rumor of the sensational development spread through the ballroom, and an awkward pall immediately descended upon the assembly. By ten o'clock all entreaties, threats, and arguments had failed to persuade the adamant Gustavus; the young king retreated to his quarters, where he barricaded himself. Catherine was dumbfounded. All the efforts she had given over to this marital alliance with Sweden, and the bright expectation for Alexandra that she had harbored, had abruptly and rudely come to naught. The audacity of the teenage king was confounding, and that these incredible events were unfolding under Catherine's own roof was a palpable insult.

The empress sat on the throne in stunned silence. When finally she rose to speak, she staggered, and her words became unintelligible. Courtiers rushed to her side and she was half-carried to her quarters. She was put to bed, and there she lay for two days;

Catherine had endured her first attack of apoplexy. Her system never recovered, and for the ensuing two months she suffered her way through the affairs of state in the poorest of health, while her condition steadily deteriorated. On November 6 Platon Zubov, Catherine's lover at the time, visited the empress. During their time together she asked to be excused for a few moments and went to "answer the call of nature" in the commode off her bedroom. Time passed, and after a while, a concerned Zubov summoned the maids. On entering the dressing room they found the empress prostrate on the floor in front of the toilet, wedged in between the two doors where she had fallen off the seat. With difficulty, the servants moved her inert body onto her bed, and there she remained, unconscious until her death two days later. It was an ignominious and pathetic end to an empress called "the Great." Moments later an elated Paul was proclaimed Autocrat of All Russia.

Within an hour of the empress's death, Paul ordered his entourage from Gatchina into St. Petersburg, and overnight the Winter Palace became a Prussian-style barracks. By morning sentry boxes had been established every few yards along the palace's perimeter, manned by guards in Prussian uniforms. The citizens viewed the transformation in bewilderment — the country was not at war, no enemy menaced the capital, yet the palace suddenly had assumed the appearance of a beleaguered fortress.

Throughout the night, with Catherine's body barely cold, there flowed from Paul's pen a stream of directives and ukases, or imperial edicts. Alexander was reduced in status to a junior officer and assigned the responsibility of organizing the sentry boxes. From that moment on, Grand Duke Alexander found himself treated more as one of his father's minor subjects than as his heir.

3

Tsar Paul's Revenge

THE ELABORATE PREPARATIONS FOR the state funeral of the late empress were overseen in every detail by the vengeful Paul. Catherine was not to be honored alone; she would be buried together with the rightful tsar, her murdered husband, now dead these thirty-four years. Paul ordered his father's body to be exhumed and the remains to be prepared for reburial. The court would do obeisance to Peter III, whose throne had been so outrageously usurped. On the day of the double funeral, as the two corteges made their way to the Fortress of St. Peter and St. Paul, the crowds observed an infirm old man painfully striding beside Peter's casket. This was Alexis Orlov, one of Catherine's favorites and the alleged murderer of the fallen tsar. On a brocade cushion the panting elder laboriously carried Peter's crown.

The joint funeral served the succession as a sort of purgative. Paul was making it painfully clear that he had come to the throne as successor to his murdered father, not his usurping mother. And he lost no time in making his mark. Catherine's favorites were summarily dealt with — some were jailed, others banished from the capital, and still others exiled from Russia. Potemkin's body was exhumed and flung into the Neva River, where the currents carried it out into the Gulf of Finland and oblivion. Catherine's foes were pardoned and welcomed back to the court, where they were showered with titles and orders and awarded estates and serfs. Then, with studied deliberation, Paul charted a course reversing most of Catherine's domestic and foreign policies.

Paul's coronation in itself was a vivid contrast to that of his mother — it contained none of the rich tradition of the Orthodox Church, none of the glorious beauty of its music or the symbolism of its ceremonial. The coronation was a stark, military affair — everyone dressed in the Prussian style, with minimum pomp and circumstance. "So enamored had he become with things military," wrote one historian, "that during the coronation ceremony he strode to the altar to take Holy Communion with a saber still swinging from the sword knob at his hip. Catherine's coronation had been festive, regal, and elegant. Paul's resembled the ceremony of a general taking command of the armies. No festive atmosphere greeted the coronation: the hearts of his subjects began to fill with fear and a dark sense of foreboding."

The foreboding was not without justification. Ukases continued to flow from the Winter Palace, frequently to be countermanded shortly thereafter; a contemporary cartoon from an underground broadsheet pictures Paul clutching a document in either hand. One is labeled "Order!," the other, "Counter-order!," while on the tsar's forehead sits a notice, "Disorder!" When he drove by in his carriage, everyone was required to dismount and bow. Anyone passing the Winter Palace was obliged to salute it, whether Paul was in it or not. "In Russia," he declared, "the only person of importance is the one with whom I speak — and then only for the duration of the conversation." St. Petersburg was placed under curfew after nine o'clock, the beginning of the evening for most people.

Paul earned the bitter hatred of his army by introducing the cumbersome Prussian uniforms and obsolete drill. Prussian perfection of parade square formations became an obsession with him, as was the minutiae of uniform orderliness. A button undone, a wig insufficiently powdered, a belt too loosely hanging — all were possible causes for a ruthless flogging. "A soldier," Paul declared, "is simply a machine stipulated by regulations."

Many nobles found themselves banished to country estates or exiled to distant outreaches of the empire. Rigid regulations characterized Paul's manner of governing, and punishment was quickly meted out for infractions. Not even foreign diplomats were immune to censure. When the Prussian ambassador arrived for a ball at the Winter Palace in a uniform that Paul found displeasing, he was summarily given back his passport and ordered to return to Berlin that same evening.

Paul came to the throne at the age of forty-two. As the years of his reign unfolded, the emperor's character deteriorated further, and much of Russia suffered, especially those in the capital. Paul's entire adult life had been filled with paranoia. The bitter years of neglect and frustration had warped his mind. Danger, conspiracy, and enemies lurked everywhere. The story is told how he once suggested to his wife that they stroll through the park after supper. The empress casually observed that there were thunderclouds and that it would likely rain. Count Pavel Strogonov, one of the finest minds in Russia, happened by. "What do you think?" the emperor asked his faithful adviser. Stroganov went to the window, looked out, and agreed that in all likelihood it was going to rain. Upon which Paul's face twitched and paled, and he flew into a mad rage. "You're conniving with the empress for the sole purpose of making me angry. I'm sick and tired of your lies. You never wanted to understand me!" he screamed. "I know that you are more wanted at your estate in Perm and I suggest your immediate departure." Thus did the emperor exile from his court one of the most important figures in the government.

Paul was not wholly mad, however; there were flashes of rationality. New laws, for example, revoked many of the traditional privileges enjoyed by the gentry. Obligations of serfs to their masters became more closely regulated. The grief Paul caused his subjects was felt particularly strongly in the capital. Moscow and the provinces viewed the emperor in a less harsh light than did the inhabitants of St. Petersburg, where the tsar's shadow was long and omnipresent.

Within months of Paul's accession to the throne, the world for him had closed even further into a web of suspicion, fear, and dread of treason and murder. Nobody could be trusted, not even his sons. Princess Lieven, wife of the Russian ambassador to the court of St. James's and a noted diarist, tells in her diary that one day Paul unexpectedly entered Alexander's rooms. On a side table the emperor discovered a copy of Voltaire's *Brutus*, open to the pages on which appeared the lines, "Rome is free: that's enough . . . give thanks to the gods." Paul became furious, and, tossing the book aside, stomped out of the room. A few minutes later, a courtier appeared at Alexander's rooms clutching a volume on Peter the Great. On Paul's orders, he read aloud to the grand duke the passage describing the agonizing torment and death of Tsarevich Alexis, whom Peter had tried for treason and had put to death. Alexander was aghast.

There was no way that Paul would live in the Winter Palace, the magnificent residence of his hated mother. He determined to build for himself a new home, one in which only he and a limited number of favorites would live in safety. The site he selected was that of Empress Elizaveta's beautiful New Summer Palace, which had been lovingly built by Rostrelli and was considered one of the jewels of St. Petersburg architecture. Paul ordered the structure demolished. In its place he erected the imposing Mikhailovsky Castle, a massive Gothic fortress complete with thick walls, double doors, moats, drawbridges, and secret underground passages. The tsar personally supervised the installation of the security arrangements. On February 18, 1797, a much-relieved Paul moved into the fortification, and within a couple of weeks, by command of their father, Alexander and Constantine had joined him; everyone would now be under the personal surveillance of the emperor. A battalion of armed guards was assigned to the castle as a security force and here, behind the battlements, Paul found solace. "I never felt happier or more at ease," he said when he took up residence in his new home, and he became more self-indulgent and autocratic than ever.

From the secure precincts of Mikhailovsky, the tsar continued to rule the vast empire, few corners of which escaped his attention. Foreign travel was prohibited, as was the importation of foreign books and publications. The handful of booksellers in St. Petersburg and Moscow were put under police surveillance. All letters leaving Russia had to pass through censors. The insidious influence of the French Revolution was under no circumstances to permeate the empire. Minute details of his subjects' lives were prescribed by Paul's regulations. Ukases provided for the cut of clothing, for the number of guests that might be hosted at a dinner party, for the depth of a curtsy. Swift and harsh punishment befell the careless tongue. A distinguished army officer received a thousand strokes of the knout for a play on words uttered in reference to Paul. Another had his tongue cut out and was dispatched to Siberia for mockingly writing a verse on the construction of St. Isaac's Cathedral. "The fear in which we are all living is indescribable," wrote Count Kochubey — one of Alexander's childhood friends — to a close acquaintance in London. "People are terrified of their own shadow. Everyone is petrified. Denunciations are a daily occurrence, and whether true or false, they are invariably accepted. The prisons overflow with captives. A profound despondency prevails and the meaning of happiness is lost to the people." Paul's moods swung from sullen silence to furious and sadistic cruelty, and the people bled.

By early 1800, Count Nikita Panin, vice-chancellor of foreign affairs, concluded that Paul must be compelled to abdicate in favor of Alexander. Russia, he was convinced, was on the brink of ruin. Panin had assumed his high post at the young age of twenty-eight. He was a brilliant man with a genuine concern for Russia's welfare, and he was particularly distressed over the new fickleness of foreign policy. Panin was as strong an Anglophile as he was a Francophobe. "The English should set an example for us," he once declared. Under Paul, Russia had rapidly drifted into a "cold war" with Britain. In his concern for the direction in which Russia was gravitating, Panin sought the counsel of his good friend Lord Whitworth, Britain's resourceful ambassador in St. Petersburg. By 1801, Sir Charles had successfully penetrated Paul's innermost circle. Not only had he managed to enlist onto the British payroll two of Paul's favorites — Paul's mistress and his valet (30,000 and 20,000 rubles respectively) — but he had simultaneously cultivated two amorous affairs "with political implications." Little went on in court without the envoy's knowledge. What advice Sir Charles had to offer Panin on the matter of an abdication is not known, but it is certain the Englishman's influence on the vice-chancellor was profound. The precedents set in the regencies of George III in England and Christian VII in Denmark doubtless loomed strong in Whitworth's mind. In the case of the British monarch, the bouts of incoherent babbling and violence from which he suffered caused him to be declared insane. The Prince of Wales assumed the regency in 1811, later becoming King George IV. In Denmark, King Christian, having given himself up entirely to debauchery, was declared mentally incompetent and a regency was established under Crown Prince Frederick, later King Frederick VI.

With elaborate care, Panin approached Admiral Ribas, a questionable figure who through intrigue and fortuitous circumstance had risen to become deputy vice president of the admiralty. In the words of a contemporary, the admiral was "an adventurer with the soul of a bandit." Ribas, ready to engage in any intrigue that might enhance his position, agreed with alacrity to Panin's proposal. The two then enlarged the conspiratorial circle by inviting Count von Pahlen to join them. Pahlen was a man of immense ambition and insecurity. Paul had already once dismissed him in disgrace, only to recall him shortly afterward. Outwardly an honest, charming, and straightforward gentleman of highest integrity, inwardly he was a fearful, self-serving, and sinister schemer. "Under that attractive exterior," wrote a contemporary, "there was an abyss of perfidy and ferocity, an iron will and a reckless audacity at the service of an ambition as boundless as it was unscrupulous." It did not require much persuasion to convince Pahlen to join the plot.

Pahlen readily convinced the other member of the conspiracy that Alexander had to be brought into their confidence before an abdication could be forced. The heir must agree to Paul's stepping down, and he had to be prepared to mount the throne. A meeting was arranged by Panin with the young tsarevich, and in the apparently casual conversation that ensued, the count skillfully reviewed the deteriorating condition of Russia and the danger it faced from the many erratic changes in government policies that were taking place. Russia could no longer be entrusted to one who had so obviously taken leave of his senses. There was but one path to the salvation of the empire: painful as it might be, Paul simply had to be forced to step down and he, Alexander, must take the throne. The precise nature of Panin's discussion with the tsarevich is not known, but it appears that Alexander was under the impression that a regency was being proposed. No doubt Ambassador Whitworth had recalled to Panin the British experience with George III. Paul would be made to retire until such time as he fully regained his mental stability; in the meanwhile Alexander would rule.

The tsarevich listened in expressionless silence, offering not a single comment. He seemed neither surprised nor indignant, but he also offered no objection to the dangerous proposal. It is said that Whitworth suggested Malta as an appropriate place where Paul could, in exile, exercise sovereign rule. The emperor had, after all, permitted himself to become the Grand Master of the Sovereign Order of Malta — a Russian Orthodox monarch heading a Roman Catholic order, a singularly odd appointment. Abdication or regency — assurance was given to Alexander that whatever happened, no physical harm would befall his father. Since everything would be done in Paul's name, there would be no breach of the oath of fealty that Alexander held so dear. For lack of negative reaction from the tsarevich, Panin assumed that Alexander supported the scheme, and he so informed his fellow conspirators.

But by autumn 1800, events had overtaken the conspirators. Paul had suddenly banished Panin to his estates for the offense of offering disagreeable advice on matters related to foreign affairs. Concurrently, Admiral Ribas suffered a heart attack and died. The British occupation of Malta so enraged Paul that he demanded the recall of Lord Whitworth. The ambassador returned home in company with the British consul, who was also expelled. By that time the conspirators had dwindled to Pahlen and an uncommitted, vacillating Alexander.

Russian foreign policy was unfolding in a frightful way. As he had done with most of his mother's directions, Paul had reversed the country's foreign policy, and the consequences were increasingly alarming. Catherine had joined Russia to Britain and others in an anti-French coalition. Now Paul deliberately set about to make friendly overtures to Napoleon. The much-admired First Consul, he felt, was best qualified to tame revolutionary ardor and to bring order to Europe. The emperor encouraged Napoleon to proclaim himself king. At the same time, without forewarning, Paul placed an embargo on British shipping. And for good measure he ordered the imprisonment of a thousand British seamen who happened at the time to be in port. St. Petersburg was stunned by these developments. Reprisals from Britain might surely be expected. Russia's trade, furthermore, was dependent on the 4,000 English and Scottish merchants residing in the capital, who virtually controlled the instruments of commerce. To add to the collective dismay, Paul impetuously dispatched 20,000 Cossacks to the Indus River, where they were to join the French for an invasion of India. Military commanders especially were horrified by this irrational order, for not only was there no hope for supply in central Asia, but there were not even maps of areas beyond what is now Uzbekistan. "My father," declared Grand Duke Constantine, "has declared war on common sense, firmly resolved never to conclude a truce."

The mood in the capital in early 1801 was one of near despair. The bustle of war preparations, the flow back and forth of people exiled, then recalled, and the surreptitious gatherings of senior military officers seemed commonplace. Colonel Nikolai Sablukov, a ranking officer of the prestigious Semeonovsky Regiment, noted in his memoirs,

> Great gloom permeated the capital's society. The diplomatic corps ceased to receive as usual. Most of the great houses, some of which kept what was called *table ouverte,* changed their style of living. Even the court itself, shut up in Mikhailovsky Castle and guarded like a feudal fortress, led a very dull and secluded life. The emperor, having his mistress in the castle, no longer drove out as he used to, and even his rides were now confined to the summer garden, which nobody else was permitted to enter.

Talk of abdication again permeated the capital; Pahlen had rekindled his efforts. A general amnesty, declared by Paul in November, brought back to the capital scores of activists, many of whom promptly rallied around the conspiratorial banner. More and more people gravitated to Pahlen, and by February his circle had expanded to more than sixty people, including senators, generals, and even two of Paul's own aides-de-camp. With the exile of Count Feodor Rostopchin, a brilliant and influential courtier from early Gatchina days who had become probably the tsar's closest friend, Pahlen's position in court was significantly strengthened, for not only did he continue as governor-general of St. Petersburg, but he was now appointed military commander of the capital and of the Baltic provinces. Since the police force fell under his direction, the conspirators were assured protection in the highest places. Protection or not, it was a deadly perilous gameplan. Was it likely that the single-minded, volatile Paul would readily agree to abdicate? If not, what then? And where precisely would the emperor retire in his exile? Above all, what horrendous fate might await the conspirators in the event they failed?

Eventually rumors of the conspiracy reached Paul's ears, and the emperor's suspicions fell on Pahlen. He summoned the governor-general and demanded to know whether he was aware of any plots against the throne.

"Yes, Your Majesty," replied the count with audacious sangfroid, "a conspiracy is in fact developing. I myself have joined it specifically to be fully informed on all its aspects. You have nothing to fear; all is under control." Paul then demanded to know whether his two elder sons were in any way involved. Pahlen assured him that they were not, but it was evident that the tsar was unconvinced.

In the next few days, Paul issued warrants for the wholesale arrest of many of the capital's notables, including a few that had but recently been amnestied. His attitude toward Alexander and Constantine became openly hostile. The perfidious Pahlen had successfully driven a wedge between the emperor and his two eldest sons by his unconvincing assurance that the grand dukes were free from involvement in the conspiracy. Orders were drafted for the arrest of Alexander and Constantine, as well as, it was also said, for the empress herself. Pahlen once more appeared before Alexander and forcefully pleaded the case for Paul's immediate removal from the throne. Not only was the grand duke's own life in danger, but the welfare of his brother and possibly his mother was jeopardized. Things were at such a perilous state that the only way the imperial family and the nation could survive, he maintained, would be the removal of Paul from the throne. Pahlen then cited England as an example, where the Prince of Wales had taken the reins of government from the mentally unbalanced George III.

In her brilliant diary, Countess Choiseul-Gouffier, wife of a French diplomat proscribed by the French revolutionary government and retired in Russia, writes of that meeting. She records that Pahlen argued that "the grand duke, employing the same moderation, could without mounting the throne take the reins of government, always being ready to return them to his father as soon as the health of the emperor is restored and when he has recovered that calmness necessary for the performance of his important duties. Such are the views of the senate, of the army, and of the nation." The emperor *had* to step down. The count then went on to assure the grand duke that after Paul's abdication in favor of Alexander, his father would quietly retreat to a country estate with his beloved mistress, Princess Gagarina. There would be no violence; Pahlen would assure the tsar's safety. The grand duke heard Pahlen out, and apparently with little or no trepidation consented to assuming the throne upon his father's abdication. He remained convinced that no physical harm would befall his father. Alexander possessed a penchant for self-deception, and logic did not always prevail in matters not to his liking. The interview over, the reassured Pahlen pushed forward and set the date for the fateful encounter — Saturday, March 11, when the Semeonovsky Guard Regiment was to assume guard at Mikhailovsky Castle. Alexander was the regiment's colonel-in-chief.

On that fateful day in March, the atmosphere in the castle was tense. To Paul, treason seemed as thick as the weather enveloping the capital. Earlier that evening, he, as noted, had ordered the door between his bedroom and that of the mistress to be locked and nailed shut — a fateful precaution. Alexander and Constantine were summoned and again made to swear their allegiance, following which the bewildered young men were put under house arrest. At this point, Pahlen appeared at the castle and requested an urgent meeting with the emperor. The governor-general appeared agitated and reported to the tsar in a knowing tone that he must immediately stand down the Horse Guard. The unreliable Sablukov, commander of the Guard, was under no circumstances to be trusted, Pahlen advised, and neither were his troops. Paul heard Pahlen out and, saying nothing, dismissed the councillor. In fact, Colonel Sablukov was perhaps Paul's most faithful and trustworthy officer within the Semeonovsky Regiment.

Early that evening, Sablukov had verified the state of the Mikhailovsky guard. Twenty-four soldiers were stationed about the corridors of the castle under the direct supervision of three warrant officers. A trumpeter was posted immediately outside the imperial bedroom. In the palace courtyard a platoon of troops from the Preobrozhenski Regiment was also stationed, together with a platoon from the Semeonovsky Regiment. The castle was well guarded and everyone was on the alert.

Just before dinner, Sablukov went to the castle to deliver his report on the state of the guard to his immediate superior, Grand Duke Constantine. At the entrance to the stairs leading to Constantine's quarters, he was greeted by a valet who asked where he was going. The colonel knew the man well and, assuming that the question was merely one of curiosity, replied that he was about to report to the grand duke.

"Please don't go," the servant asked, "for I must immediately inform His Imperial Majesty of that."

"I can't help that," replied the irritated officer. "I'm the duty colonel and I'm obliged to report to His Highness. You may tell that to the emperor." As Sablukov mounted the stairs, the valet scurried off to the opposite stairwell, presumably to inform the tsar.

"I found Constantine three or four paces from the door looking very excited," recalls Sablukov. "I began to deliver my report when Alexander entered through another door looking like a frightened hare. At that very moment the back door opened and in came Paul I *in propria persona,* booted and spurred, carrying his hat in one hand and a stick in the other. He marched to our little group as though he were on parade. Alexander scampered away like a lamplighter into his own apartment. Constantine stood transfixed, hands flopping in his pockets as though facing a bear unarmed." Sablukov turned to Paul, intending to deliver his report, but the emperor cut him short and mumbled, "Oh, it's you who's on duty." He then marched out of the room, slamming shut the door. No sooner had the door closed than Alexander "sneaked in again like a crouching pointer." Only after the second set of doors banged shut did the grand dukes understand that their father had in fact left them and that it was now safe to speak. Both the young men had obviously been unhinged by the bizarre encounter. They expressed admiration of Sablukov for his lack of fear of their father; it was obvious that they themselves had been terrified. After rendering the report to Constantine, Sablukov left the castle and returned to his own quarters.

"That evening," recalled General Mikhail Ilarionovich Kutuzov, hero of the latest Turkish war and Russia's future defender against Napoleon, "we dined with the emperor. There were twenty people at the table. He was in a lively state of mind and joked quite a bit with my eldest daughter, a lady-in-waiting, who was seated opposite him. As we left the dining room after the meal, the emperor and I fell into conversation. We happened to pass by a large mirror, whose glass was imperfectly formed, thus distorting the reflected image. Paul glanced at the mirror and said jokingly, 'A peculiar mirror: I see it wringing my neck.'" And, Kutuzov added, "An hour and a half later he was a corpse."

4

Courage from the
Cognac Bottle

KUTUZOV LEFT THE EMPEROR at about the same time that Sablukov returned to his private quarters. The colonel barely had time to
undo his tunic before a breathless messenger knocked at the door,
bearing the urgent message that Sablukov was to report to His
Majesty forthwith. All highly irregular; it didn't bode well. He
hurriedly ordered his sleigh and went off to present himself to his
sovereign.

Sablukov entered the tsar's anteroom, where Paul awaited
him, and stood smartly at attention. The emperor marched up to
him, stick in hand, and, coming face-to-face, cried out, "Vous êtes
des Jacobins!" Taken aback by this unexpected volley, the startled
officer found nothing better to reply than, "Oui, Sire!" The red-
faced Paul then sputtered that he didn't really mean that Sablukov
himself was a Jacobin; what he meant was that the Semeonovsky
Regiment was a nest of traitors. The colonel tried to object, but
Paul cut him short, shouting that he knew better. He then informed
the distressed officer that his regiment was to be disbanded; orders
had already been drawn up for the distribution of his troops
among several provincial cities. Would the colonel be good enough
to muster the regiment at 0400 in full kit and marching order and

attend to the task? The emperor then turned to the two valets who were in attendance and informed them that they would assume guard duty instead of the disgraced guardsmen. The bewildered Sablukov was curtly dismissed, and with that Paul marched out of the anteroom. The treacherous advice Pahlen had given the tsar about the maligned Sablukov and his regiment had not fallen on deaf ears; Paul had acted. The wily count now had the satisfaction of having the emperor's bedroom guarded by nobody more threatening than two unarmed servants.

The anxiety within Mikhailovsky Castle that evening was not exclusive to the fortress — tension seemed to permeate the city streets. The conspiracy that Paul's fine-tuned antennae sensed was no illusion. The conspirators' plot was now in motion, headed by the insidious Pahlen. Earlier, as the imperial family dined with Kutuzov, assemblies of determined men had gathered in the warmth of various homes to share dinner and to draw strength from one another's company — and from the free-flowing brandy. It was an uncommon night in every respect. "That night," remarked Sablukov of the conspirators, "more than one of them discovered his courage at the bottom of a cognac bottle."

The main group left General Talyzen's home shortly after midnight and, as stealthily as their alcoholic circumstances permitted, made their way by foot to the dreaded fortress through the frigid night. The new leadership now included General Leonty Bennigsen, a Hanoverian-born officer who had spent half his life in Russia. Bennigsen feared and despaired of Paul's unpredictability; the tsar's capricious whims offended his logical and orderly mentality. In addition, there were the three Zubov brothers, one of whom — Platon — had been Catherine's last lover. After her death Paul had sent him into exile but recently had recalled him to the capital. None of these conspirators, or any of the others, was a personal friend of Alexander, although among them were numerous officers from the Semeonovsky Regiment, of which he was colonel-in-chief.

General Talyzen had arrived in advance of the main body and now awaited within the castle the appearance of his conspiratorial colleagues. Very shortly the main group reached its destination and entered Mikhailovsky's summer garden. As they passed under the park's trees, they were startled by a tremendous noise, described later by one of the conspirators:

> The old linden trees of the garden served as a night roost for thousands of crows. When in the unaccustomed hour there passed such a large military troop, the roused birds set up an incredible hue and cry. We were all quite certain that the emperor could not have failed to be awoken. We froze to the spot, but the bedroom windows remained darkened. Had the emperor heard the bedlam he could have saved himself and our enterprise would have come to naught. The crows in that case would have gained the same notoriety as the geese on the Capitol.

The cacophony of the startled birds notwithstanding, the conspirators managed to penetrate the fortress without incident, thanks to Pahlen's meticulous spadework. A majority of those on night duty in the castle had in one way or another become party to the plot. The lead group that included Bennigsen and Platon Zubov made its way up the stairs toward Paul's bedroom. Lieutenant Argamakov, adjutant of the grenadier battalion of the Preobrozhenski Regiment, approached the valet-sentries and demanded entry into the bedchamber, saying that he had documents that required the tsar's urgent attention. Clearly unsure of themselves, the servants objected to the unreasonably early hour, but finally acquiesced when the officer reminded them that it was already six o'clock and all was in order. Thus so simply and easily did the group gain entry into Paul's bedroom.

What happened in the next few minutes is not totally clear, as the accounts that have come down to us are contradictory. Bennigsen tells it as follows:

> Twelve of us entered the room. Pahlen and Valerian Zubov were not with us [they were with Alexander in the grand duke's quarters], but Platon and Nikolai Zubov

were there. The noise of activities outside the bedchamber awoke the emperor and he sprang out of bed. Had he not earlier taken his own security precautions, he might have saved himself by escaping down the secret stairway that led into Princess Gagarina's bedroom. That door, however, had earlier been nailed shut on his own orders, acting on the suggestion of Count Pahlen. The tsar panicked and he hid behind the fireplace screen.

Platon Zubov approached the bed and, finding it empty and in disarray, shouted, "He's escaped!" Bennigsen, who presumably had had less to drink than the others, coolly surveyed the room and discerned Paul's feet peeping out from behind the screen. He pushed the fire screen aside and found the emperor standing barefoot, dressed in a nightshirt, bed-jacket, and nightcap. "Your Majesty, you have ceased to reign," Bennigsen declared in French. "Alexander is now our emperor. We are arresting you on his orders. You must renounce the throne. Be reassured, nobody wishes to kill you. I'm here to see to that. Face up to your fate, for if you offer the least resistance I cannot vouch for your safety."

Paul made no answer, and Platon Zubov repeated in Russian all that Bennigsen had said. "What have I done to you?" asked the tsar. One of the guardsmen replied, "You have tortured us for four years!" At this point another group of conspirators who had gotten themselves lost in the fortress finally found their way to Paul's bedroom. The noise of the approaching troop frightened those who were already there. "Everyone in the room took flight," continued Benningsen. "I was left alone with the tsar, and with my sword prevented him from moving. Those who had fled met the others of our group and everyone reentered the room. There was much excited pushing and shoving by the large crowd and the fire screen toppled over, thus knocking over the chamber's only lamp, and we were plunged into darkness. I left the room to get a light and in the few minutes which followed, Paul met his fate."

While Bennigsen was out of the room, Paul tried to make his way to an adjoining room. His path was blocked and the trapped emperor cried out hysterically, "Arrest! Arrest! What does this mean?" He again lunged for the door, to no avail. The conspirators pinned him down and a scuffle ensued.

"What have I done to you?" the tsar cried out once again, struggling to free himself from the clutches of one of the conspirators. The entangled pair fell to the floor. Someone grabbed a sash and thrust it around Paul's neck. At this point, those who were pressing in on the struggle fell, and in the ensuing melee the emperor was strangled. Although Colonel Sablukov was nowhere near the scene, based on "the best authority, quite fresh at the time," he reported that Paul had spoken so loudly and excitedly that Nikolai Zubov, a gigantic man, had "struck the emperor on the hand and said, 'Why do you shout so?' [using the familiar *tu* form rather than the formal *vous*]. At this insult, Paul brusquely pushed away Zubov's left hand. In retaliation, the intoxicated officer swung a powerful blow at Paul's left temple with his right hand in which he clutched a heavy gold snuffbox." It was this blow that felled Paul, and once the emperor was on the floor, someone grabbed Paul's sash that hung from a bedpost and strangled him. Here, several people "revenged themselves of personal insults they had received from the emperor by kicking and trampling on and in every possible way mangling the unfortunate corpse. So much so that it was no easy matter for surgeons and painters to render it fit to be exhibited to the public, as it was during several weeks, according to the usual etiquette."

Sablukov recalls that he subsequently stopped at the casket of the emperor, lying in state in the throne room of the Winter Palace. "His face was black and blue, although skillfully painted. His cocked hat was placed on his head in such a manner as to conceal as much as possible the left eye and temple, which had been knocked in." When the diplomatic corps was permitted to view the body, the French ambassador leaned over the railing and, pulling down the cravat, exhibited the red mark around the emperor's neck that the sash had left.

Another, poignant account has it that Paul, realizing that the end was at hand, pleaded with the conspirators for a few minutes to pray. This was hotly denied him, and just then, according to some accounts, the emperor appeared to notice his son Constantine among the conspirators. "What!" he exclaimed in bewilderment. "Your Highness is here?" Had in fact the grand duke been in the room, Paul's final moments would have been all the more agonizing. There is little reason to believe, however, that Constantine had been present. As these fateful moments were unfolding, he was apparently in his own quarters, either asleep or pretending to be. So it was that Tsar Paul I met his death in the fifth year of his reign and the forty-seventh year of his life.

As these momentous events were unfolding, Alexander, in the company of Pahlen, had cloistered himself in his own quarters. The young, inexperienced, and timid heir to the throne required the moral support of a hard, strong-willed person such as the governor-general. Only three hours earlier Alexander had dined at his father's table; after he had been dismissed he went directly to his quarters. There he signed a manifesto agreeing to accept the throne upon his father's "retirement." By affixing his name to the document, Alexander formally became a party to the conspiracy, and now in the precincts of his quarters he awaited word of the outcome.

In due course, a flushed Nikolai Zubov appeared at the grand duke's door and announced the stunning news that Paul had died in a fit of apoplexy. Initially, Alexander did not grasp what he was being told. But then the full impact of the dreadful message sunk in. He collapsed in a chair, stunned and incredulous, in complete dismay. All along he had truly, perhaps naively, believed that a peaceful abdication was possible; he certainly did not countenance his father's death. Alexander continued to sit mutely, transfixed, refusing to accept the awful news. His face was ashen and his lips trembled. Again, it was Pahlen who took charge. He spoke sharply to the young man and ordered him to take hold of himself; he was now the tsar and must behave as such. "I cannot," cried Alexander. "I cannot go on with it. I have no strength to reign. I resign my power and give it to whomever wants it! Let those who have committed the crime be responsible for the consequences!"

"Stop behaving like a child!" retorted the count. "The fate of millions now depends on your firmness. Go and reign. Show yourself to the guards!" A shaken but more composed Alexander finally did as he was told, and early on the morning of Sunday, March 12, he appeared on the balcony overlooking the parade square and, choked with grief, made the following terse announcement to the assembled soldiers: "My father is dead. He died of an apoplectic seizure. During my reign everything will be done according to the spirit and principles of my grandmother, the Empress Catherine." And with this, he reentered the fortress, a man never again to be the same. "How shall I have the strength to rule with the constant memory that my father has been assassinated?" Alexander pathetically demanded of his wife, the Grand Duchess Elizaveta, whom he had married seven years before.

Whatever shocked state Alexander might have been in, that same day, two ukases were issued to the country. Coming as they did, just hours after Paul's death, it is clear that Alexander had for some time pondered the prospect of an accession; he was not totally unprepared. Despite the grief and emotion of the hour, the new tsar was collected enough to issue his first official acts. The first ukase read:

> We, by the grace of God, Alexander the First, Tsar and Autocrat of all the Russias, etc. declare to our faithful subjects: It has pleased by the decrees of the Almighty to shorten the life of our beloved parent, sovereign, Emperor Pavel Petrovich, who died suddenly of an apoplectic stroke, at night, between the 12th and 13th days of this month.
>
> We, on receiving the imperial hereditary throne of all the Russias, do also receive at the same time the obligations to govern the people committed to us by the Almighty, according to the laws and the heart of her who rests in God, our most august grandmother, sovereign, Empress Catherine the Great, whose memory will be dear

forever to us and the whole country. Following the steps of her wise intentions, we hope to arrive at the object of carrying Russia to the summit of glory, and to procure an uninterrupted happiness to all our faithful servants, whom we do, hereby, invite to seal their fidelity to us, by oath, before the face of all-seeing God, whose assistance we implore to grant us power to support the weight now resting upon us.

ALEXANDER
Given at St. Petersburg, 13 March 1801

The second ukase made a broad sweep of things. In reading it, we can better appreciate what Pososhkov meant when he declared that "the tsar is master of his country . . . in the domain assigned to him he can create, like God, what he likes." The document provided for the following:

1. All prisoners of state are set at liberty; 2. All the late laws relative to contraband are abolished; 3. The tariff of tolls and customs of 1782 is reintroduced; 4. The English seamen are released from confinement; 5. All societies and clubs are permitted; 6. The Orders of St. Vladimir and St. George are restored and that of Malta to be repressed; 7. Everyone may dress as he pleases, provided he does not offend common decorum; 8. The importation of books and literary publications of every sort is again permitted; 9. The regiments are to bear their old names and the former regiments are to be reorganized; 10. Every person, whether native, foreign or exile shall freely enter or quit Russian dominions, without any molestation or difficulty on the frontier.

Within an hour of Paul's death, Sir James Wylie, privy councillor and chief physician to the court, arrived at Mikhailovsky to attend to the imperial body. He worked the dead man's face, and, with careful application of cosmetics, the cuts and bruises incurred in the scuffle were cleverly disguised. The body was "clothed in his uniform, booted and spurred and with his hat placed on his head so as to hide the right temple. It was laid out in the coffin in which he was to be exposed to the public, according to the usual etiquette." All was now in order: the corpse had been made ready for funeral display and the job was completed as skillfully as circumstances permitted. The physician then issued a certificate attesting that the cause of death was apoplexy. There was nothing extraordinary in these artificial arrangements: deceit and cover-up in the deaths of Russian tsars was a regular pattern. The services rendered by Wylie further endeared him to Alexander. A special bond now developed between the emperor and the physician, and the trust placed in the stalwart Scotsman became implicit.

The empress's initial reaction to the death was one of hysteria. After she had collected herself and the body had been prepared, Maria Feodorovna insisted on viewing the remains. Until she saw her dead husband with her own eyes she would not recognize the new emperor. Sablukov describes the scene. The pale, cold, and "marble-like" empress entered Paul's room with Alexander and Elizaveta.

> Approaching the corpse, the empress stopped in dead silence and fixed her eyes on it steadily without shedding a tear. Alexander, who now for the first time saw his father's mangled face, whitewashed and painted, was horrified and stood transfixed. The empress mother then turned toward her son and with becoming gravity and the most dignified air it is possible to imagine, said, "I now wish you joy. You are emperor" . . . at these words Alexander fell to the ground. Those who stood by thought for a moment that he had died.

Maria Feodorovna exited the room, vowing no longer to have anything to do with the son she deemed guilty of murder.

One account has it that she openly cried out, "You're covered by the blood of your father!" By noon, however, the empress had significantly calmed down. Her son's intense grief appeared so genuine that she now judged him innocent of the terrible death. She kissed Alexander and spoke soothingly to him. And it was more than a momentary reconciliation — the relationship between the two soon became firmly cemented. For the rest of his life, Alexander lavished unabated filial love on his mother, and that love was generously reciprocated. As for Grand Duchess Elizaveta, now empress, she proved a tower of strength and comfort as she stood by her distraught husband. At twenty-three, he had now been propelled in one terrible night onto one of the world's mightiest thrones; he was soon to be crowned emperor and Autocrat of All Russia.

The stunning news of Paul's death was not long in reaching the population. That it was of "an apoplectic stroke" seemed plausible — after all, it was of this same condition that Alexander's grandmother had died. (When Talleyrand learned the news, he commented sarcastically, "Russians should invent another illness to explain the deaths of their emperors.") For the imperial family it was a dark moment, but outside, as Mistress of the Robes, Princess Lieven observed, "a superb sun broke over this great and terrible day . . . there were shouts of deliverance and joy."

For weeks thereafter, Alexander became a virtual recluse, attending only to the most urgent duties. He received nobody and dined alone with his wife in the familiar surroundings of the Winter Palace. The mental images of what had taken place in Paul's bedroom on that fateful night, and particularly the manner of his father's death, would remain with him for the rest of his life. True, he had not been directly involved with those horrible events, yet he knew he was far from innocent. "His sensitive soul will be tortured by it forever," wrote Elizaveta to her mother. Adam Czartoryski, a Polish aristocrat who was one of Alexander's closest friends and who eventually rose to become Russia's deputy foreign minister, wrote that "the grief and remorse which he was continually reviving in his heart were inexpressibly deep and troubling. In the midst of pomp and the festivities of [his own] coronation . . . he saw in his imagination Paul's mutilated and blood stained body on the steps of the throne which he was now himself to ascend. . . . His mental tortures never ceased."

The torments were indeed real. But to what extent were these agonies deserved? Was the young grand duke a key player in the tragedy, or was he merely the pawn of a coterie of determined men? At one time Alexander Pushkin commenced work on a biography of Alexander, and in his notes he clearly defined the tsarevich's complicity in the murder. In the first place, those involved in the conspiracy — Alexander, above all — knew Paul well enough to realize that there was no way he would freely and calmly walk away from the throne, simply at their behest. An abdication would have to be imposed; one way or another, force would be required. Alexander's stipulation to Pahlen that no physical harm should befall his father was as naive as Pahlen's assurance that such would be the case. A struggle was inevitable, and it is difficult to accept that anyone might have thought otherwise. Furthermore, the fact that many of the conspirators had generously imbibed before setting off to the palace that night did not augur well for a peaceful conclusion.

In principle, an abdication required a proper document and signature. Yet at no time is there any record of such a document having being presented to the unfortunate tsar or, for that matter, of one having ever been drawn up. A number of accounts of the murder exist, some of which vary in detail, but not one speaks of anybody bringing along either a prepared statement of abdication or writing implements. Surely, these desperate men were not planning to rely on Paul's verbal accord. The excited conspirators burst into the tsar's bedroom and announced that "you have ceased to reign. . . . Alexander is now our emperor. We are arresting you on his orders." Legally, an order of arrest by Alexander could not take place until an abdication was signed. In fact, the whole encounter was an absurd charade. What were the conspirators thinking?

That a docile Paul would acquiesce to their demands, serenely go off into exile, and then, sometime in the future, formalize the deed by signing an instrument of abdication? Hardly. And there is no way that any of this could have escaped Alexander's attention. The grand duke knew far more than we are led to believe. Pushkin was right in charging him as an accomplice in the murder.

"Until the end of his life," writes another British historian, Alan Palmer, "there would come, now and again, black days of despair when [Alexander] was unsure of himself or his purpose; alone with his doubts and reflections, his conscience would again begin to turn round itself and the tsar of Russia became a squirrel in a cage, thrown into torment by the shadows of parricide."

5

The Crowned Hamlet

RUSSIA ENTHUSIASTICALLY EMBRACED its new emperor. Alexander was the very picture of regal bearing — tall, blond, strikingly handsome, and possessed of a most affable charm. His immaculate manners and courteousness immediately put people at ease, and virtually all who met him found his company delightful. Over the coming decades, he would break scores of female hearts across Europe, and many a ruler and statesman would fall under the spell of this captivating and at the same time enigmatic, complex monarch.

Alexander had been brought up by his grandmother. Catherine had coddled him as a baby, fussed over him as a child, lavished upon the strapping youngster every sort of attention. Nothing was too good for the boy. She loved her grandson with a maternal passion, and Alexander reciprocated with the warm filial love denied his parents, whom he barely knew. The boy's education was in the hands of the empress, and she was determined to mold the young grand duke in accordance with her own principles. Catherine saw in her grandson a successor to the throne, an instrument for the continuation of her enlightened policies. Her own son, she had long ago concluded, was simply unfit to carry the imperial crown.

To prepare Alexander physically and mentally for the strain of rule over a vast and militarized empire, the empress directed that the boy be brought up in spartan conditions. His bedroom windows were thrust wide open, regardless of the weather. From his days in the crib the child slept on a tough straw-filled mattress of thick morocco leather, a practice he kept up the rest of his life. In his many travels and campaigns as emperor, Alexander's baggage invariably included just such a mattress, which, even in the most luxurious palaces, was laid out for him on the floor. To accustom the child to the sound of cannons, his Winter Palace bedroom was deliberately located near the battery of ceremonial guns. The artillery roared on numerous festive occasions, and although Alexander became used to the roaring cannonades, the delicate membranes of his inner ears were sufficiently damaged to cause significant deafness in one of them. As the boy grew, vigorous physical exercise became an important aspect of his training, and Alexander eventually developed into a sturdy, muscular, robust young man.

When he turned twelve, the responsibility for Alexander's education was given over to Colonel Frédéric La Harpe, a noted Swiss scholar, who was both a liberal and a republican. Working with La Harpe were other tutors who, in addition to physical education, taught Russian language and history, the classics, philosophy, and the humanities. Catherine had directed that her grandson be educated in the manner of the fashionable teachings of the Enlightenment, "according to reason and nature, and on the principles of rational and natural virtue." Rousseau's *Émile* served as the pedagogic handbook of the day. La Harpe carefully guided his young charge through the works of Plato, Demosthenes, Plutarch, Tacitus, Locke, Descartes, and other thinkers. Abstractions such as justice, equality, and the power of reason were painstakingly explored. The boy was made to wrestle with the concepts of liberty and servitude, more than one lesson being given over to such weighty matters as the origins of society and the evils of despotism and serfdom. Philosophic discourse came naturally to La Harpe, and his dutiful pupil permitted himself to become enveloped in the enlightened principles he encountered. But although Alexander appeared enthralled with all this, it is unlikely that a twelve- to fourteen-year-old could fully comprehend and digest much of it. Many of La Harpe's lessons were undoubtedly grasped less as intellectual constructs than as artistic expressions. The Swiss tutor emphasized the humanities; science and mathematics were of secondary importance. Logic, analysis, and problem solving lost out in favor of idealistic concepts and abstract ideas. Historical perspective was totally missing. The training Alexander received from his earliest days focused on how to feel and behave rather than on how to think and act. However attentive and willing to please the boy appeared, he was in fact an uninspired student. One tutor complained of his "ease, tardiness, sloth, and reluctance to make an effort." Still, he managed to acquire a comfortable command of five languages. Whether or not Alexander received full value from the lessons offered by La Harpe, the influence of the Swiss tutor on the youngster was profound. The two established a lifelong friendship, and their correspondence over the years was voluminous. In his outlook, Alexander eventually developed a thoroughly European perspective. He was more at home in the French language than he was in Russian, and in fact, if the conversation was sufficiently sophisticated, Alexander simply could not keep up in the tongue of his own people.

Brought up in the Winter Palace, the young grand duke was surrounded by exquisite paintings, sculpture, mosaics, and priceless collections of books. Even at this time, the palace was virtually a museum. The beauty of the surroundings was not lost on the boy, and his tastes in luxury and the fine arts took root early on. By the time he was thirteen Alexander began to make public appearances, the empress taking great pride in parading the handsome boy on ceremonial occasions. She delighted in providing Alexander with the finest clothes: embroidered waistcoats, fine silk stockings, delicate Italian lace collars, velvet and brocade. Turned out in this finery and with his naturally "enchanting blue eyes, exquisite mouth, and fair silken hair," the young grand duke readily won over the court with his charm and grace. Alexander was not unaware of his physical attributes and, more importantly, of his position in court.

In her determination that Alexander should inherit the throne, Catherine was concerned that the grand duke should be suitably married. The continuation of the dynasty had to be secured above all. Casting her eyes on all the courts of Europe, the empress finally settled on Princess Louise of Baden — Grand Duchess Elizaveta Alexeyevna, as she came to be called. The beautiful and charming princess was then fifteen, one year younger than the groom. On September 28, 1793, a twenty-one-gun salute announced to St. Petersburg that the young couple had married. "It was a marriage between Psyche and Cupid," an ecstatic Catherine wrote later. "They looked like a pair of angels."

Even as a youngster, Alexander was fascinated by women, in whose company he found greater comfort than with men. In the course of his life, a bevy of women came and went, some of whom exerted a significant influence on his development. With Elizaveta, however, the young grand duke was initially shy and ungiving. "He did not come near me," wrote the young wife to her mother, "and he stared at me in an unfriendly manner." But it did not take long for bashfulness to dissipate and fondness to develop. Still, their relationship was more one of friendship than of love. Nonetheless, it survived for more than a quarter century. The apparent intimacy between Alexander and Elizaveta in the tranquillity of their youth and in the quiet weeks of the emperor's last days was by no means part of a lifetime continuum. For the majority of their years together their marriage was rocked by scandalous infidelities, as Alexander took on a succession of mistresses and she sought solace in the arms of lovers. As the years passed, Alexander slept with his wife only as a matter of duty. Sex to him was "a many-roomed mansion" and there was nothing pejorative in multiple partners. From his grandmother in the Winter Palace and his father in Gatchina — each with a variety of partners — the example of marital fidelity simply did not exist. Through most of their married lives, Alexander and Elizaveta lived apart, and only a year or two before their deaths did they come together again.

Catherine had begun to permit Alexander to spend more time at Gatchina with his parents. Eventually he and his brother Constantine grew to be as much a part of the scene in Paul's estate as they were in the Winter Palace. But that decision was not the result of Catherine's having mellowed. On the contrary, by permitting Alexander to see his parents, she had hoped that the Gatchina experience would demonstrate to the youth not only his father's shortcomings but also his unsuitability to reign. At first the young grand duke and his brother had difficulty adjusting to the demands of the Gatchina court, but in time they began to discover in the rough life of the estate certain attractive qualities. Every Saturday the troops were mustered in immaculate full-dress uniform and an elaborate parade was held under Paul's critical eye. Alexander and Constantine each commanded a battalion, which they were required to drill mercilessly into perfection. The highest expectations were had of every individual on parade, and soon Alexander was deriving satisfaction from the successful execution of Paul's intricate military drill. Furthermore, at Gatchina, the young grand duke grew closer to his mother, whom he barely had known in his childhood, and they passed many happy hours together in conversation and in chess. As for his father, Alexander soon discovered that his grandmother's judgments were somewhat severe: Paul, he saw, could be gentle at times, even generous; he was not always cruel, angry, or suspicious. A certain bond began to form between father and son. In the salons of the estate and in the tumble of the barracks, the empress was regarded with open hostility, and the grand duke heard many disparaging comments about her. Eventually, Alexander began to sense that, in the denial of succession of his father, a real injustice had been committed. Some of his respect for his grandmother began to wane, but he kept his opinions to himself and Catherine never knew any better.

Father and grandmother lived in two different worlds: one, within a disciplined military atmosphere, austere, almost puritanical; the other, in an ambience of intellectual and artistic pursuits, with its dissolute, libertine ways. In Gatchina: high boots with spurs, Prussian tricornered hats, trumpets and drums, and much rude barrack-room behavior. At the Winter Palace: wigs, laces and curtsies, fashionable French plays, and witty repartee with elegant jests. One court was rife with jackbooted militarism and strict absolutism; the other with sensitive intellectualism and enlightened liberalism. Life in the two courts stood in stark contrast, and Alexander, the born courtier, appeared, at least on the surface, to move effortlessly between them. La Harpe's lessons, however, bathed in idealism and virtuous expression, found little basis in the reality of either world. What the future Autocrat of All Russia required most in his formative years, he did not receive: an appreciation of hard work and an understanding of the realities of the empire over which he would one day reign.

In his monumental *A History of Russia* V. O. Kluchevsky wrote:

> Alexander never was trained to perceive the existence of actuality, or to adopt anything of a practical outlook. Such perception and such an outlook call for, before they can be acquired, persistent toil in life's constituent dross. And Alexander had no love either for dross or for stubborn, independent drudgery and movement in it. True, he knew well the showy, elegant dross which was to be encountered in the *salon* of his grandmother, even as he did the dross which was to be encountered in his father's barracks; but of the healthy muck in which God bade men immerse themselves with the words, "Earn ye your bread in the sweat of your brows," he had absolutely no knowledge at all. No; his spiritual possessions, when he ascended the throne, were limited solely to a stock of virtuous, lofty aspirations designed instantaneously and automatically and without the least trouble or hindrance, to introduce, as at a magic "Now!" a general freedom and prosperity.

Alexander's character was as complex as it was elusive. Within his lifetime he acquired such appellations as "the sphinx" and "the enigmatic tsar." After his death, some referred to him as "the crowned Hamlet," whereas popularly he became known as "the Blessed." Emotionally and psychologically, he was a person of many and often conflicting contradictions. Exuding humility and humbleness, he also reveled in pomp and circumstance. A declared pacifist who consorted with Quakers, he was an unabashed aficionado of all things military. Hailed by some as a liberal, he was equally damned by others for being a reactionary. Alexander invoked Christian charity and the brotherhood of man, yet like his father he drilled his troops unmercifully and approved the establishment of military colonies, a move that later in his reign would become a political hardball. He could be earnest in serious studies, yet he enjoyed the most trivial frivolity. The inescapable, dominating trait in this chameleonlike character, however, was his open manner and consummate social grace. Innately warm and kind, he knew precisely how to handle every sort of person; few failed to fall under his spell. Alexander was as much a born diplomat as Napoleon was a born general.

Despite his charm, however, Alexander was restless, inconsistent, and above all secretive. Nobody fully understood his mind, including himself. He often said one thing and did another; contradictory views were held with equal conviction. "Like a rudderless ship," wrote one historian, "he veered before the changeable winds of his enthusiasms, which were usually in contradiction with both his own inherited beliefs and the logic of events." But once a decision was made, Alexander stuck to it. He possessed a certain shrewdness and a penchant for hypocrisy. He baffled many of those who worked with him — there was something askew, but nobody could define it. "A cunning Byzantine," Napoleon called him. But then he went on to remark, "Something is missing in his character, but I find it impossible to discover what it is." Chateaubriand declared that Alexander "had a strong soul and a weak character." And Metternich, writing in language that reflects the attitudes of the times, went further: "Alexander's character represents a strange blending of the qualities of a man and the weaknesses of a woman." A onetime French ambassador to St. Petersburg, Count de la Ferronays, added, "If Alexander were to be dressed in female clothes, he would have made a shrewd woman."

In 1816, General Alexander Mikhailovsky-Danilevsky, one of Alexander's close companions on his many travels, wrote of his sovereign as follows:

> I spent . . . evenings in the same room with the emperor, and not being fond of dancing or a seeker of new companions, I was able to observe him constantly and I found little sincerity in his actions. As usual, he was lighthearted and talkative. He danced much and, through his simplicity and openness, he sought to have people forget his rank. His inimitable amiability and extreme charm notwithstanding, I observed him from time to time casting glances, which indicated to me that his soul was troubled and that his innermost thoughts were far removed from the ball and the women who appeared to have captured his attention.

"Something is missing in his character . . ." One element Napoleon found wanting was emotional and spiritual stability; it was the "troubled soul" of which Mikhailovsky-Danilevsky wrote. Particularly in the decade preceding his death, Alexander showed great and increasing restlessness, as though seeking to find refuge from himself. In the period from 1816 to 1825, he made fourteen extensive tours to the outposts of his empire, in addition to trips in the vicinity of St. Petersburg and journeys in Europe to such places as Aix-la-Chapelle in France, Troppau in Austrian Silesia, and Verona in Italy.[†] In fact, during this decade the emperor spent two-thirds of the time away from his capital, and when he was in St. Petersburg, it was mostly in the relative seclusion of Tsarskoye Selo. The peace and tranquillity of the summer residence was com-

---

[†]Aix-la-Chapelle is now Aachen, Germany. Troppau is Opava, Czech Republic.

forting to one who was permeated by the profound inner torment and gnawing sense of inadequacy to the challenges of the throne that Alexander had developed over the years, despite the power in his hands. He plunged more and more deeply into the abyss of religious mysticism and the quest for salvation. Images regularly flashed back to him of that fateful March night in 1801. The murder of his father weighed ever more heavily upon him.

Of all those who exercised spiritual influence on Alexander, the earliest and perhaps most profound was his lifelong friend Prince Alexander Golitsen. As children the two had spent countless hours happily playing in the palaces of St. Petersburg; as adults, they continued to lean on one another. Upon Alexander's accession, Golitsen was appointed Procurator of the Holy Synod, in effect the lay head of the Russian Orthodox Church. The prince's friendship with Alexander was so intimate that, we are told, over a ten-year period he dined with the emperor nearly every night.

In his youth, Golitsen had been viewed as shallow, frivolous, and certainly worldly. After coming to his high church office, however, the prince, much to everyone's surprise, plunged into the study of the Bible. From there, he moved into mysticism. He had formed a close friendship with Rodion Koshelev, Grand Master of the Imperial Court,[†] who was deep into occultism. In addition, Koshelev carried on a wide correspondence with a variety of sects, including the Quakers and the Moravian Brothers, a pietistic sect founded in Romania. Koshelev influenced Golitsen and he in turn Alexander. Pamphlets and tracts on sects, mysticism, and the occult flowed into the emperor's study, each being acknowledged by Alexander with the salutation, "Dear and tender friend," and signed, "Yours, heart and soul in Our Lord the Savior."

Koshelev and Golitsen founded the Russian Bible Society, and Alexander was readily persuaded not only to become its patron but also to donate a large sum of money to it. Under Golitsen's guidance,

---

[†]As such, he was the overseer of the court's daily operations, including daily schedules, appointments to court, and staff supervision.

Alexander immersed himself in the study of Scripture and his attention to the Bible took on a renewed devotion. In early 1813, he wrote,

> My faith is fervent and sincere. It is not possible to describe the value of what I receive from my readings of the Holy Scriptures, which before I knew only superficially . . . Address your prayers to the Supreme Being, to Our Savior and to the Holy Ghost, which emanates from them, so that they will guide me and strengthen me in the only path, which leads to salvation. And pray that they shall give me the strength required to fulfil my earthly tasks, thereby making my people happy . . . it is the cause of hastening the true reign of Jesus Christ that I devote all my earthly glory.

The declared object of the Bible Society was to combat superstition among the populace and to reveal evangelical truth. The Society developed rapidly, and soon two hundred chapters blossomed throughout the empire. Before long, however, and much to the discomfort of the Orthodox Church, it developed a sectlike organization, and offered ecstatic prayer meetings.

Golitsen next became attracted to Freemasonry, and despite his high church office was initiated into the movement. By the eighteenth century, Masonic lodges had become firmly rooted in Russia. Suppressed by Catherine, they were reestablished during Paul's reign and in the first years of Alexander's. Despite the censure of the church, the movement gained in numbers, and by 1815 it was at the height of popularity in political, literary, and court circles. In addition to Golitsen, Grand Duke Constantine was inducted, as were others of the tsar's close friends, including such intimates as Adam Czartoryski, Pavel Strogonov, and Victor Kochubey. These three men, as will be seen, together with Alexander, eventually formed the so-called Committee of Friends, an informal group devoted to discussion of the issues of the day and to strategic planning. Spurred by Golitsen, Alexander was inexorably drawn to the brotherhood — particularly to its secret teaching and mystical aspects. The emperor, of course, as the Lord's Anointed and Head of the Church, could never submit to the secret rites of initiation, and there is no conclusive record that he ever did. Many believe, however, that he had been secretly inducted. In any event, he certainly tolerated the brotherhood, if not favored it.[†]

Golitsen then dabbled with the Skoptsy, a peculiar sect noted for its sadism, over which a certain Kondrati Selivanov presided. Initially the group was known for orgiastic feasts and for self-mutilation. To rid themselves of carnal desire, men were castrated, originally by red-hot pokers but later by sharp blades. Women sought infertility by undergoing gruesome operations and the cutting off of breasts. By the time Golitsen came in contact with the sect, these practices had all but disappeared. Selivanov, perched on a golden throne and proclaiming himself "the dwelling-place of the Holy Ghost," attracted all kinds of people: merchants, professionals, army officers, even ladies of high society. He claimed the gift of prophecy, and his utterings were reported to the emperor, who appeared interested in them. One of Selivanov's disciples, Catherine Tatarinova, eventually broke away from the sect and gathered her own religious followers, whose rites included spinning dances resembling those of the whirling dervishes. The participants spun like tops and in their ecstasy reveled in blissful visions. Tatarinova's mother had been an imperial governess who lived in "grace and bounty" in Mikhailovsky Castle, and now her apartment was made available to the newly founded group. Golitsen frequented their meetings, and Alexander was known to have consulted Tatarinova on interpretations of certain biblical passages. He provided her with a hefty pension.

In his search for spiritual truths, Alexander turned to most anyone — Golitsen, Koshelev, Tatarinova, whoever — who bore a divine message or offered the gift of revelation. Perhaps the most extraordinary of all his spiritual advisers was Baroness Julie von

---

[†]In 1822, however, Alexander banned the Masonic lodges, along with all other secret societies.

Krüdener, who firmly held the emperor under her spell for a brief but eventful year in 1815. A Livonian by birth, Krüdener was the widow of an eminent Russian diplomat. During her married life she had become well connected within many of the glittering courts of Europe. Within a couple of years of her husband's death in 1804, however, she had withdrawn from society and taken up spiritualism. She was "converted" by a Moravian cobbler, under whose guidance she discovered her "mission": to act as an intermediary between the material and spiritual worlds. In Germany she chanced upon a simple peasant, one Adam Müller, whose gift of prophecy was well-known. Muller informed the ecstatic baroness that a man from the north, "from the rising sun would soon arise to destroy the anti-Christ [Napoleon] and that the true millennium would then begin."

For over a decade, the baroness searched Europe in vain for the man "from the rising sun." At a court soiree in Heilbronn she met Alexander and wasted little time in enchanting him. She instructed him to surrender his soul to God and revealed to him his formidable destiny. What, everyone wondered, could he possibly see in the singularly unattractive, blotched, elderly, and bewigged baroness?

What Alexander saw in Julie von Krüdener had nothing to do with the physical. In her he found inspiration; she was both a guide and a judge. She admonished him to repent. "You have not yet approached God . . . you have yet to renounce your sins and you have not humbled yourself before Christ. That is why you have not found inner peace!" Alexander inferred from her words the sin of parricide, and the rekindled memory of Tsar Paul's death shattered him. No one had ever dared to speak to Alexander as Krüdener had, and yet he rejoiced in her utterings. "All your words have found a place in my heart!" he exclaimed, thanking the baroness for being forthright and honest. So rapidly was he taken by this incredible woman that he asked her to join his court and follow him on his travels. He desperately required the spiritual sustenance she offered. In the months that followed, the baroness delivered uplifting sermons and engaged in edifying conversation. She interpreted Scripture as nobody else, chastised the emperor for his errors, and roundly denounced his pride. For slightly over a year she was Alexander's closest companion, holding complete sway over him, allowing him to do little without consulting her. He was so taken by her, in fact, that at one time he paraded a vast portion of his army in a special military review around altars especially constructed for her benefit. Eventually, however, the ardor of this bizarre relationship with the prophetess waned, particularly after it was reported to Alexander that Krüdener was attributing to her influence many of the Russian emperor's acts, not the least of which being the Holy Alliance. By 1822, the hostility toward the baroness on the part of the church's hierarchy and the court was such that Alexander broke off the relationship and ordered her barred from court. Subsequently, she retired to the Crimea and died there on Christmas Day, 1824.

Alexander's spiritual life, therefore, was a kaleidoscope of revelations, mystical experiences, religious encounters, and piety of diverse nature. "After the regicide," writes the biographer Henri Troyat, "Alexander had felt terror, despair, and remorse, but without coming closer to God. Having himself become emperor and as such administrative head of the Orthodox Church, he had proved respectful of rites, no doubt, but indifferent to dogma." Increasingly he became convinced that the elusive peace he so desperately sought could only be won in quiet retirement.

Long before coming to the throne, Alexander had already been concerned about his future. As early as 1796 he confessed to his friend and confidant Count Victor Kochubey, "The thought that one day (and that day is not far off), when I shall be placed, thanks to fate, at the head of the empire, makes my very hair stand on end. I am not made to govern . . . I am so unhappy . . . The day will come, I say again, when they will salute me Caesar! Sad lot for a man who wishes to live!"

On May 10, 1796, the eighteen-year-old tsarevich wrote Kochubey again. This time his words are alarmingly desperate and frank. On the one hand, his letter is telling, that of a romanticizing youth swept up in idealism. On the other hand, it is an honest assessment of the situation as he saw it at the time. But the point is that, even as a youth, Alexander decried and deplored the future that awaited him.

I repeat, my dear friend, what I told you earlier: I am quite displeased with my situation. It's entirely too brilliant for my character, which is more drawn to quiet and tranquillity. Court life is not for me. I suffer every time I must appear before the court.

My blood riles every time I come in contact with those who seek ostentatious distinctions, which to my mind are totally worthless. I feel miserable before such people, whom one wouldn't wish to have near one even as waiters. At the same time, these same people occupy the most important positions in the Empire, Z . . . , Y . . . , B . . . , M . . . , both S . . . , for example, and many others whom it's not even worth mentioning — they who are haughty with those of lower rank but cringe before them out of fear. In short, my dearest friend, I am aware that I was not born for the lofty position I now occupy and even less for the one that awaits me in the future. I have sworn to myself to renounce it, one way or another.

So, my dearest friend, this is an important secret that I wished to share with you for quite some time. Obviously, it's unnecessary for me to ask that it not be passed on to anyone. As well you might understand. I could pay for it dearly. I asked Mr. Garrik [a valet] to burn this letter if he was unable to deliver it to you personally.

I have considered this matter from all viewpoints. I must tell you that the first thoughts along these lines developed before I ever met you. Since then I have not lost time in coming to my decision.

Our affairs are in unbelievable disarray. Embezzlement is everywhere; all departments are badly administered; order everywhere seems to have been banished. But the empire does not cease in further expansion. How is it therefore possible for one man to govern it, and still more, to remove all its abuses? To my mind, it is beyond the powers of a genius, much less of a man of ordinary capacities, like me . . . My plan is, once having renounced this scabrous place (I cannot say when), to settle with my wife on the banks of the Rhine to live the life of a private citizen, devoting my time to the company of my friends and to the study of nature.

You laugh at me and I know that you'll judge me. However, I can't do otherwise, for my first principle in life is to have a clear conscience. Could it be at peace if I took upon myself tasks that are beyond my strengths? There, my dear friend, all this I wanted to lay before you for a long time. Now, having laid everything before you, there remains for me only to let you know that wherever I might be, happy or unhappy, rich or poor, your friendship for me will always remain one of the greatest consolations for me. And mine, for you, please believe, will end only with my death.

Life between the two courts — one in St. Petersburg and the other at Gatchina — brought a confusing duality into Alexander's life, one that took a toll. Rather than becoming strengthened by the experience, he was weakened. Flexibility and adaptability became so much a part of his life that often he did not know what he actually wanted or which path to follow. Vacillation and indecisiveness increasingly became a part of his character. As discussion of Paul's possible disinheritance began to surface openly in the salons of St. Petersburg, Alexander became more and more terrified at the prospect of one day assuming the throne. He spoke repeatedly to family and close friends of his intention to renounce any rights, of his fervent desire to retire to some tranquil corner of Europe or America where he could lead a simple, pastoral life of meditation and thought.

But by 1803, two years into his reign, the lack of confidence reflected in the Kochubey letters had dissipated. To his surprise,

Alexander found himself quite at home with "the lofty position" he now occupied, which had so frightened him earlier. His "dear friend," in fact, now stood at his side as one of the Committee of Friends that fervently plotted the rise of the new Russia. Alexander was beginning to feel that it might be possible, after all, "for one man to administer the state, even more to reform it and to abolish all the ingrained evil." After Paul's dark reign, the country was reveling in the fresh climate created by its new ruler. Yet, despite his brilliant debut and idealistic visions for the country, in 1803 Alexander wrote to La Harpe, now living in retirement in Switzerland, "When Providence shall bless me with bringing Russia to the degree of prosperity that I desire, I shall deem it my first duty to cast aside the burden of rule and to retire to some remote corner of Europe whence I shall be able to watch and to enjoy the felicity of my country."

Before coming to the throne, after the accession — in fact throughout his reign — Alexander spoke repeatedly of abdication and retirement. His 1796 and 1803 letters were not isolated pronouncements. As late as 1817, at a large dinner party in Kiev, Alexander declared, "When anyone has the honor to be the head of a nation such as ours, he must have the courage to face danger. He must not remain in place any longer than his physical strength will permit him nor, one might say, longer than he is able to mount his horse. After this he must retire. As for me, I feel well at present, but in ten or fifteen years, when I shall be fifty, then . . ."

In 1819, Alexander's sister, Grand Duchess Helene, who was married to Frederick Louis of Mecklenburg-Schwerin, noted in her diary that during an intimate family meal, Alexander announced, "I have decided to free myself from my present obligations and to retire from this sort of life. More than ever, Europe needs young monarchs, strong and energetic, and I am no longer what I was. Therefore, I deem it my duty to retire in time."

That same year Alexander informed Constantine, "I must tell you, brother, that I want to abdicate. I am tired and I have little strength to shoulder the burden of government . . . when the time to abdicate comes, I shall inform you and you will then tell Mother."

Nicholas's wife, Grand Duchess Alexandra, noted in her diary of a meeting held in the summer of 1819 between her husband and Alexander, at which she was present. For the first time they learned of Constantine's intention to renounce his rights to the throne.

Further, at the time of her coronation, the grand duchess entered in her diary, on August 15, 1826, "As we appeared before the people, I recalled the words of the deceased emperor when he spoke of his abdication: 'Oh, what joy I will have when you [as empress] will be driven past me and I, as part of the crowd, will raise my hat and cry "Godspeed!"'"

In 1825, the Prince of Orange, future King William II of the Netherlands, the husband of Alexander's sister Anna, visited St. Petersburg. The intimate friendship between the tsar and his brother-in-law was touching. "I have great confidence in William's heart and head," declared Alexander. And Anna wrote of William, "He has the deep feeling of being misunderstood [at home] and often ill-appreciated. He finds in you, dear brother, more kindness and more support than in his family." So taken was William with Alexander that in announcing the birth of his son, he declared his decision to name the boy after him, "since the name brings such happiness."† Early in the St. Petersburg visit, Alexander confided in William his intention to abdicate and to retire from the world. "The prince was horrified and tried to dissuade the emperor from such action. But Alexander stood firm in his intention and the efforts of the prince came to naught; he was unsuccessful in budging the emperor from his determination."

---

†The current Prince of Orange also bears the name William Alexander. His mother, Queen Beatrix, is the great-granddaughter of William III, son of Anna Pavlovna, who was the first Romanov bride to leave Russia for a non-Germanic king. Thus today the Dutch queen is the reigning sovereign closest in descent from Catherine the Great and Paul I. And, speaking of names: Queen Victoria was in fact named Alexandrina Victoria, after Alexander I, her godfather.

6

A Riddle Wrapped
in a Mystery

By THE EVENTS OF that fateful night in March 1801, Alexander acceded to the throne of one of the greatest empires in modern history. Through the determined efforts of Peter the Great and Catherine, the already enormous realm had been further expanded and was brought into the European family of nations. It seemed a land without limit and its population was as diverse as its topography and climatic condition.

Russia has invariably held a peculiar fascination for the Western European, and coming to terms with it has been an ongoing challenge — then and now. Russia, wrote Winston Churchill, is "a riddle, wrapped in a mystery inside an enigma." For the European of the nineteenth century it was particularly enigmatic. Its vast expanse, its extremes of climate and nature, its millions of single-minded serfs, the fathomless Slavic character — all this stretched the Western imagination. There was something un-European, strange, and magnificently terrible about the relatively unknown land that rolled east, seemingly without limit.

Such was the empire that Alexander spontaneously rejected upon learning of his father's murder. "I resign my power and give it to whomever wants it!" That initial hysteria, however, was short-lived, and within hours he had taken hold of himself and the situation. He would go on to rule effectively for the next twenty-four years. Many excellent biographies have detailed and explored the tsar's manifold political successes and failures, as well as the decisive role he played in the Napoleonic Wars. Our task here is to try and ferret out the truth about his death in 1825.

Still, to understand the sovereign's character and frame of mind during the last months of his life, one must at least summarize certain key aspects of the reign. By the autumn of 1825 Alexander was in a fragile psychological state and spiritual turmoil. And much of this had to do with the conditions in which his country found itself — largely through his own actions, or rather lack of action.

Alexander's reign might be viewed as three periods of peace broken by two wars against Napoleon. However devastating these conflicts were, they propelled the tsar conspicuously onto center stage of European politics and international affairs. The periods of peace in themselves were unsettled, as they seesawed erratically between idealistically tinged liberalism and reactionary conservatism.

The beginning of Alexander's reign was brilliant. The day following his father's death, as we have seen, the new sovereign, by the stroke of a pen, in a single ukase, brought profound changes to the country: freedom of the press was restored, as was the right of assembly; political prisoners were released from jail and the right of travel, which had been severely restricted under Paul, was restored. The dreaded Secret Chancellery, in charge of state security, was soon abolished. The enlightened ideas of Alexander's youth, so carefully inculcated by La Harpe, found form at the very start of his reign.

Within days of his accession to the throne, the young emperor gathered about him a select circle of four friends, all liberal, reform-minded thinkers. Count Pavel Strogonov had lived in Paris during the French Revolution and was a member of the

Jacobin Club. Nicholas Novosiltsev was a confirmed Anglophile and an enthusiastic supporter of the British parliamentary system. Prince Adam Czartoryski was a liberal and a well-known Polish patriot, and Count Victor Kochubey was a brilliant, forward-thinking Russian who had received much of his education in England. The "Committee of Friends" or the "Secret Committee," as they were then called, met regularly at leisurely dinners, after which they adjourned to a drawing room where, over coffee and brandy, they debated the issues of the empire.

Constitutionalism and serfdom were the two burning concerns that monopolized these deliberations. As for the first, the Committee concluded that while a constitution was highly desirable, it could not be framed at the expense of the emperor's autocratic power. On the second, they enthusiastically agreed that serfdom was evil, but were in accord that little could be done about it, for fear of alienating the nobility.

The Committee of Friends, as well as similar groups in the reigns that followed, clearly identified Russia's problems, but they all lacked the capacity, or the will, to deal with them except under extreme pressure. Alexander and his successors were well aware not only of the issues but also of the solutions. The autocratic sovereigns, furthermore, possessed the power to force these solutions if only they possessed the fiber to do so. The tragedy of that massive and magnificent country was that it lacked the collective will to tackle the issues.

Although the Committee failed to come to terms with the two foremost concerns of the day, it did manage a reorganization of government administration, one that flirted with a separation of power. Peter the Great had established an administrative structure that, apart from foreign affairs and the military, functioned poorly. By 1801, the instruments of government had pretty well broken down and things were chaotic. Five years earlier, in 1796, Alexander had complained to Kochubey, "Our affairs are in unbelievable disarray . . . order seems to have been expelled." Eighteen months into his reign, Alexander issued an ukase that brought a number of significant administrative changes to the structure of government, thus giving substance to the Committee's deliberations. Central to these was the establishment of eight distinct ministries: Finance, Foreign Affairs, War, Navy, Justice, Education, Interior, and Commerce (later a Ministry of Police was established but then abolished). A minister headed each division and had direct access to the tsar. Together they formed the Committee of Ministers, an advisory body to the tsar. While this group had the power of counsel and recommendation, it was not empowered to formulate policy. The emperor continued as chief legislator as well as chief executive. The new ministries consolidated their functions surprisingly quickly, and the overall efficiency of government improved significantly. An imperial bureaucracy had now been established that functioned reasonably well until 1917 without impinging on the power of the tsar.

Alexander was well versed in the 1789 French Declaration of the Rights of Man — "Men are born and remain free in rights" — that committed France to a constitutional government within which were provisions for an elected assembly and a separation of powers — and, it might be added, for the representatives of the people to fix taxes. In America, President Jefferson learned of the early reforms undertaken by the tsar and sought to offer encouragement. In their admiration for each other, the two heads of state developed a considerable correspondence. Jefferson wrote of Alexander, "The apparition of such a man on a throne is one of the phenomena which will distinguish the present epoch so remarkable in the history of man. But he must have a herculean task to devise and establish the means of securing freedom and happiness to those who are not capable of taking care of themselves. Some preparation seems necessary to qualify the body of a nation for self-government."

Encouraged from abroad and inspired by the Declaration of Rights, Alexander established a commission to draft a new code of laws and to review the powers of the Senate, particularly as they might relate to taxation. In Russia he received support from many quarters, but particularly from Pahlen and his coterie of co-conspirators. The men who had engineered Tsar Paul's downfall and assassination remained active in court, participating in their various capacities. Alexander's involvement, however passive, mitigated their situation; trial or punishment was out of the question. In the end, however, one by one the principals found themselves disgraced and exiled. In October 1801, Panin was sent to his estates; in December, Platon Zubov was posted abroad; Bennigsen was ordered away from St. Petersburg. Pahlen outlasted the others, but then he too found himself exiled from St. Petersburg in June 1802. During the first couple of months of Alexander's reign, Pahlen exerted a commanding influence on the young sovereign, so much so that many people maintained he was the one who was really in charge. It was Pahlen, the Zubovs, and Panin who pressed hard for a constitution, and as long as they were in court Alexander appeared committed to constitutional reform.

By June however, Alexander was sufficiently self-confident to dispense with Pahlen's services and force him to retire to his estates. He now reversed himself on most of the issues his avowed liberalism had espoused. The proposals he had advocated for a new code of law, for increased powers for the Senate, and for the administration of taxes were quietly shelved. It was one thing to give the country a constitution; it was another matter to share power with elected representatives. As tsarevich, Alexander had told La Harpe that he was prepared to lay down his life for the gift of a constitution. Now he balked and all was put aside.

In the period of peace between two Napoleonic Wars, from 1807 to 1811, fresh initiatives were taken to frame a constitution. This time the remarkably talented Mikhail Mikhailovich Speransky stood at Alexander's side, a visionary and reformer whose indelible stamp shines conspicuously from the pages of Russian history. Speransky was the son of a village priest from the province of Vladimir, and very early on proved to be an unusually capable student, with a particular talent for languages. By the time he had completed studies he knew Latin and Greek, had a perfect command of French, and possessed a flawless mastery of his native tongue, both written and spoken. By his honed intellectual curiosity and gift for analytical thought, in his youth he acquired a close familarity with a wide range of thinkers, such as Voltaire, Diderot, Newton, Locke, Kant, and Benjamin Franklin. Young Mikhail began his career as a tutor to the children of Prince Kurakin, a high functionary in the Ministry of Foreign Affairs. Speransky's intelligence and talents were quickly recognized, and Kurakin moved him into civil service, where he rose meteorically.

By 1806, Speransky had become personally known to Alexander, whom he impressed profoundly by his breadth of mind, efficiency, and attention to detail. The two often spent time together discussing matters of state, eventually coming to focus on the modernization of government administrative structures. The tsar was so taken by Speransky and his ideas that he appointed him deputy minister of justice and later raised him to secretary of state. The new secretary was given the onerous commission of first drawing up a code of laws, and then formulating a plan for the complete reorganization of the government from top to bottom. After two years of unremitting toil, the inspired secretary of state submitted to the tsar a comprehensive blueprint for just such a project.

Based on the French constitution of 1789, the plan provided for a centralization of power in the sovereign through fresh administrative structures. Speransky proposed that the operation of the empire be conducted by a legislative body, the State Duma; a judiciary, the Senate; and an executive in the form of a council of ministers. A series of legislative-type bodies commencing at the lowest cantonal level and progressing through provincial levels would culminate in the State Duma, the supreme legislative authority. No law could be promulgated without the majority vote of the State Duma, and, once it was passed by the emperor, the government would be required to conform to it. A State Council, drawn from the aristocracy, would advise the emperor on draft laws for consideration by the Duma. The same body would also oversee the various administrative branches of government in the execution of the country's laws. The proposal was basically a pyramidal structure, with the emperor at the apex, immediately below whom was the State Council, then the Dumas and the ministries. In effect, Speransky was proposing a constitutional monarchy.

Alexander received Speransky's proposals with enthusiasm and assured the faithful minister that he intended to adopt them. "Such ideas have never before been proclaimed from the throne of Russia," he declared. Having thanked his dedicated adviser, the emperor stowed away the document, kept it entirely to himself, and put into effect only minor portions of the recommendations. On New Year's Day, 1810, he promulgated the formation of the State Council and appointed Speransky its chairman. In time the Council developed into an important advisory body that lasted until 1906, to which Russian sovereigns frequently turned for counsel on proposed laws. But with the formation of the Council, Alexander stopped. The balance of Speransky's inspired work continued to rest on the emperor's shelf.

Speransky was at the height of his career, and the power and influence he wielded were the envy of St. Petersburg. The Sardinian ambassador described him as "the almighty Speransky, secretary-general of the empire, and in fact the prime minister, if not *the* minister." He had immediate access to the emperor and dined alone with him on frequent occasions. His intimacy with the sovereign was probably greater than that of the tsar's old friends of the now-defunct Committee of Friends. The spectacular rise of this impoverished provincial from Vladimir was more than the jealous courtiers could tolerate. It was inevitable that the great man was headed for a fall, and tumble he did. Grand Duke Nikolai Mikhailovich wrote of Speransky's decline from power:

> It is in the personal relationship between Alexander and Speransky, daily and genuine relations full of living trust, that one should look for the cause of misunderstanding that eventually led to the final dishonor. By lavishing such incredible favor on one person, by allowing him such

power, having placed Speransky at the head of a variety of institutions, from Chancery of the Empire to Chancellor of the University of Äbo, Alexander had alienated all the people, without exception. Speransky found himself in isolation. He had no friends and all about him enemies lurked. But he paid not the least heed to enemies (in fact he was totally naive in withstanding intrigue) and did not look for friends; all his talent, creative energy and the whole of himself he gave over to his emperor. All the time he firmly trusted in his protection and gave not the slightest thought to the possibility of losing it. For two years all went smoothly, everything and everybody submitting and bowing to the tsar's favorite, a former seminarian and son of a poor priest. At that time Speransky indeed governed Russia.

After Alexander decreed that anyone wishing to join the civil service had first to pass entrance examinations, there was a vehement outcry from the embittered aristocracy, who rightly blamed Speransky for conceiving the ukase. This was followed by a further decree that titles of nobility awarded for service would not automatically confer rank within the civil service. Scores of lesser nobles, many of whose education was limited, now had the door of advancement virtually closed to them. Rumor circulated that Speransky was also advocating the abolition of serfdom. Then word spread that a tax was to be imposed on the nobility, and that high duties on luxury goods were about to be instituted.

From all quarters, Alexander's secretary of state came under vicious attack. Even Speransky's French-imported clothing and lavish lifestyle were scrutinized. "The arrogant upstart has pretensions of equality with us! And furthermore, he wishes to ruin us!" cried the envious critics. The scorn and vitriol culminated in the accusation of treason — Speransky, after all, had used French legislation as the basis of his varied reforms; he was Napoleon's admirer. What, in fact, the maligned minister had once declared was, "I look upon the emperor of the French not as the victor at

Wagram, but as the restorer of religion, the author of the Civil Code, and the creator of an exemplary administration, unequaled anywhere in the world." Treason, indeed. No doubt the nobles had something serious to worry about if Speransky had his way, and their outcry against him was as understandable as it was predictable.

One influential historian of the time, Nikolai Karamzin, indignantly pontificated, "Russia really does not need solemnly to acknowledge her ignorance before all of Europe and to bend graying heads over a volume devised by a few perfidious lawyers and Jacobins. Our political principles do not find their inspiration in Napoleon's Code of Laws or in an encyclopedia published in Paris, but by another encyclopedia infinitely older, the Bible." He reminded the emperor that the best government for Russia lay not in radical reforms but in a good autocrat. The vehement reaction from the nobles was as much out of fear as it was of resentment. A peculiarity of the Russian character is to resent the success of a neighbor, particularly if he is an outsider. Speransky was an outsider.

So hysterical and unrelenting were the attacks on Alexander's councillor and right hand that Alexander soon came to feel that his own popularity was in jeopardy; public opinion of him was souring. Some of the accusations, furthermore, appeared to have enough credibility to cast doubt on Speransky's integrity and faithfulness. In early 1812 Baron Armfelt, a close adviser to Alexander on military matters, told him, "Guilty or not, Speransky must be sacrificed. It is indispensable to rally the nation together around the chief of state. The war we are about to engage in with Napoleon is not an ordinary war. If we are not to succumb, it is essential that we make it a national war." The baron went on to add, "Observe how the public attacks him; let them uncover a conspiracy; that is precisely what we need!"

In March 1812, Alexander received word that the secretary of state had allegedly established a burgeoning network of personal secret agents, not only abroad but within the empire, agents who spied on the minister of foreign affairs, among others. This imprudence was too much to bear, and when the rumor spread throughout the city, Alexander determined to act firmly, if not through conviction then through expediency. The emperor summoned Speransky and accosted him with the allegation. Speransky did not deny it, but defended himself by pleading that Alexander had recently instructed him to become well informed on the activities of his diplomatic corps, "using all necessary means." He had further been requested to report confidentially on anything untoward. The secretary protested that in no way was he acting treacherously; the accusations, he claimed, were fabrications and pure slander.

For two hours the exchanges between tsar and minister continued, and those waiting in the anteroom heard Speransky's voice fade from a loud, clear tone to a hoarse whisper. "I sympathize with you in your dilemma, Mikhail Mikhailovich, but you must understand my situation," Alexander pleaded. "The enemy is knocking at the doors of my empire. I realize that the accusations levied against you are outrageously exaggerated, but the situation in which you find yourself, placed there by the suspicions you have aroused by your behavior and the various remarks you have permitted yourself to make, what can I do? You must understand: it is essential that I do not appear weak in the eyes of my subjects by continuing to put my faith in a person under suspicion of treason . . . even an autocratic ruler must heed the voice of public opinion."

And then Alexander brought the discussion to an end. "I am exceedingly sorry, Mikhail Mikhailovich, but I must sacrifice you for the sake of bringing our Russian people together in order to face the deadly danger before us . . . sovereigns cannot be judged by standards of private morality. Politics requires me to perform certain duties, unpleasant as they may be, in cold blood, even when my heart condemns it. Nevertheless, my severity, necessitated by the situation, will be tempered by generosity. You will reside in Nizhni-Novgorod,[†] not an unpleasant town, on the banks of the Volga. Your pension will be sufficient to cover the expenses of a

---

[†]Renamed Gorky under the Soviets, it has reverted to its original name.

household worthy of a former minister, and you may take with you all your belongings, including your vast library. Farewell, my dear friend."

Eventually a shaken and pale Speransky emerged from the emperor's study accompanied by an equally upset Alexander — both were in tears. The emperor embraced his friend warmly and with great emotion said, "Farewell, once again!"

Speransky, clutching his portfolio under his trembling arm, turned and walked out of the palace. On his arrival home, General Alexander Balashov, the minister of police, one of those who for months had vilified him, greeted him. The official was there to seal Speransky's documents and to attend to his departure out of the city. Too distraught even to face his wife and children, Speransky gathered a few belongings and within an hour was on his way out of the capital, under escort to his place of exile in Nizhni-Novgorod. The all-powerful minister was no more.

After Speransky left him, Alexander reentered his study and closed the door. Sometime later he summoned Prince Golitsen. The tsar was in tears, and when Golitsen inquired about the reason for his grief, Alexander replied, "If you had your arm cut off, you would doubtless scream and howl from the pain. I have lost Speransky; he was my right arm." It was a tremendous personal sacrifice — all in patriotic duty.

"Politics requires me to perform certain duties," he added, "even when my heart condemns it." Doubtless, in these words to his faithful friend he was referring to the memories of Mikhailovsky Castle, which continued to haunt him, as we know from a number of contemporary accounts.

The brilliance of Speransky's meteoric passage across the pages of Russian history faded almost as suddenly as it appeared. With his tragic fall, the promising period of liberal reform in Russia came to an abrupt halt and the country found itself unchanged in its autocracy. In the face of solid court opposition, Alexander, the self-styled liberal reformer, proved himself incapable of carrying through decisively what he knew in his heart was right. An outpouring of congratulations on his action, however, flowed into the Winter Palace from all corners of the country. "What a glorious day," wrote a contemporary. "God has shown his compassion and our archenemy has been overcome . . . Speransky aimed to deliver our emperor and our country into the hands of our worst enemies."

Such was the passage of the liberal and reform-minded tsar at a time when war clouds were gathering in the west. Speransky's inspired proposal was a workable scheme. Had Alexander embraced it fully, perhaps future Marxist-Leninist ideas would have found Russian soil insufficiently fertile and the evolution of twentieth-century history might have been very different.

By 1812, Napoleon's conquest of most of the Continent was complete, and intelligence reports now began to filter into St. Petersburg that the insufferable Corsican was massing armies on the frontiers of Poland and Prussia. Danzig was being developed into a massive military depot. There was no mistaking Napoleon's intention — he was looking east.

By the time Alexander came to the throne in 1801, Napoleon had successfully consolidated his coup d'état. Within months of Alexander's coronation he was named Consul for Life, and two years later he had himself crowned emperor. The great battles of the Pyramids, the Nile, Zurich, Novi, and Marengo had already been won. Among other territories, Napoleon's burgeoning empire now included Italy, Belgium, Holland, Switzerland, and the west bank of the Rhine — all were under his direct or indirect control.

On December 2, 1804, Napoleon's magnificent coronation was solemnized in Paris's Cathedral of Notre Dame. The pope was brought in from Rome for the colorful consecration, but at the climatic moment of the service, following the example of Charlemagne, Napoleon grasped the crown from the hands of the Holy Father and placed it on his own head.

As emperor, he now pressed on with the work of expanding his empire. One war followed another: with Russia in 1805, and with Austria that same year. The war with Britain had been going steadily since 1803. The battles of Austerlitz (Russia-Austria), Jena and Auerstädt (Prussia), Friedland (Russia), the Peninsular Campaign (Britain-Spain-Portugal), and Wagram (Austria) were all victories for the apparently invincible Napoleon. In just over a decade since his coronation, Bonaparte had expanded his empire to include Spain, the Papal States, Naples, Illyria, the Rhine States, Bavaria, Prussia, the Duchy of Warsaw, Austria, Denmark, and Norway. Through direct conquest, arranged control, or alliances, virtually all of Western Europe was now under his domination.

7

The Defeat of the
Grande Armée†

ON JUNE 23, 1812, Alexander attended a glittering gathering under
the midnight sun in the park of the home of General Bennigsen in
Lithuania's capital, Vilnius. "The evening was beautiful," wrote
Countess Choiseul-Gouffier, "the whole place was ornamented
with orange trees in full bloom which perfumed the air . . . the
musicians of the imperial guard played choice bits of music in different parts of the grounds. The sight of this brilliant assembly of beau-
tifully dressed women and the military in splendid uniforms with
their diamond decorations; this company scattered over the green
lawns, the old trees forming masses of verdure; the villa that
reflected in its winding course the blue heavens and the colors of the
setting sun; the hills whose tops disappeared in the soft clouds — all
offered a sense of enchantment. But when the emperor appeared, no
one saw anything but him."

Over this seemingly idyllic gathering, however, war clouds
hung heavy. French armies were assembled on the borders of the
empire — some within half a day's ride of Bennigsen's garden
party — and the threat of invasion was alarmingly real. Over the

---

†The dates in this chapter are reported according to the Gregorian (Western) calendar.

years, as Napoleon's successes and power grew, Alexander had drawn ever closer to Britain. In 1805, he had consolidated the friendship by a formal alliance, one that was joined by Austria and Sweden. Within months, the alliance found itself at war with France, and at the battle of Austerlitz on December 2, 1805, the Austro-Russian forces suffered a resounding defeat. Austria sued for peace, and Alexander, who headed the allied forces, re-treated — only the vast distances of his immense country saved Russia. The state of war between the two countries continued, but hostilities were in abeyance for some eighteen months. Then, in 1806, Napoleon attacked Prussia, took Berlin, and proclaimed a blockade of Great Britain, known as the Continental System. His aim was to close the Continent to British trade, effectively isolat-ing and impoverishing the island nation and thus bringing it to heel. Once more, Alexander committed his troops to a stand against the insatiably ambitious Napoleon. On June 14, the two armies met at the battle of Friedland and again the French proved victorious, with the Russians forced into retreat.

By his victory, the triumphant Napoleon added fresh lands to his burgeoning empire — all of Prussia, to the very border of Lithuania. The French Empire now abutted the Russian Empire, and only the narrow Niemen River separated the two. For the moment, Napoleon was pleased to rest on his laurels — in fact, he desired an armistice as much as Alexander did. The Russian army was exhausted and demoralized; little assistance or encourage-ment came from Britain or Sweden; and, most importantly, there was virtually no patriotic support from within Russia — the pop-ulation was suffering from war fatigue. As for Napoleon, his pri-ority was to consolidate the organization of central Europe and to nail down the isolation of the archenemy, Britain. At this juncture, he had no heart to pursue the Russians in what would have been a lengthy and costly undertaking.

Emissaries from the opposing camps were exchanged to engage in preliminary discussions of peace. Napoleon received Alexander's envoy, Prince Dimitri Lobanov-Rostovsky, a seasoned field commander, and at a dinner he proposed a toast to the tsar with the words, "The interests of our two empires are reciprocal and call for an alliance between them." Pointing to the Niemen River on a wall map, he declared, "Here is the boundary of our two empires. Your master must dominate one side and I the other."

Prior to his mission, Lobanov-Rostovsky had met with the tsar to receive instructions. "In a mixture of bravado, idealism, vanity and sheer cheek," observes the British historian Janet Hartley, Alexander had ordered his envoy as follows:

> Inform [Napoleon] that this union between France and Russia has consistantly been what I desire. I am convinced that this alone will assure the happiness and tranquillity of the world. An entirely fresh system must replace the one that we have had to date and I flatter myself in thinking that we can readily come to an understanding with the Emperor Napoleon, provided that we meet without intermediaries. A permanent peace might well be concluded between us within a few days.

The envoys conferred and, after elaborate negotiations, details were hammered out for a face-to-face meeting of the two sovereigns. On June 25, Napoleon and Alexander met and embraced in a pavilion on a hastily erected raft that was anchored in the middle of the Niemen, the closest thing at hand to neutral territory. Following an hour and a half of closeted conversation, the two emperors emerged, wreathed in smiles and radiating goodwill. Both seemed enchanted with each other — Alexander with Napoleon's decisiveness, and Napoleon with Alexander's charm. "If only I had seen him sooner!" lamented Alexander. "The veil is torn aside and the time of error past." That night Napoleon wrote to his wife, Empress Josephine, "I have just seen Emperor Alexander. I am well pleased with him. He is a handsome and good young emperor. There is more spirit in him than one usually imagines."

For over a week, the two sovereigns and their advisers conferred and negotiated at the nearby city of Tilsit, amid a setting of colorful parades, inspections, and carefree excursions into the countryside. From time to time, as though by afterthought, King Frederick William, in whose Prussian territory all this was taking place, was invited to join the social activities; he was excluded, however, from the deliberations. The formal treaties were agreed upon, and on July 9 they were ceremoniously signed by the two rulers: France and Russia had became formally linked in an alliance. Alexander bestowed on Napoleon the riband and glittering Cross of St. Andrew, and the French emperor reciprocated by removing from his own chest the Grand Cross of the Legion of Honor, which he draped over the tsar. Amid embraces, cheers, and gun salutes, the two emperors parted company. But beneath the surface of all that magnificent pomp and warm bonhomie, suspicion and distrust continued to simmer in both camps. How genuinely sincere and reliable was the other side? Whatever the mistrust, peace between the two nations had been established, at least for the moment.

In February 1811, Napoleon made an unusually frank declaration to Joseph Fouché, Duke of Otranto, the man who, as minister of police, really guaranteed the tranquillity of France while his emperor waged war abroad. "How can I help it if a great power drives me on to become dictator of the world? . . . I have not yet fulfilled my mission, and I mean to end what I have begun. We need a European code of law, a European court of appeal, a uniform coinage, a common system of weights and measures. The same law must run throughout Europe. I shall fuse all the nations into one . . . This, my lord duke, is the only solution that pleases me." (First-person singular aside, it was a statement of remarkable vision and eerie prophecy.)

By the time Napoleon passed this remark to Fouche, the Franco-Russian alliance of Tilsit had all but disintegrated, and in European capitals speculation was rife, not on whether there would be a war between the two nations, but rather when it would start. Napoleon's political ambitions were transparently in opposition to Russia's territorial security. Furthermore, the opposing economic interests of the two countries were in fundamental conflict, with the Continental System a particular source of vexation. Napoleon sought steadfastly to maintain and strengthen the blockade of Britain, but for Russia the system was proving painfully damaging to its trade and prosperity. In December 1810, Alexander withdrew his support of the blockade by announcing the imposition of heavy duties on goods imported by land and the reduction of duties on goods arriving by sea. This, in effect, penalized French exports — particulary wines and luxury goods — and favored British imports, goods that all along had been arriving with impunity on ships of the neutral United States (in 1810, 120 American vessels discharged cargo in St. Petersburg alone). In view of these fundamental differences, whatever minor contretemps arose in the relations between the two countries invariably became exacerbated and mushroomed into insurmountable obstacles. The collapse of the treaties of Tilsit seemed inevitable — and crumble they did on that balmy June evening when Bennigsen was hosting his garden party.

Just as supper was about to be served in the candlelit park where the band played, an agitated General Balashov, minister of police, appeared before Alexander and whispered into his ear that the French had crossed the Niemen. Napoleon's invasion of Russia had begun. The shaken tsar thanked his aide and ordered him to maintain silence so that the festivities would not be disturbed. The countess relates what happened next: "The emperor left the ball at the end of supper. He did not sit down at table but moved from one table to another with the appearance of perfect enjoyment. I say 'appearance' because he played his role marvelously, having already been notified that at this very moment while the ball was going on at the villa, a scene much more magnificent and solemn was being enacted some twenty miles from there. Napoleon crossed the Niemen with six hundred soldiers."

The anxious Alexander took leave of the Bennigsens and hurried to his headquarters. There he composed a manifesto in which he informed his countrymen that hostilities had commenced, albeit without a formal declaration of war. "I will not lay down arms so long as a single enemy soldier remains in my empire . . . God's wrath be on the one who starts." As a last-ditch attempt to ward off war, he sent General Balashov to meet with the French emperor. The discussions between the two were as tumultuous as they were unfruitful. When it became evident that the talks had broken down, Napoleon angrily sputtered, "Which is the road to Moscow?" Tradition has it that the uncowed Balashov calmly replied, "There are several roads which lead thither, and you can go by way of Poltava." (This city's name is synonymous with the rout of the Swedish armies by Peter the Great in 1709, which saw the annihilation of Charles's forces.)

The *Grande Armée* that Napoleon led into Russia originally numbered approximately 420,000, but ultimately with reinforcements it grew to 600,000, probably the greatest military force ever assembled up to that time. It was a patchwork force the majority of which was made up of unwilling conscripts from Italy, Poland, Holland, Switzerland, Germany, and Austria. But among the Frenchmen, particularly in the Imperial Guard, were some of the best-trained troops in the world, supplied with what was then state-of-the-art equipment, including vast quantities of light and heavy artillery. In command of the whole was the military genius whose legendary successes made him appear invincible. Napoleon entered Russia in early summer, counting on a swift and decisive campaign.

Before crossing the Niemen, the French ruler dispatched Count de Narbonne to meet with the tsar, as much to gather intelligence on Russian preparedness as to submit a proposal for peace. An unyielding Alexander rebuffed the French envoy with the words, "I have no illusions. I know how great a military leader Napoleon is. But, you see, I have space and time on my side. In all this land hostile to you there is not one single spot, no matter how distant it may be, which I shall not defend rather than conclude a dishonorable peace. I shall not attack, but I will not disarm so long as a single enemy soldier remains in Russia." And then, almost as an afterthought, Alexander added, "If Napoleon attacks and if fortune

smiles on him, notwithstanding the legitimate goals pursued by
Russia, he will have to sign the peace on the Bering Strait."

And now Napoleon was in Russia. To reinforce the invasion,
his staff had provided for a system of logistical supply, but in the
planning they relied heavily on the availability of local food
sources the captured territories would provide. "An army crawls
on its stomach," Napoleon once quipped. The farther the expedi-
tionary force penetrated into the country, however, the more inef-
ficiently the supply system worked. And before the path of the
advancing Frenchmen, the inhabitants retreated, all along the way
burning crops and food stores and carting off or slaughtering the
livestock. The scorched-earth policy made feeding the vast army a
horrendous problem, and the farther it moved into the interior,
the more miserable it became. In his memoir, General Caulaincourt, Napoleon's aide-de-camp and onetime ambassador to Russia, offered this impression: "There were no inhabitants to be
found, no prisoners to be taken, not a single straggler to be picked
up. We were in the heart of inhabited Russia, and yet we were like
a vessel without a compass in the midst of a vast ocean, knowing
nothing of what was happening to us."

Deeper and deeper Napoleon plunged into that enormous
country, all the time hoping for battle. He had supreme confidence
that only one decisive engagement would be required to bring the
tsar to heel; Russia would certainly be his, and soon. But the retreat
of the Russians continued, as much to the chagrin of the impatient
Russian populace as to the French emperor. Alexander was in no
position to challenge the invader, for not only did he lack numeri-
cal superiority but at that juncture his forces were stretched widely
along the country's lengthy western border, from Lithuania to
Moldavia. Days passed into weeks, and for the weary Frenchmen
the Niemen's crossing became a distant memory. In the first days of
August, news was brought to a delighted Napoleon that the Russians had called a halt to their retreat at Smolensk and that they
were preparing for battle. The engagement took place on August
16 and 17, and despite a heroic resistance, the Russians proved no

match to the superior enemy forces. They were forced to abandon the city, which first they put to the torch. The retreat continued.

The leadership of the Russian forces was in an obvious state of disarray, and it seemed that the ranking generals were as much in conflict with one another as they were at war with the enemy. Alexander contemplated assuming the supreme command of his forces himself. "I plan to place myself at the head of the armies," he informed Count Karl Nesselrode, a young staff member who years later rose to become minister of foreign affairs. His sister, Grand Duchess Catherine, however, urged him to forget any such notion. Not only did she fear the negative consequences to the tsar's popularity in the event of defeat, but, she argued, the sovereign's primary duty was to the affairs of the empire, not the battlefield. "Your role is not merely that of captain, but of a ruler as well."

The country's population had by this time bonded in a patriotic response against the French, in a swelling support of the war effort. The six percent treasury bond that had been issued in April, however, had proved insufficient to meet the emergency needs. The cry went out for voluntary financial support of the war effort, and donations from every part of the country and from all sectors of society poured into the state coffers. The merchants of Moscow alone, for example, raised eight million rubles. The province of Kaluga, south of Moscow, collected over a quarter of a million rubles, while the diocesan clergy contributed a further 9,204 rubles, together with more than ten pounds of gold and silver vessels. The country's population so determinedly rallying around the cause now cried for the immensely popular General Kutuzov to head the Russian forces.

Sixty-seven-year-old Mikhail Ilarionovich Kutuzov was a distinguished veteran of French, Polish, and Turkish wars and had an enviable reputation not only for sagacity and valor but for invincibility. He was known as "the unkillable soldier." Twice bullets had passed through his head without in any way affecting his speech or thought, although one eye had become blinded. Physically, a more unlikely field commander could not have been. The general was so grossly overweight that he found it impossible to mount a saddle — troop inspections were carried out from the ease of a horse-drawn vehicle. Despite his advanced age, Kutuzov continued to base his life around beautiful women, good food and wine, and plump easy chairs, in which he spent much time napping. After retiring from the military, he moved from one diplomatic or high administrative post to another, in each of which he distinguished himself. The edge of the shrewdness for which he had gained such fame had never become dulled; he seemed invariably to achieve what he wanted. In May 1812, for example, he returned from Bucharest, where he had successfully persuaded the Turks to sign a peace treaty after six years of hostilities — despite concerted French pressure on the sultan to continue the war. In the process, incidentally, he gained for Russia the province of Bessarabia.

Between the tsar and the general, however, there was not only an age difference of thirty-two years but also a burning animosity. In 1805, contrary to Kutuzov's explicit advice, Alexander had committed Russian forces to a joint stand with the Austrians against Napoleon at Austerlitz. They were soundly defeated, and the general never fully forgave the tsar. Nevertheless, as Henri Troyat observes, the "old General Kutuzov, bloated and one-eyed, bowed before his young master. A man of preceding reigns, he had an almost religious respect for the imperial will."

Alexander heard his country's cry, and on August 20, perhaps heeding the advice of his sister, he brought the aged general out of retirement and appointed him commander in chief. "The public wanted him," the monarch confided to General Komarovsky, a trusted member of the imperial staff, "and I made the appointment. As for me, I wash my hands of it."

Despite the personality clash between the new military commander and his sovereign, the partnership, as it were, of the two men worked to the country's advantage and ultimate victory. While Kutuzov and his subordinate generals took charge of defense, Alexander threw his energies into rallying public opinion and consolidating the support of the nation. He quit the field headquarters and went to Moscow, where he was greeted with an outpouring of enthusiasm and patriotic fervor. At the palatial home of Countess Orlov, where Alexander dined one evening, a delirious crowd gathered at the garden gates and chanted for their emperor. Alexander stepped out of the house and plunged into the crowd, which roared its approval. Countess Choiseul-Gouffier, witness to the scene and others similar to it, made the following observation:

> These spontaneous impulses on the part of the people, impossible to counterfeit or provoke, are grand and sublime. They can exist only among those nations whose hearts continue near to nature and who are deeply impressed with religious ideas. Nations where the people are accustomed to seeing in their sovereign the representative of God whom they adore and upon whom they build their hopes of future happiness — all in the sentiments of obedience and fidelity to which they have consecrated themselves.

In the days following his apppointment, Kutuzov ordered the continuation of the unpopular retreat. He was unwilling to engage the enemy until Moscow was under direct threat and until such a time that he could take a stand in a location where success had a chance. The strategy of the wily marshal was, first, to extend even farther the French supply lines, and, second, simply to exhaust the enemy. Summer's fierce heat, dysentery, and shortage of supply were already taking a toll, and in some units of Napoleon's army discipline was breaking down. In a twelve-day period after Smolensk, it is estimated, one-tenth of the French forces had been depleted through sickness and desertion. The state of the *Grande Armée* was visibly deteriorating.

Kutuzov's strategy, however, did not meet with universal approval. Many of the ranking officers as well as soldiers were becoming impatient for battle, and the public in general was demanding a halt to the galling retreat. Sacred Moscow, further-more, was looming ever closer. Near the little village of Borodino some seventy miles west of Moscow, the commander-in-chief finally ordered a halt on Friday, September 4, and instructed redoubts to be thrown up in preparation for action. That same afternoon, from four o' clock until darkness fell at ten, a murder-ous battle raged, one that continued for three days. Despite fatigue, depletion of equipment, and sickness, and notwithstand-ing the valorous defence by the tsar's forces, the French prevailed; the tsar's forces quietly withdrew farther inland. The ghastly en-counter proved to be one of the world's bloodiest — all in a futile struggle to satiate one man's driven ambition. The French lost some 40,000 men, including 47 generals, while the Russians lost approximately 45,000 troops, a third of Kutuzov's forces. "When it was all over and mist and drizzle enveloped the crumpled plain," writes Alan Palmer, "there was no elation in either camp — only weary relief mingled with apprehension that at dawn the futile folly would begin once again."

The following day, however, there was no more battle. Kutu-zov had yet again withdrawn his forces and was pulling back to Moscow. At one time the country had enthusiastically clamored for the one-eyed general, but now there was universal bewilder-ment and disappointment in his seemingly never-ending, humiliat-ing retreat. To his aide-de-camp, however, Kutuzov confided, "I consider this retreat providential, for it will preserve our army. Napoleon is like an impetuous torrent, but Moscow will be the sponge which will absorb him." And later he declared, "To save Russia we need an army. To save the army we must give up the idea of defending Moscow. Moscow is not the whole of Russia; better to lose it than the army and Russia."

The strategy of retreat was deliberate, and in this Kutuzov received the tsar's full support. In the days following his departure from Moscow, Alexander, rather than heading for St. Petersburg as originally planned, wisely chose to travel to Äbo, on Finland's southwestern coast, in order to meet with Crown Prince Charles of

Sweden. The prince was in fact Count Bernadotte, a brilliant marshal of France and a onetime close associate of Napoleon's. With no heir to their throne, the Swedes in 1810 elected him to succeed King Charles XIII, which he did eight years later. In traveling to Äbo, Alexander sought to secure Sweden's assurances that it would not take advantage of Russia's perilous situation by seeking to regain Finland. The Swedes agreed, and the tsar was thus able to transfer to Kutuzov the 14,000-man garrison that had been stationed on the northern frontier. More importantly, Alexander received from Bernadotte not only moral support but valuable practical advice. At all costs, counseled the former marshal of France, avoid major battles. Concentrate on the enemy's flanks, thus forcing him to detach troops. Tire him out with marches and countermarches, the thing French troops dislike most and where they are most vulnerable. Above all, bring in the Cossacks, the Russian troops most feared by the French. Continue the retreat, Bernadotte advised, and draw the enemy ever deeper into the country.

Within a week of Borodino, Napoleon stood triumphant at Moscow's walls, and there, at Dorogomilov Gate, he awaited the tsar's deputation of surrender with the keys to the city. Hours passed but no deputation came. And then the startling news filtered in: Moscow was deserted. Refusing to accept these unbelievable reports, Napoleon rode into the city and passed through the eerily silent streets. Only the cooing of doves and the echoing clatter of his party's horses' hooves broke the stillness. No evidence of the inhabitants could be found. Shops, residences, government buildings, palaces — all stood lifeless and still. French intelligence had failed to note that since the fall of Smolensk, Moscow's 200,000 inhabitants had been leaving their beloved capital; for many days the roads leading east and north had been jammed with every imaginable type of vehicle, loaded with the most precious household items. Now there was stillness; it was hardly a triumphant entry for a conquering hero.

With wild abandon, the French troops took possession of palaces and shops. Sleep that night, however, was not to be theirs.

As early as nine o'clock, reports began to filter in to Napoleon's headquarters that fires had been observed in various parts of the city, particularly in its northern reaches. Within hours, the small blazes had spread in numbers and had gained significant momentum. By midnight, the skyline was bright with leaping flames and the streets were choked with smoke. One witness saw "trails of fire follow their dreadful course while other furnaces roar up and new torrents flow from them. Driven by the wind, they fill in the gaps that the previous streams of fire had not managed to reach." For four days the conflagration continued, during which time the looting and disorder that had started on the first day of occupation spiraled out of control. Wine cellars were invaded and the streets were filled with intoxicated troops in every state of dress and undress. They scurried about the piles of broken furniture, emptied chests, and slashed paintings that littered the pavements. A certain Captain Labaume of the French army was a witness: "Soldiers, convicts, and prostitutes ran through the streets, entered deserted palaces, and snatched everything that could gratify their greed. Some covered themselves with stuffs woven of gold or silk, while others put over their shoulders, without choice or discernment, the most highly prized furs. Many covered themselves with women's and children's skirts and even the convicts hid rags beneath court garments. The rest, flocking to cellars, broke down the doors and, drinking the most precious wines, staggered off with immense booty." The sky over the city was so brightly reddened that the glow was visible, it was said, for well over one hundred miles. Since nearly all the buildings had been constructed of wood, eighty percent of the city's residences were ultimately reduced to ashes.

Who had started these fires? The French held no doubt that blame for the conception and execution of the devastating act lay squarely at the feet of Count Fyodor Rostopchin, Moscow's governor-general. It is true that, prior to the entry of Napoleon's forces into the city, the governor had evacuated the firemen and carted off all the water pumps. The Russians, however, were convinced that the French had deliberately sought to destroy their beloved capital, the sacred cradle of Orthodox civilization, in an act of barbarous revenge. There now could be no peace settlement with Napoleon, for how could one negotiate with the anti-Christ?

With the fall of Moscow, the French invasion of Russia took on a fresh complexion. From the moment that Napoleon crossed the Niemen — through Smolensk, Borodino, and his entry into the ancient capital — not only had there been an enemy to drive back, but above all, there had been a genuine expectation of imminent surrender. Now Napoleon had established himself as master of Russia's sacred capital — but the enemy was not before him. How much farther would he have to chase it? Surely not to the Bering Strait. The tsar had suffered a resounding defeat, but he showed no signs of acknowledging it. There was no surrender, no emissaries pleading peace — only an icy and obdurate silence.

As for the Russian forces, Kutuzov had withdrawn them some fifty miles southwest of Moscow and taken up defensive positions at the small village of Letacheva. The old general now rested and, it was said, spent much of the time asleep on his down-filled mattress — up to eighteen hours a day. The French and the Russians waited. Meanwhile, as is common in that part of the world, summer passed dramatically into winter. French records have it, for example, that by September 14, the army suffered badly from many days of "dry, scorching heat." In the next few weeks, the days were generally warm but the nights cold — the whole weather system inexorably passing into freezing temperatures and cold winds. On October 13, it snowed.

During all this time, Alexander remained quietly at work in St. Petersburg, keeping in constant communication with Kutuzov. During the weeks following his meeting with Bernadotte, his mood had been one of despair, particularly after receiving the news of Moscow's fall. "The taking of Moscow has brought the feelings of exasperation to a climax," his sister Catherine wrote to him. "The dissatisfaction is at the highest point, and your person is far from being immune . . . You are accused loudly of the misfortunes of your empire, of its ruin in general and in particular, and finally for having lost the honor of your country and of your person." Despair turned to despondency. One evening, Alexander happened to be sitting with Golitsen, who by then had become even more enveloped in mysticism. During their discussion regarding the enemy's successes, the prince drew from the table a heavy Bible, which he clumsily let fall to the floor. The pages happened to fall open at Psalm 91: "The Lord is my refuge and fortress, my God: in him will I trust . . . He shall cover thee with his feathers and under his wings you will find refuge." That the Good Book opened as it did was clearly the will of God, explained Golitsen. Alexander was much taken by this chance revelation. A day later he was attending a church service for troops about to depart for the south when he heard these very same words once more. At the conclusion of the service, the priest informed the tsar that he had been directed by God to select that particular passage. Twice, within barely twenty-four hours, Alexander had been exposed to the same verse. This was no mere coincidence — the prophetic text was the manifest work of the Divine. Although Alexander had always had a strong spiritual bent, to that point of his life he had not been particularly religious in the strict sense of the word. But now he plunged headlong into the Scriptures, which provided him the comfort he so fervently desired. His latent mystical inclinations found gratification in the discovery of the Bible. In speaking of the period, Alexander later noted that "I simply devoured the Bible, finding that its words poured an unknown peace into my heart and quenched the thirst of my soul. Our Lord, in His infinite wisdom, inspired me in order to permit me to understand what I was reading. It is to this edification, to this internal light that I am indebted for all the moral well-being that I have acquired by reading the Scriptures."

In his biography of Alexander, Professor Leonid Strakhovsky explains the emperor's spiritual state in those early days of Napoleon's invasion: "Alexander spent his days plunging deeper and deeper into a sort of superstitious mysticism. But in reading the Bible he found not only an explanation of the terrible events, which, like a nightmare, enshrouded Russia, but also he persuaded himself of his own weakness and moral inferiority. What was he before these formidable forces gathered against Russia? Had he the right to be ruler of this empire, the master of this valiant nation? Was he not predestined to expiate the sins of past generations? His own sins . . . lost in contradictions, deep in a mystic haze, Alexander struggled with himself while Russia struggled with Napoleon."

The mood in St. Petersburg swung wildly. The adulation with which the population had beheld Alexander in August, in September veered to disapproval. Moscow had fallen, the army was supine, and the tsar appeared uninvolved. Alexander, on the other hand, freshly bathed in spiritual enlightenment, became reenergized in a newfound confidence and sense of purpose. The despondency in which he had allowed himself briefly to wallow was dissipated. "My people and I stand united as never before," he wrote to Bernadotte in early October, "and we would rather perish under ruins than make peace with the modern Attila."

For over a month Napoleon occupied Moscow, waiting for the tsar to sue for peace. But the deafening silence from St. Petersburg was palpable. Kutuzov calmly continued to bide his time. And wait he did, while the occupying forces suffered from lack of supplies, illness, cold, and then fire. The French passed through a gamut of moods — confidence, concern, anxiety, and, finally, desperation. In early October, Napoleon dispatched an envoy to Kutuzov in order to propose an armistice while peace was negotiated. The general referred the matter to Alexander, who reacted angrily, as upset with the gall of Napoleon's suggestion as he was with Kutuzov's having received the French envoy in the first place. "Peace?" he thundered. "We have not yet made war. My campaign is just about to begin." To Kutuzov he wrote, "My firm resolve is that at present no proposal from our enemies will persuade me to cease in our struggle. By so doing, we fail in the hallowed obligation to avenge our transgressed motherland."

In the end, Alexander's determination prevailed. On Monday, October 19, Napoleon and his staff quit Moscow, joining the thousands of troops that had already begun the evacuation. After an occupation of thirty-two days, they were leaving behind a city that had been pillaged, burned, and desecrated. The *Grande Armée* bore little resemblance to the disciplined force that had entered Russia four months earlier. Loaded down with wagons carrying every imaginable sort of goods, and bearing heavy sacks of booty, this was a motley collection of the half-starved, the sick, and the dispirited. "They were not regiments on the march," comments Henri Troyat, "but twenty tribes of nomads, weighed down with booty and united by fear, dragging themselves across the steppes."

The painful retreat of Napoleon's ragtag army is one of the more sorry episodes in military history. Suffering profoundly from a lack of supply, the ill-fed, sick, snow-covered force saw its morale plummet. "Generals January and February" were on Alexander's side. The exit of the *Grande Armée* rapidly developed into a catastrophic rout. Deprivation and starvation, deep snow and freezing temperatures, illness and the wounds of battle — through all this, the French struggled on in ignominy. And all along the way, their retreat was encouraged by fresh Russian forces and determined partisans, all of whom wrought additional havoc and misery on the haggard invaders. Of the 600,000 men who had entered Russia some weeks earlier, three-quarters succumbed to starvation, sickness, wounds, and the elements.

8

The Crown:
An Increasing Burden

ON NOVEMBER 13, the last of the French troops departed Russian territory into Prussia. Napoleon had been expelled, and Alexander stood the victor; he had achieved the seemingly impossible. Europe now looked to him to free it finally from the scourge of French domination, or, as one unnamed Prussian exile put it, "to deliver the human race from the most absorbed and degrading of tyrannies." In the first months of 1813, Alexander brought Prussia, England, and Sweden into an alliance and soon thereafter successfully persuaded the Austrians to join. The tsar was a man with a mission, determined to see the end of Napoleon and propelled by a conviction that God was on his side. To Golitsen he wrote, "Placing myself firmly in the hands of the Almighty, I submit blindly to His will. Each day it grows firmer and I experience joys I had never known before . . . It is difficult to express in words the benefits I receive in reading the Scriptures, which previously I knew only superficially . . . all my glory I dedicate to the advancement of the reign of the Lord Jesus Christ."

Throughout the spring and summer of 1813, the allies and the French were locked in a series of engagements, the climax of which came on October 16, near Leipzig at the "Battle of Nations." The combined armies of Russia, Austria, and Prussia, a body of 360,000 men, soundly defeated a French force of 185,000 in a three-day engagement that saw some 60,000 perish on the first day. Throughout the battle, Alexander steadfastly rode with his entourage from one area of the fighting to another, issuing orders and encouraging wavering troops. At one point, as though possessed, he led a successful charge of Cossacks against a body of French cavalry. When it was all over, in the quiet of early dawn of the fourth day, a fatigued tsar, joined by King Frederick William of Prussia and Emperor Francis of Austria, found himself on a hill, observing to the west the dust of the withdrawing French forces. Within days, Napoleon was crossing the Rhine and reentering France, while the allies, for the moment, rested. Two months later, they too crossed the river, and after a series of bitter engagements, on March 31, 1814, they made their way into Paris, in a triumphant parade down the Champs Elysées. Twelve days later Napoleon abdicated and was exiled to the tiny island of Elba, off the western coast of Italy.

That same day, Alexander issued a proclamation: "The armies of the allied powers have occupied the capital of France. The allied sovereigns respect the wishes of the French nation. They declare that if conditions of peace are to have the strongest guarantees the ambitions of Bonaparte must be curbed . . . they respect the integrity of France such as she was under the legitimate kings . . . they invite the senate to form a provisionary government . . . and prepare a constitution which will be agreeable to the French people."

The events that followed that triumphant entry into Paris are all too familiar. Napoleon abdicated and was exiled to Elba, after which the Congress of Vienna assembled to work out a lasting peace. Then came Napoleon's hundred-day return to power, culminating in the battle of Waterloo. And that, in turn, resulted in the decisive fall of Bonaparte and his lonely exile to St. Helena, a forlorn island in the middle of the South Atlantic.

In Europe, the eight-year period 1814–22 is sometimes referred to as a system of "government by conference." The greatest statesmen of the day gathered at one international meeting after another in the challenging effort to guarantee a lasting peace. Metternich, Castlereagh, Talleyrand, and Alexander I were the four decision-makers, but the assemblies on the whole were as large as they were glittering. At the drawn-out Congress of Vienna, balls, banquets, hunting parties, and concerts were as much a part of the proceedings as the diplomatic negotiations. "The Congress dances but does not march," one diplomat quipped. The purpose of the congresses was not to punish the French for past transgressions, but rather to prevent a new Robespierre or a fresh Napoleon from again appearing on the world stage. Castlereagh declared that the purpose of his own presence was "not to collect trophies but to bring the world back to peaceful habits." The liberal experiment in Europe, launched by the French Revolution and inherited by Napoleon, had proven itself a failure, and the reactionary forces assembled in Vienna were now in ascendancy.

Alexander was in his element. He was the conquering hero, savior of Europe, restorer of the Bourbons. The Parisians, completely under his spell, sang his praises. In acknowledging the honors bestowed on him by the *Académie française,* he declared, "My happiness and my one desire is to be useful to the human race." From France, he traveled to England, where again receptions, balls, festivities, and honors befell him, albeit from a populace less demonstrative than in France. In responding to the Lord Mayor of London's laudatory remarks, the tsar declared in fluent English, "Europe has gained a peace which I hope will be conducive to the happiness of the human race. Say to your compatriots from me that the English nation has every right to my esteem . . . I shall be her constant friend."

By September 1815, Alexander had become saturated with a religious romanticism. Prayer and the Bible were now an integral part of his daily life and he grabbed any opportunity to discourse with mystics and fundamentalists. Baroness von Krüdener had now reached the apex of her influence over the tsar, and it was with her encouragement that he drew up his proposal for a Holy Alliance. This was an innocuous guideline for sovereigns concerning the manner in which their subjects should be treated, and, more importantly, how they should treat one another. Francis I of Austria and Frederick William III of Prussia readily accepted the document. "Consistent with the words of the Holy Scripture," the paper read, "the three contracting monarchs will remain united by the bonds of a true and indissoluble fraternity." They agreed to abide by "the precepts of justice, Christian charity, and peace, which far from being applicable only to private concerns, must have immediate influence on the council of princes and guide their steps." Eventually, all the rulers of Europe signed on except the pope, the sultan of Turkey, and the prince regent of Britain. British foreign minister Castlereagh scorned the document as "a piece of sublime mysticism and nonsense." Initially Metternich called it a "loud-sounding nothing," but later he helped to edit the wording, thus propelling it into a deeper nothing, that being his intention.

One significant development that eventually negatively affected Alexander's mental state during this period of "government by conferences" was what would come to be called the Greek Question. In March 1821, the Hellenes revolted against their Turkish overlords. The movement was led by Prince Alexander Ypsilantis, an enterprising Greek who had for years served in the Russian army and was an aide-de-camp to the tsar. The Turks reacted quickly and vigorously, and before long the entire country was embroiled in insurrection. Ypsilantis appealed to his mentor and coreligionist: "Save us," he wrote to Alexander, "save our religion from those who would persecute it, return to us our temples and our altars whence the divine light once spread its beams to the great nation you govern." Under normal circumstances there would have been no doubt about the tsar's reaction: as champion of the Orthodox world, he could hardly have rejected such a plea. The circumstances at the time, however, were anything but normal. Central Europe was being held captive to the views of Austrian chancellor Metternich, to whom any hint of insidious liberalism — revolutionary movements in particular — was anathema. The Holy Alliance of which Russia was an enthusiastic signatory and its driving force was to assure this. Despite his personal sympathy for the Greeks and antipathy to the Turks, there was no way the tsar could let down the established new order. It was a conundrum that he painfully resolved by disavowing and censuring Ypsilantis. There was to be no Russian help for the Greeks. Massacres followed slaughters — particularly in the Peloponnesus — and for the following nine years Greece was embroiled in war. Alexander never forgave himself for having failed his coreligionists.

For over four years Alexander had preoccupied himself with Napoleon and international affairs. With Napoleon languishing on St. Helena and Europe at reasonable peace, he now refocused his attention on Russia's domestic affairs. He had willingly left the administration of his country in the hands of a wallowing, unimaginative, dogged bureaucracy, and the nation did indeed wallow. The French chargé d'affaires in St. Petersburg — with certain bias — shared his views.

> Russia is enjoying the glory which she won in her victories. Dazzled by these successes, the Russian Empire puts itself in the front row and proclaims its sovereign the arbiter of Europe and half of Asia. Meanwhile, the country itself is devoid of laws, of decent administration and is almost completely lacking in industries . . . Arbitrary authorities govern the interests of ninety-nine percent of the entire population . . .
>
> To sum it all up, everything comes up to the decision of this primitive power which is crushed under the burden of its endless attributions; 250,000 unsettled questions await the supreme decision; mistakes and inequities complement each other and like the courts of justice the administration lags . . . Four hundred million francs constitute the revenues of this empire which occupies one-seventh

part of the entire globe; 300 millions are appropriated for the needs of the army whilst the sciences, the arts, all that makes peace glorious is left undeveloped.

A tributary of entire Europe for its needs and fantasies, Russia is unable even to clothe her soldiers by whose support she exists . . . Seen from a close angle this country is far from offering the aspect of one of those nations which through successive development of wise institutions, of virtues and the most noble faculties of mankind have rested their glory and their power on a solid foundation.

Alexander seemed in despair. After the glitter and adulation of Paris, London, Vienna, and the rest of the West, so much needed attention at home: the realities of homecoming appeared overwhelming. "One cannot do all things at once; events did not permit me to busy myself with the affairs of government as I should have," he lamented. "The army, the government are not as I should like to see them, but how can I remedy it? One cannot accomplish everything in a single gesture; I have no collaborators."

The apparent hopelessness of it all made him despondent. He found excuse after excuse to avoid shouldering the increasing burdens of state demanded of him. "It is from this time that Alexander became visibly tired of living," wrote Metternich. And it was at this point that Mikhailovsky-Danilevsky made his observation of the tsar, that "his soul was troubled and that his innermost thoughts were directed to objects far removed" from day-to-day matters. As an escape, Alexander turned into an inveterate traveler — one trip followed another, both within Russia and outside. And, as noted, when he remained at home, he closeted himself a good deal of the time at Tsarskoye Selo.

The pendulum of Alexander's political views had swung to reaction, and this provoked growing opposition. Particularly disaffected were the thousands of army officers who had gotten a healthy taste of liberalism in the West. Secret organizations attracted the discontented, with the Northern Society in particular coming to prominence. Favoring a constitutional monarchy and the abolition of serfdom, this group eventually precipitated the Decembrist uprising of 1825 that came on the heels of Alexander's untimely — or presumed — death.

In granting a constitution to the Poles in 1818, the tsar told his brother Constantine, "Soon also this great moment of joy will arrive for Russia, when I will grant a constitution to her and when, like now, I will cross Petersburg with you and my family to return to my palace surrounded by joyous people."

Constantine was tongue-tied at this declaration. He replied, "If Your Majesty puts aside absolute power, I doubt whether this will conform to the wishes of the people." To which the "constitutionalist" tsar replied curtly, "I do not require your advice, but I will explain my will to you as to one of my subjects." But despite these high-minded declarations, considerations of a Russian constitution were put aside for another day.

Alexander's religious attitudes brought him into contact with a variety of sects and religious societies. He continued particularly to favor the Bible Society and supported it handsomely — eventually it went through seventy-nine editions of the Bible in twenty-five languages. He received a two-man delegation from the Quakers with whom, hand-in-hand, he prayed and afterward embraced. He delved into questions related to the Old Believers, the Holy Synod, and the status of Jews. In his work on educational reform, Alexander embraced the philosophy of Joseph Lancaster. The Englishman's system provided for teachers to instruct and for the most gifted pupils to pass on the learning to the other children, all by rote. The advantage of this approach was that it reached out to a vastly expanded student enrollment, through fewer teachers, at less cost. The structure offered the further benefit of helping to assure that religious instruction reached greater numbers.

Since his Gatchina days, and for the entire length of his reign, Alexander had at his side an indomitable administrator in the person of Count Alexey Arakcheyev. It was the count who now provided the broad shoulders to which the sovereign transferred much of his burden. This son of a poor provincial landowner had risen rapidly from a modest start as an artillery officer to become one of the most powerful figures in Russian history. He had faithfully served Catherine, Paul, and Alexander in a variety of offices, and by 1824 he had acquired so much power that in the eyes of the people he was virtually "vice-emperor." All the business of the country passed through his hands. He had become the very symbol of autocracy, and in his time he grew into a legend. It was he who reorganized Russia's military, and contributed significantly to the strategy that defeated Napoleon. He made all political appointments. While the restless emperor indulged in his insatiable thirst for domestic and international travel, Arakcheyev took charge of virtually every aspect of Russian internal affairs.

The count was as clever and intelligent as he was harsh and barbarically cruel. He was held in universal awe and fear. "His name should be written not in ink but in blood," remarked a priest who served him at Gruzino, Arakcheyev's vast estate awarded him by Paul. "Industrious as an ant and venomous as a tarantula," noted one associate. "The evil genius of Russia," another called him. Nonetheless, Alexander loved this man, doubtless because he could not do without him. "Alexander knew that in Arakcheyev he had a servant who would never defect and never be indiscreet," writes Troyat, "an automaton ready to assume all responsibilities that the emperor refused to take."

Foremost among Russian's unresolved problems was that of serfdom. Even before coming to the throne, Alexander had written, "Nothing could be more degrading and inhuman than the sale of people, and a decree is needed that will forbid this forever. To the shame of Russia, slavery still exists." In the pre-Napoleonic period various reports on the abolition of serfdom had been submitted and projects proposed, but nothing happened. The Committee of Friends had grappled with the question but were at a loss how to proceed. In 1818, Alexander entrusted Arakcheyev with drawing up a plan for the resolution of the problem. The task was made all the more daunting by the tsar's clear admonition to the court that in solving the problem the nobility should not be offended. The tireless Arakcheyev responded by a proposal in which the government would annually purchase parcels of land from the nobles, including the serfs living on it — in effect, a buyout. The costs involved were so outrageously high that the plan was never seriously considered. Before long the file on the liberation of the serfs joined the constitutional file on the shelf.

One project greatly favored by Alexander did get off the ground, thanks to Arakcheyev's determination and ruthlessness: the infamous military colonies. The scheme called for soldiers and their families to be paired off with farmers on agricultural plots within specially set-up colonies. The soldier in time of peace would thus not be deprived of family life, and the farmer would benefit from discipline and military training that was part of the program. The two would work jointly, living off the land, and sparing the state the vast cost of maintaining a military machine. The scheme provided modern health facilities, community sanitation systems, and relief from taxation. It also provided for compulsory uniforms, parade training, and military precision in farm management. The families would live in identical blue or pink cottages, generally built on the sites of razed farm properties. The children, also in uniform, would form children's battalions in which they would receive schooling and disciplinary training. Marriages were to be arranged by the military authorities or by lot. Ruling over all would be the virtues of orderliness, cleanliness, elegance, and symmetry.

Such a radical and restrictive organization was the antithesis of everything the peasants had ever known, and their resentment was universal. Wherever the colonies were set up, the population was drawn into them kicking and objecting. Nonetheless, Arakcheyev doggedly pressed on, smothering all opposition, and eventually nearly a million souls were caught up in the experiment. In Chuguev, one such military colony rebelled. Arakcheyev hurried to the scene and immediately arrested, tried, and found guilty the ringleaders. The condemned men — 250 of them — were punished barbarically. Every prisoner was stripped to the waist and dragged twelve times through rows of a thousand soldiers, each armed with a birch rod. As the prisoner passed the soldiers, heavy blows were administered to the back. Many of the victims died, while others never fully recovered. In reporting to Alexander on all that had transpired, Arakcheyev wrote that "the events which took place here have much disturbed me." Alexander sympathized with him. "I understand entirely what your sensitive soul must have undergone in the circumstances in which you found yourself. Moreover, I appreciate the good judgment with which you acted in the face of these grave events, and I sincerely thank you for all you did. The event was, of course, unhappy. But once it had unfortunately taken place, there was no alternative but to allow the force of the law to take its course."

The continued toleration of serfdom, the lack of progress on constitutional reform, and the spread of military colonies had by 1824 caused disenchantment with Alexander not only within segments of the nobility but also among the peasants. In early summer, near Novgorod, upset peasants stopped the carriage of the dowager empress and presented her with a petition demanding relief from their heavy burdens. She referred them to the emperor, whose own carriage followed closely. When the tsar's vehicle came into view, they prostrated themselves in front of it and successfully presented their grievances to their sovereign. An agitated Alexander made little comment and continued on his way, probably as upset with the demonstration as with his own failure fully to respond to the people's needs.

For the restless Alexander, the weight of the imperial crown was proving increasingly burdensome.

9

God Is Punishing Us
for Our Sins

BY THE AUTUMN OF 1824 Alexander's frame of mind was precarious. For some time now the sovereign had generally shown himself to be morose, apathetic, inwardly centered, and at times seemingly indifferent to life about him. Countess Edling, a longtime lady-in-waiting to Elizaveta, wrote of the tsar's mental and emotional state at the time: "Alexander, discouraged and unhappy, found consolation only in solitude, which brought him to a higher level of consciousness, away from this world full of disappointments and miseries." And then, to compound his private problems, the floodgates quite literally opened, and in the onrush of turbulent waters Alexander was propelled into the final dramatic moments of his reign.

In the early days of November, the Baltic was beset with hurricane-force winds and heavy seas. Storms blew unremittingly from the southwest into St. Petersburg as the waters of the Neva swelled, backed up, and by the seventh had caused a catastrophic flood. The river's raging waters overflowed the banks and mercilessly battered all that stood in their way. No street or building was spared, as the capital became deluged as never before. Mud, animal carcasses, debris of every sort beat against the walls, as water cascaded into basements and then flooded ground floors. Within five hours more than 500 people had drowned in the city; 324 houses were destroyed and another 3,600 severely damaged, together with bridges, sidewalks, and embankments. In the suburbs, another 100 people lost their lives and over 300 houses were destroyed or damaged.

Countess Choiseul-Gouffier described the flood:

People were surprised in the midst of their occupations by an enemy which they were unable to resist; the laborer, at his work, the merchant in his shop and the sentinel at his post. A number of persons driving about town on business became a victim of the tempestuous flood. The first stories of the houses were submerged and in a few hours the water rose in some parts of the town to the height of seventeen feet. The court quarter, by its proximity to the river, was most exposed and the imperial yacht was ready to receive the emperor, who with the royal family had taken refuge in the most elevated part of the palace, where he was forced to contemplate the disasters of his people, whom he would have been willing to save at the expense of his own life.

Rowboats traversed the streets of the city and picked up many unfortunates who were being drowned in trying to reach their homes. A sentinel was carried in his sentry box by the current as far as the Winter Palace. Seeing his sovereign at the window, the poor soldier, who even at the approach of death could not forget military discipline, presented arms. They succeeded in rescuing him. A funeral cross was transported by the force of the water from a cemetery on the other side of the river and deposited opposite the palace. This was regarded as a fatal omen.

As soon as the waters receded, Alexander toured the muddied streets. What he saw appalled him. Death and devastation were everywhere, and the clinging smell of dampness pervaded the city. The calamity of the desolation spread before him was overwhelming. He harked back in his mind to the flood that had hit St. Petersburg so severely in 1777, the year of his birth. And now this, an even greater deluge. Was this another divine sign? At the base of Nevsky Prospect, the tsar alighted from his carriage and stood silently, surveying the terrible damage while pedestrians passed by, wailing and crying. For many long minutes he was plunged deep in thought as tears streamed down his cheeks. And then an old man limped by and, when within a few paces of the emperor, cried out, "God is punishing us for our sins!"

Alexander looked up and replied, "No, not for *our* sins, but for mine!"

The tragedy wrought by the flood touched the monarch, and there is little doubt that he truly believed what he had said. The sin was his, unforgotten and unexpiated — parricide. In surveying the desolation around him, Alexander saw clear evidence of God's wrath in all its fury. At that moment, as in many in the past, the specter of his father hovered over him. Over the years it had kept coming back to torment him. Virtually everything he did recalled that March night in 1801. Now the vision of the floodwaters further exacerbated his guilt.

As the waters raged outside the Winter Palace, the empress was inside in her sickbed, suffering from a rapidly worsening pulmonary ailment. She had developed a persistent cold, with a rasping cough, and sometimes had trouble breathing. The physicians especially worried about her rising fever. During the course of their marriage, the imperial couple had mostly lived apart, but in the past year or so, Alexander and Elizaveta appeared to have rediscovered each other. For weeks, the tsar had been preoccupied with his wife's deteriorating condition. "We're terribly concerned about the health of the Empress Elizaveta Alexeyevna," wrote a courtier, "who from a cold has developed a heavy cough and temperature. I've observed the emperor in great anxiety."

Throughout his life Alexander had always enjoyed robust health; sickness was unknown, foreign to him. But earlier that year he had come down with a high fever, nausea, and splitting headaches. The court physicians diagnosed the peculiar condition as "glowing fever." The doctors also discovered an inflammation in his left leg, in the thigh area, where a horse had once kicked him. The leg pained him greatly, and the doctors even talked of an amputation. Both conditions slowly improved, however, and eventually dissipated. Elizaveta's illness and his own health problems doubtless brought home to him, perhaps for the first time, visions of mortality.

By early December, the empress's condition had improved slightly. Alexander was able to report to his longtime confidant Count Nikolai Karamzin, "Although there is some amelioration in the health of my wife, it is far from sufficient to cause me freedom from concern. Her cough has not lessened and she suffers many complaints. What's more important is that she is unable to get down the medication prescribed for calming the heart and arteries." There were intermittent periods, however, when the empress seemed clearly on the mend. During one such interval, Alexander felt sufficiently reassured about her physical state to take a trip to Poland. By the arrangements concluded in 1815 at the Congress of Vienna, Russia had been handed most of the Grand Duchy of Warsaw, which Alexander organized as an autonomous kingdom of Poland, in permanent union with his country. Within three years he granted the Poles a constitution and appointed his younger brother Constantine as viceroy. The charter guaranteed Polish as the official language, established a legislative assembly, and provided for a separate army. It was an exceptionally liberal concession, one that the tsar really viewed as an experiment. If it took root successfully, a similar, perhaps expanded constitution might be granted in Russia. But this never came to pass. Alexander was now eager to open the third Diet of Warsaw. On April 4, he left Tsarskoye Selo and seven days later was in Warsaw, having en route paid official visits to the cities of Vitebsk, Orsha, and Brest-Litovsk.

On May 1, the Diet of Warsaw assembled, and Alexander appeared before it, resplendent in a white tunic with the sash and star of the Polish Order of the White Eagle gleaming on his chest.

He certainly cut a dashing figure, and several parliamentarians and spectators subsequently commented on the strikingly handsome appearance of the forty-seven-year-old tsar. The new constitution provided the Poles with a legislative assembly, which he now addressed. "Representatives of the Kingdom of Poland!" spoke the tsar, "proceed in your deliberations calmly and free of all influence. The future of your country is in your hands." Here stood the Russian emperor, ruler of Poland, addressing in such words the democratically elected representatives of the people. In Russia, the citizens vented jealous anger at their sovereign for establishing such a body in a foreign dependency, while at home similar institutions were denied. For their part, the Poles, despite the favored position in which they found themselves, were also bitter about the tsar and resentful of the Russian presence in their country. In essence, the tsar's army was one of occupation. What was more, despite the presumed protection of a constitution, the presence of the secret police was as disturbing as it was evident. Above all, the Poles deeply resented the fact that many former lands of the Polish commonwealth remained under Russian control. And, understandably, they found the appointment of Grand Duke Constantine as head of the Polish army especially galling.

Despite the brilliance of the occasion, Alexander felt little triumph — it was more a sense of defeat. He had given them so much, yet they were still displeased. It seemed to him that no matter how hard he sought to serve the people, however much good he tried to do, his subjects always appeared dissatisfied or ungrateful.

On June 2, after a dizzying round of inspections, parades, and balls, Alexander bade farewell to Warsaw and to Constantine. Eleven days later, having visited Riga, Revel, and some of the battle sites of the Napoleonic Wars, the emperor returned to Tsarskoye Selo, literally overnight. On the very next day he set off for Novgorod and a whirlwind inspection tour of the latest industrial and educational developments in that area. He seemed propelled by some invisible force within him into a frenzy of travel and activity. It was as though he was purposely avoiding a return to the capital and the grim realities of rule. During that ten-day trip, he stopped at Gruzino, the estate of his old friend Count Arakcheyev, who, although in semi-retirement, continued to wield profound influence not only in the affairs of state but on the tsar himself.

Shortly after Alexander had taken leave of Arakcheyev, a courier caught up to him bearing an urgent message from the count. Apparently a certain Warrant Officer Sherwood of the Ukrainian Uhlan Regiment had just reported that he had vital information to pass on to the emperor concerning a conspiracy developing in the army. Under no circumstances would he reveal anything but to the sovereign. Arakcheyev had dispatched the officer under escort to await Alexander's return to St. Petersburg.

On arriving in the capital, Alexander received the young officer alone in his Winter Palace study. It turned out that the twenty-seven-year-old Sherwood was an Englishman in the emperor's service, whose father had been invited by Paul to emigrate from England and take up a post as an instructor in the newly established mechanics' school in St. Petersburg. Ivan Vasilivich, or "John" as he was called, proved to be a quick-minded, well-educated person who, in addition to Russian and English, also spoke French, German, and Latin. Alexander immediately took a liking to the young man. Sherwood succinctly and systematically delivered his well-prepared report without the least evidence of being awed in the august presence of the tsar. He warned Alexander that certain officers within the army of the Ukraine, together with accomplices in St. Petersburg, were plotting an uprising in the military. The object was the overthrow of His Majesty's government. Alexander received these tidings without visible surprise. He merely asked, "And what do these people wish? Are they so badly off?"

"Overfed dogs are ones more likely to catch rabies," replied Sherwood. The officer went on to explain that he did not know the extent to which the conspiracy had developed but that he was prepared to keep an eye on it and to investigate further. The emperor authorized Sherwood to do just that and instructed him to report on any developments through Arakcheyev.

It is not surprising that the emperor's reaction to Sherwood's startling news was so passive. The tsar was well aware that revolutionary elements existed not only in the army but in the civil service as well. The Englishman's report merely confirmed that the subversives were developing into an organized force. If Alexander appeared so little concerned, it was doubtless because he knew that the young men who now were agitating and conspiring were imbued with the very same ideals that he himself had so ardently embraced only a couple of decades earlier. He confessed to this openly. "You know that I have shared and encouraged these illusions and errors. It is not for me to be harsh [with them]." Nevertheless, this was clear evidence of his subjects' serious dissatisfaction. He could not ignore that the throne was under threat, both in Poland and at home.

The cruelest blow suffered by Alexander that year was the death of Sophia, his favorite daughter through a liaison with Maria Naryshkin, a Polish-born beauty of great wit and culture. The eighteen-year-old girl had long suffered from tuberculosis, and during the summer, after prolonged discomfort, she finally succumbed. The news was broken to the emperor just as he was dressing for a ceremonial review of the guard's artillery. The shattered Alexander collapsed in stunned silence and wept profusely. It seemed to those in attendance that there was no way that the sovereign could carry on. But within a quarter of an hour, the grieving monarch managed to pull himself together, and, after greeting the assembled generals, he mounted his horse and galloped off toward the review. A man of duty, Alexander attended to his. He inspected the troops, took the salute, and received the parade's cheers, "Long live the emperor!" The ceremonial over, he changed out of his dress uniform and ordered his faithful coachman Baykov to hurry to Tsarskoye Selo. After dinner, he locked himself into his study and spent a sleepless night. The pain of Sophia's loss was long in leaving him.

In the weeks that followed, Elizaveta's condition continued to deteriorate, and by midsummer her fever was no longer intermittent but persistent, as were her rasping cough, heart palpitations, and anemia. By August she was spitting blood. Dr. Stoffregen, the empress's personal physician, and Dr. Wylie initially diagnosed Elizaveta's condition as angina pectoris and later as tuberculosis coupled with a cardiac condition. It is evident, however, that uncertainty prevailed as to the precise nature of the illness, despite the experienced medical team. Whatever it was, there was general agreement that an escape from the capital's harsh, damp winter would be beneficial. The doctors advised Alexander to move his wife to a warm climate — possibly Italy, southern France, or even southern Russia — before cold weather set in, and he concurred. The matter of location was carefully discussed and a variety of possibilities were suggested. Then Alexander, in his own enigmatic manner, took everyone by surprise by announcing that the empress would winter in Taganrog, of all places. Why Taganrog? "I can't believe it," complained Prince Volkonsky, the tsar's personal secretary, freshly returned from Paris, where he had attended the coronation of Charles X. "How could the doctors possibly have chosen such a place, as though no better places exist in Russia?" If it were to be southern Russia and not southern France or Italy, why not the sunny coast of the Crimea? Yalta, for example, had a Mediterranean climate. In addition, there were a number of splendid villas in the area. But Taganrog — really!

But no — despite everyone's urging, Alexander was determined it was to be Taganrog; he seemed fixated on the place. It might fairly be asked whether, in choosing a remote locale, the emperor had his wife's best interests at heart, or whether he was driven by his own agenda. And if the latter, what possibly might it have been? If at the time Alexander had been actively contemplating an escape from the Russian throne, then an exit from the country by sea to some far-off land would have been the surest way. Unlike Odessa or the populated shores of its vicinity, Taganrog offered an obscure springboard for a maritime departure. The provincial town had a simple society that could more easily be managed — fewer of the curious and gossips. In any event, Elizaveta accepted her husband's decision.

Alexander's singular choice of location was a sleepy commercial port on the northern reaches of the Sea of Azov, not far from the mouth of the Don. Peter the Great, anxious to strengthen his sovereignty over the area, had founded it in 1689 as a lightly fortified citadel. The town was located near a vast swamp, and the saltwater air was known to be anything but wholesome. Azov was referred to as "the putrid sea." An Englishman visiting there in 1854 wrote, "The sea is not navigable after the beginning of October, two years ago all the vessels were frozen up in this month." Taganrog was also often buffeted by violent gales, which sometimes lasted several weeks. At one time, the city's population had grown to 60,000, but after its return in 1771 to the Turks following Catherine's first war against the Ottomans, it was virtually destroyed. In Alexander's time there were fewer than 5,000 inhabitants in the town. The harbormaster's archive for 1825 records the arrival into port of 212 ships that descended the river networks to discharge cargo for export — mostly grain, leather, oil, tar, copper, and caviar. Because of the port's shallow nine-foot draft, there were no wharves along the waterfront, so everything had to be loaded onto the anchored seagoing vessels by lighters. An 1825 census shows that Taganrog had 197 stone houses and 896 wooden ones. The town sported a couple of schools, ten churches, a municipal garden, and a small garrison. It did not have quarters suitable to accommodate a lengthy stay by the emperor with a large entourage. Furthermore, the town was some 1,400 miles from the capital and was accessible only over poor roads. "The idea of founding a capital in a place so unfortunately situated," wrote one of Alexander's contemporaries, "can certainly be reckoned among Peter the Great's least happy projects."

In the nearby Crimea, on the other hand, the southern shores are sheltered from the winds, and the winter weather is generally balmy, certainly more so than Azov's northern shore. There were delightful villas and palaces situated on some of the world's most beautiful shorelines, an ideal setting for those seeking an escape from the harsh northern winter. Alexander was fully familiar with the delights of the "Russian Riviera," so much so that earlier he had purchased a magnificent parcel of land at Orianda, where he planned to build a private residence. Furthermore, had the emperor selected the Crimea, he would have had the practical advantage of being near a large city, Odessa. And from the Crimea, communication with St. Petersburg would have been far simpler.

The tsar announced that he would accompany his wife to the remote outpost. He would return to the capital by New Year's, but the empress would likely remain on. The physicians were no doubt correct in recommending a more favorable climate, and now a decision on a location had been taken. Again, Alexander took the court by surprise by announcing that they would leave immediately. The physicians' concern had been to have the empress escape the cold and humidity of St. Petersburg's winter, but it was now only late summer and the weather was still mild. For some reason, there seemed an urgency on the part of the emperor to depart. Was the empress so ill that she required an immediate change of scene? Was St. Petersburg's autumn that arduous?

Prince Volkonsky was ordered to prepare for an imminent departure south. He was detailed to escort the empress and attend her for the duration of her stay there. An architect was dispatched to Taganrog to prepare quarters for the imperial party. Given the empress's health, the long journey would be both difficult and exhausting. She was not the seasoned traveler that her husband was, the roads were relatively primitive, and coach stops generally offered only rudimentary hospitality. It was decided that the emperor, who liked to travel fast, would leave St. Petersburg two days before his wife. Because of her fragile health, hers would be a leisurely journey, with a retinue of attendants and physicians.

In preparing for his own departure from St. Petersburg, Alexander ordered Prince Golitsen to sort out the papers and documents in the imperial cabinet. In the course of this assignment, Golitsen remarked to the emperor that there appeared to be no formal documentation concerning a succession to the throne in the unlikely event of the tsar's death. Should such a tragedy occur, the absence of provision would have profoundly serious repercussions on the country. In view of His Majesty's lengthy and distant absence from the capital, might it not be prudent to make appropriate provisions? The question startled Alexander. He pondered the matter in silence, and then, raising his hand to the heavens, replied, "Let's rely on the Almighty. He'll provide better than any of us feeble mortals can."

On August 31, on the eve of his departure from the capital, Alexander paid a visit to his mother, the dowager empress, in Pavlovsk. After dinner the two strolled through the silent park. They passed the Rose Pavilion, where twelve years earlier the emperor had been gloriously feted after his victorious return from Paris. Now, in the autumnal colors of the changing leaves and the sadness of the barren rose beds, the mood of the setting was entirely different. It seemed to correspond to Alexander's melancholy frame of mind. He bade farewell to his mother and kissed her good-bye.

In the early hours of September 1, the emperor left his capital. A heavy stillness hung over the city as his solitary troika distanced itself from the palace. For the first leg of his trip, Alexander was accompanied only by his coachman, Ilya Baykov, a faithful servant who had been at his side for thirty years. At a quarter past four in the morning the coach arrived at the gates of Nevsky Monastery, where, by prearrangement, there awaited him Metropolitan Seraphim — the presiding bishop of Novgorod and St. Petersburg — priests in full vestments, and the monks. Alexander descended from the troika, kissed the proffered cross, had holy water sprinkled on him, and made his way into the church as the monks sang the familiar "Save, O Lord, Thy People." He took a place by the tomb of St. Alexander Nevsky, where he stood motionless throughout the long liturgy. The monks standing closest to him observed through the candlelit gloom that Alexander was in tears for a good portion of the service. When the moment came for the reading of the Gospel, he approached the metropolitan and requested that the Bible be placed on his head. He then knelt down before the high churchman and the lesson of the day was read from the heavy book reposing on the bowed head of the Autocrat of All Russia.

Following the service, the tsar accepted the metropolitan's invitation to stop by at his quarters. There he was told of a particularly holy monk who resided in the monastery in self-imposed solitary confinement, spending virtually all his day in prayer. Alexander promptly requested to meet the holy man, who made no objection to receiving the tsar. On his arrival at the monk's cell, a somber sight greeted the emperor: the floor and all four walls were covered in a coarse black material. Through the dark gloom there stood a solitary bench. A few candles flickered in front of icons.

After greeting the emperor, the monk fell to his knees before a crucifix and, facing the august visitor, cried out, "Pray, Tsar!" Alexander knelt and the two prayed together. After a while, Alexander ceased his prayers, but the monk continued for some time. In a whisper the emperor asked the metropolitan whether all the monk's belongings were in the room. Where, for example, did he sleep? "He sleeps on the floor at the base of the crucifix where he prays," replied the churchman.

"Not so," interrupted the monk, who had overheard the exchange. "I do have a bed. Come, I'll show you." He beckoned Alexander behind a screen that divided the cell, and there on a table Alexander was startled to find an open black coffin. In it lay a shroud and various burial accoutrements. "Look! That's my bed," cried the monk, "and not mine only. In it we shall all someday lie, and then we shall sleep deeply." The emperor stood in stunned silence, contemplating the bizarre sight before him.

"Emperor," said the holy man, "I am an old man and I have seen much. Be good enough to listen to me. Before the great plague, ethics in our land were far better and the people were God-fearing. But after the plague principles deteriorated. The year 1812 should have been a watershed, a time for renewal and godliness, but with the war's end morality sank lower than ever. You are the emperor and you should oversee morality. You are a son of the

Orthodox Church and you must love it and protect it. That's what our Lord wishes." Having delivered this admonition, the monk turned away and lapsed into silence.

Alexander was visibly touched. Turning to the metropolitan, he whispered, "In my lifetime I've had many long and flowery speeches addressed to me. But none can compare in beauty to the simple words I have just heard." To the monk he said, "What a pity that I haven't met you sooner." He asked and received the monk's blessing. With that, Alexander and the metropolitan left the cell and made their way to the waiting troika. The tsar mounted the carriage and, with tears in his eyes, bade farewell to the metropolitan and the assembled monks. "Pray for me and for my wife," he asked them. Baykov cracked the whip and off the troika sped. For some time Alexander stood on the coach step, looking back, gazing at the monastery's receding spires. He crossed himself occasionally. Only when the buildings had disappeared from sight did he finally take his seat.

The gloomy cell and the open coffin with its folded shroud — these were the final impressions that Alexander carried away with him as he took leave of St. Petersburg. At the outskirts of the city, he ordered Baykov to stop. Once more he stood up in the carriage and for a long time silently gazed at the city. It was as though he was saying farewell to his capital.

Equestrian portrait of Alexander I painted in the 1820s. It depicts the emperor at the height of his power and fame, after the defeat of Napoleon. EQUESTRIAN PORTRAIT OF ALEXANDER I BY FRANZ KRUGER, COURTESY OF THE STATE HERMITAGE MUSEUM, ST. PETERSBURG.

Baroness von Krüdener, 1815. A mystic and fundamentalist, she, for a brief period, insinuated herself into Alexander I's good graces and wielded enormous influence over him.

In the early days of November 1824, hurricane winds caused the waters of the Neva to back up into St. Petersburg, causing a catastrophic flood. Alexander, increasingly beset politically and personally, saw it as a sign of retribution for his participation in his father's death.

Alexander I praying at Alexander Nevsky Monastery, September 1825, shortly before he left for Taganrog.

A view of Taganrog in the early nineteenth century. Because of his wife's declining health, Alexander decided to move her—and the court—south to this little town on the Sea of Azov.

Dr. James Wylie, Alexander's faithful physician and friend, who accompanied him to Taganrog and was chief physician during his "final" illness.

General Diebich, Alexander's chief of staff, who accompanied him south to Tananrog.

An artist's rendition of Alexander's death in Taganrog, 1825. PAINTING BY
I. KULAKOV, 1827.

The funeral cortege of Alexander arriving at St. Petersburg after the long
journey north from Taganrog.

Alexander's younger brother, Grand Duke Constantine, who might have succeeded to the throne but deferred to his younger brother, Nicholas.
ENGRAVING BY H. BENNER.
AUTHOR'S PERSONAL COLLECTION.

During the confusing period between the death of Alexander and the coronation of Nicholas I, a small group of revolutionaries headed by Sergey Trubetskoi fomented what became known as the Decembrist revolt, which was quickly put down. (The prince, by the way, was an ancestor of the author.)
AUTHOR'S PERSONAL COLLECTION.

The only known portrait of
the starets Feodor Kuzmich.

Feodor Kuzmich's "cell" on the Khromov property in Tomsk, Siberia. FROM
GRAND DUKE NIKOLAI MIKHAILOVICH'S *Legenda o kochine imperatora Alexandra.*

The chapel over the grave of Feodor Kuzmich, Tomsk, Siberia. AUTHOR'S PERSONAL COLLECTION.

Grand Duchess Olga, sister of Tsar Nicholas II. She said: "we have no doubt" that her ancestor Tsar Alexander I and the starets Feodor Kuzmich were one and the same. PAINTING BY A. S. RÖMER, 1950. COURTESY OF OLGA KULIKOVSKY-ROMANOFF.

Alexander I at age 24, a year after he acceded to the throne.

Alexander I in full military uniform. His patience and his courage in battle contributed to the defeat of Napoleon, making him the hero of all of Europe. ENGRAVING BY H. BENNER. AUTHOR'S PERSONAL COLLECTION.

Peter III, who succeeded his mother, Elizaveta, in 1761. A strange, troubled man, he reigned for only 197 days. ENGRAVING BY H. BENNER. AUTHOR'S PERSONAL COLLECTION.

Catherine II, known to history as Catherine the Great, wrested the throne from her husband by a palace coup in 1762 and ruled Russia for the next 34 years. ENGRAVING BY R. WOODMAN. AUTHOR'S PERSONAL COLLECTION.

Paul I. His mother, Catherine II, repressed and ignored him throughout most of his life. She never intended for him to succeed her. When she died suddenly in 1796, leaving no explicit orders concerning succession, Paul assumed the throne at the age of 42 and ruled for the next five years. ENGRAVING BY J. CHAPMAN. AUTHOR'S PERSONAL COLLECTION.

Empress Maria Feodorovna, Paul's second wife. Theirs was a happy marriage, despite Paul's instability and bitterness toward his mother. Paul and Maria had ten children, the eldest of whom was Alexander.

Elizaveta Alexeyevna. She was married to the then Grand Duke Alexander in 1793, when he was just 15 years old. Theirs was not a happy—or faithful—union.

Mikhail Speransky, a visionary and reformer who rose from humble origins to become the most powerful personage in Russia, referred to by some as "Secretary-General of the Empire." The negative reaction of the Russian nobles, however, forced the emperor to oust him in March 1812.

ENGRAVING BY P. WRIGHT.
AUTHOR'S PERSONAL COLLECTION.

By 1807, Napoleon's conquests were such that the French Empire now abutted the Russian, with only the Niemen River separating the two. On June 25, Napoleon and Alexander met on a hastily constructed raft in the middle of the Niemen to sign an alliance between France and Russia.

In 1812, only five years after the peace treaty had been signed, Napoleon's *Grande Armée* invaded Russia, reaching and occupying Moscow by mid-September. Russia's persistent refusal to engage in combat totally frustrated the French emperor. On October 13, it started to snow, and he and his troops abandoned Moscow and headed west. Less than a month later, the last French troops departed Russian territory. PAINTING BY P. FESSE. AUTHOR'S PERSONAL COLLECTION.

10

Retreat to Taganrog

ALEXANDER HEADED SOUTH with all due speed. There were none of the customary military inspections, parades, or visits with local dignitaries along the way. The emperor's only concern was to arrive at his destination as soon as possible and do whatever he could to assure the comfort of Elizaveta's forthcoming journey along the same route. On exiting the capital, he was joined by the remainder of the imperial party: chief of staff Baron Diebich, aide-de-camp Colonel A. D. Salomka, and two doctors — the ever-present Wylie and Tarasov. In addition to these gentlemen, the suite included six court officials — an Englishman by the name of Miller, who was the maitre d'hotel, a couple of valets, and four servants: seventeen people in all, including the coachmen and attendants of the baggage train. The imperial party would be absent for three months at the very least. No military escorts accompanied the group, and no police. Despite the known activities of subversive groups seeking the overthrow of the government, security did not seem a concern. One wonders in which of today's major countries might a head of state, particularly an absolute monarch, travel so openly for such long distances under such casual arrangements!

Covering nearly sixty miles a day, the tsar's party arrived at Taganrog on September 13, a little over three weeks after leaving

St. Petersburg. It was a hard, fast-paced trip, and everyone was delighted when it was over. In his notes for the day, Wylie makes this curious remark: "Here ends the first part of our journey." Precisely what did he mean by that? It would seem to imply that, at the time of writing, the doctor expected that there would be further legs to the journey.

The residence selected for the imperial quarters was a modest, single-story stone house with basement accommodations for the servants. The portion of the building assigned to the empress consisted of eight small rooms, two of which were given over to the ladies-in-waiting. One of the rooms accommodated the portable chapel. In the center of the building was a large foyer that served as the dining room and reception hall. On the other side of this hall were the tsar's quarters — one reasonably large room that served as his bedroom-study, and another equally spacious one with a view on the garden that served as his dressing room and washing room. Outside these was a corridor where the duty valet made his headquarters. The closets and wardrobes were in the basement. The house had a walled garden with unattended fruit trees that Alexander, immediately upon his arrival, ordered pruned and cleaned up. The furniture throughout was of the simplest sort.

At Taganrog, Alexander's priority was to make the place as comfortable as possible for Elizaveta. He personally attended to almost every detail, even helping to move the furniture about and hammering the hooks for the picture frames. In anticipation of her arrival, he supervised the cleanup of the municipal gardens and, spade in hand, directed the relocation of certain paths within the park.

Elizaveta had set off for the south accompanied by Prince Volkonsky, State Secretary Longinov, and two ladies-in-waiting — Princess Volkonsky and Katerina Valueva. In addition, her party included her trusted physicians Drs. Stoffregen, Dobbert, and Rheingold; Mr. Prott, the court pharmacist; and two chambermaids. The party made relatively good time and arrived at Taganrog on September 23. Alexander rode out from town to the first relay station to meet the group.

As anticipated, it had been a fatiguing journey, hardly the sort of trip that a woman in Elizaveta's condition should normally have made. Yet she alighted from the carriage as though returning from a brief excursion in the gardens of Tsarskoye Selo. "It is extraordinary," comments Nikolai K. Shilder, Alexander's official biographer, "that the empress, whose weakened condition prevented her in St. Petersburg from making the barest unnecessary movement . . . descended from the carriage effortlessly and unassisted." It was a joyous reunion but brief, for there still remained a bit of travel before dark. By seven that evening the carriages had pulled up in front of the Greek monastery on Taganrog's outskirts. The abbott, clergy, and monks were lined up on the steps as Elizaveta descended unaided from her coach. The empress seemed in high spirits and good shape, despite the obvious fatigue of the three-week trip. The imperial party entered the monastery's church, where a service was held in thanksgiving for the safe arrival.

At the conclusion of the service, Alexander and Elizaveta drove to their new "palace," where all stood in readiness. Familiar picture frames adorned the walls; the curtains and carpets smelled of freshness, and a profusion of fresh flowers decorated the cozy rooms. Outside, two platoons of Cossacks from the local garrison had taken up guard around the grounds. Baron Frederiks, from the same garrison, was appointed commander of the imperial household. The modesty and simplicity of that Taganrog court was remarkable. "It was no more elaborate," writes Shilder, "than the home of a prosperous provincial landowner."

Within days of his own arrival at Taganrog, Alexander had written to his devoted Arakcheyev: "Thank the Lord: I arrived at my destination, my dearest Alexey Andreovich, in good shape and after an agreeable journey — the roads and weather were excellent . . . my quarters here are fairly pleasing. The air is superb, we have a view on the sea, and the pace of life is agreeable. I do hope that you will come and see for yourself."

No sooner had the emperor dispatched his letter than he received a report that Arakcheyev's mistress of nearly a quarter century, Nastasia, had been brutally murdered. Her abuse of her household staff was legendary. The servants seethed with hatred and resentment, and resorted to all kinds of subterfuge to try and better their miserable condition. Once, for example, a selection of herbs was secreted under Nastasia's mattress, in an effort to mollify her brutal character. When the grasses failed, more radical possibilities were contemplated and discussed. During one of the count's absences from the estate, a chambermaid named Praskovya and several others were particularly harshly beaten on the orders of their mistress. That afternoon the incensed girl and her brother stole into Nastasia's bedroom while she was napping and stabbed her to death, repeatedly plunging a kitchen knife into her chest and face. The bloodied corpse was so mutilated that "her head was only hanging on by the skin."

The count, in a state of shock, lapsed into such anguish and despair that for a time he appeared on the verge of insanity. Three days after the murder he was sufficiently collected to write to the emperor: "My little father, Your Majesty! I have suffered a personal tragedy and have lost my faithful friend who shared my home for twenty-five years. My health and state of mind have been so shattered and weakened that I desire and seek only my own death. I have no strength of mind to attend to business matters. Farewell, little father, remember your servant. My friend was butchered by servants and I don't know where I will take my orphaned self, but for certain I shall leave." Arakcheyev resigned all responsibilities; the emperor thus lost his most trusted and perhaps most devoted colleague.[†]

Alexander's grief over his friend's tragic loss was profound, and the murder created an indelible impression on him. Diebich

---

[†]Praskovya, her brother, and thirty-two others were arrested for the murder and sentenced to the knout. Praskovya received 125 blows of the lash and her brother 175. The execution of such a harsh sentence was unlawful inasmuch as all the arrested were under the age of eighteen. By an 1807 law, minors involved in murder could receive no more than 30 strokes of the knout.

tells us that when the news from Gruzino was received, "the emperor supposed that Arakcheyev's mistress was killed not for hatred of her but for hatred of the count and to force him to abandon his post." The joy of Taganrog was deeply clouded by the Gruzino murder; the peace that Alexander appeared to be enjoying in his new pastoral environment was shaken to the roots.

For the next two weeks the weather in Taganrog continued mild and bright. Elizaveta was in good form and seemed to gather strength. Alexander was so pleased with her improved condition that he decided he could safely leave her for a few days. Always eager to travel, he decided to carry out an inspection of the local provinces. On October 11, he bid farewell to his wife and left Taganrog to visit the centers of Rostov, Nahichevan, and Novocherkask, three towns lying to the east, on the banks of the Don River. The brief tour was successfully completed, and before returning home he even managed to inspect the forces of the Don Cossacks. The tsar was absent a mere five days, but his wife greeted his homecoming as though he had been missing for months. It was a happy trip and an even happier reunion.

Shortly after his return, Alexander received an anxious General de Witte, commander in chief of the southern armies. The agitated officer had arrived to report on the activities of a certain secret society that was, he revealed, plotting to overthrow the government. The general presented a list of the subversive leaders. For some time Alexander had been well aware of the existence of such societies, but he appeared to accept the fact with surprising passivity. De Witte's report, however, was especially disturbing, for evidence showed that revolutionary action was actually developing. Despite the clear evidence and the burgeoning danger, Alexander ordered that, for the moment at least, nothing be done except to continue surveillance. A bewildered and frustrated de Witte returned to St. Petersburg, empty-handed of arrest orders.

Alexander's inspection of the local hinterland had been such a success, and was greeted so enthusiastically by the populace, that a more ambitious tour was planned, this time of Crimea. Count I. Vorontsov-Dashkov, the governor-general of Novorossisk, urged an

early departure in order to permit a reasonably comprehensive itinerary, one that would permit a return home before the autumn rains
and cold set in. Since the empress's health continued to improve and
she appeared happy in her setting, the emperor decided in favor of a
more extensive tour, this one of seventeen days.

The tsar left Taganrog on October 20, accompanied by Chief
of Staff Diebich, Drs. Wylie and Tarasov, and Colonel Salomka. On
the eve of their departure, an incident occurred that created a lasting
impression on Alexander. The emperor was at his desk in the afternoon working on state papers when a thick rain cloud settled over
the town. The room grew so dark that he ordered his valet Anisimov to bring in candles. Shortly afterward the sky cleared and the
sun shone once more. The servant reentered the room with the
intention of removing the candles. Alexander asked why, to which
the servant replied that in old Russia it was considered an ill omen
to sit in daytime with lighted candles. Flaming candles in daytime,
he explained, stood only by coffins of the dead. "You're right. And I
believe this too," agreed the tsar. "Take them away!" To the ever
superstitious Alexander, however, it seemed a portent of ill. "I could
do very well without this trip," he later confessed to Elizaveta, "but
everything is arranged and people are expecting me. I must go
through with it." In the days to come the exchange with Anisimov
came back to him, and more than once the emperor mentioned it to
Elizaveta and other members of the royal household.

For most of the tour all went well, and Alexander was in
high spirits and unusually talkative. The first night was spent at
Mariupol, where the emperor visited the Mennonite colonies on
the banks of the Molotchnaia River. These people were pacific
fundamentalists, stemming from a sixteenth-century Swiss Protes-
tant sect, and they had made their way into Russia nearly a century earlier. Alexander was impressed with what the "industrious
and talented Germans" had been able to carve out of the desolate
steppe. A warm reception was accorded him, and he came away
delighted with the orderliness of these productive villages.

During the third day of the tour, a stop was made at
Orianda, the property recently acquired by Alexander from Count

Koushelva-Bezborodka. Some years earlier he had visited the spot and had been instantly taken by it. Here was the special corner of Europe for which he had long searched, and here it was that he would someday erect a comfortable palace, eventually perhaps to retire and live out his days.

Since coming to Taganrog, the emperor had continued to make references to quitting the throne. "I'll soon move to the Crimea," he announced one evening, "and I'll live the life of a private citizen. I've earned my twenty-five years, and every soldier earns his right to retirement after those years." And to Prince Volkonsky he added, "and you will retire with me and become my librarian." There was nothing startling in this declaration; for most of his adult life, Alexander had been uttering similar expressions of intent — he would someday fade away from public view into quiet retirement. (One might, however, imagine that the loyal secretary was surprised to find himself included in the emperor's plans — surely he did not share the monarch's enthusiasm for exile in Orianda's rural setting.) However much Alexander might have wished to retire, his oft-declared intention was empty. Russian monarchs did not voluntarily retire. Autocrats had been deposed, perhaps forced into a monastic exile. Some had been murdered or "died of apoplexy," but none had simply resigned to live a secluded life of peaceful retirement. God anointed the sovereign. It was not for mortals to undo His work; only the Almighty could wipe away the sacred coronation ointment. Deep in his heart, did Alexander truly expect one day to realize his declared dream? Or this time, while giving utterance to such desires — now that he was at the southern fringe of his empire with access to the sea — did he perhaps have an alternate plan in mind?

By October 29, the tsar's party had arrived at Bachtchysar, the ancient capital of the Crimean Khans. He visited the old palace of the Khans, the mosque, and the Turkish baths. The Tartar mufti invited the emperor to attend a service in the mosque, a celebration of prayers for the emperor's long life. Alexander agreed, but did not appear with the public in the main body of the mosque. Instead, he stood behind the screens, out of sight of the praying public. That evening, he asked Tarasov to prepare the same rice drink he had once received when he was with a fever. The doctor did as requested and then went to report to Wylie that the sovereign appeared feverish and seemed to have an upset stomach. "It might be noted, however," Tarasov wrote later in his diary, "that the emperor complained neither to me nor to Wylie of any disposition. That day, however, he ate sparingly — only some barley soup and a cutlet."

Despite the tsar's stolid stoicism, the doctors became increasingly concerned. Alexander was not his own self; he was coming down with something. Perhaps it was the oysters he had eaten en route or the fatty fish at Balaklava; or it might simply have been a cold caught during that exhausting ride to St. George's Monastery when he was inappropriately dressed. From one so robust and rarely ill, the signs were not to be lightly dismissed.

In the morning, Alexander complained of nothing. Observed Tarasov, he "appeared entirely healthy and was in high spirits. With everyone he was as sociable as ever." Accompanied by his suite, he set off on horseback for Tchufout-Kali, in the depths of the Bachtchysar pass. Atop a vertical cliff, deep within the pass, was a Karaite settlement said to have been founded in 480 B.C. The Karaites were a local Jewish sect that opposed Talmudic Jews, upon whom they looked as heretics. They rejected all tradition and rabbinical teaching and adhered solely to the Old Testament. "It's hard to understand why the Karaites selected for their home such a forlorn and unlikely place, so far removed from any known place, where there is no water, which is perched on a cliff towering over the pass . . . totally inaccessible without a guide," noted Tarasov.

As he traveled toward Tchufout-Kali, the emperor passed numerous gypsy encampments. Squalid and unkempt, these settlements created a sad impression; everyone in the party was pleased to leave them behind. The Karaite settlements, on the other hand, were diametrically different. These were enterprising tradesmen, and their affluence showed in their large, richly decorated houses of a Far Eastern design. "All the inhabitants except the women" turned out to greet the tsar, and the enthusiasm of the crowd was evident. The emperor visited the principal synagogue, an impressive stone building of considerable size. After touring the high school that was attached to the synagogue, he spent some time with the chief of the Karaites, where an elaborate tea was served "with every sort of sweet delicacy the East can offer." According to custom, the chief presented to his honored guest his wives and children, all of whom lived in a separate building. "Some of the wives," observed Tarasov, "were beautiful but incredibly pale. With them were a number of small children. The entire harem was richly dressed in the Eastern style."

On November 1, Alexander was at Perekop, where he toured at length the town's hospital. He seemed particularly interested by the malaria wing, where he tarried, posing a number of questions about the disease.

As the tour progressed, the emperor continued in good health, and his entourage had the impression that the earlier scare had been a false alarm. "Since the time His Majesty ordered the rice soup at Bachtchysar," Tarasov noted in his diary, "neither I nor Baron Wylie had any reason to complain about his health. In a small town midway between Znamensky and Orehov the party stopped off for dinner. During the meal Alexander turned the conversation to the hospitals of the Crimea, inquiring particularly about the local malaria. He seemed especially curious about quinine, which he recognized was truly effective against the disease but which, he lamented, tasted utterly unpleasant. In defense of the medication, Baron Wylie informed the tsar that its taste wasn't unpleasant, simply bitter. "The emperor, as though disbelieving the doctor, then and there ordered me to get him some quinine from the pharmacy. I gave him a jar of the medicine and the emperor put a touch to his tongue. He made a terrible grimace and said, 'You and Wylie certainly don't go out of your way to spoil patients with pleasant-tasting medicines.' And later, when he returned the jar to me, he asked, 'And how do you administer this medication?' I replied that patients receive the medicine either as a powder or as a pill. 'Thanks for the treat,' he answered, 'please replace it where it belongs.'" It is curious that Alexander took such a detailed interest in the subject of malaria, but from this impromptu lesson, he certainly became better acquainted with the disease.

Following the meal, the party continued its journey, planning to make it to Orehov before dark. At the final change station before Orehov, a courier from St. Petersburg intercepted the emperor's entourage. A certain Major Maskov carried dispatches that required the tsar's attention. Alexander thanked the major and ordered him to join the party. The weary rider was invited to make himself comfortable in an empty carriage that was at hand. The officer gratefully accepted the offer, mounted the vehicle, and the troika's coachman gave the horses free rein. They galloped off at full speed. Hurtling down the uneven road, the vehicle unexpectedly hit a soft clay pothole and the jolt unseated Maskov, so that he was hurled from the carriage and hit the stone road with tremendous force, landing on his head. Alexander, whose carriage was just behind, witnessed the accident and ordered a halt, asking Tarasov to look after the unconscious man. Darkness was fast approaching, and so while the physician and two officers attended the prone figure, the rest of the party sped on to Orehov.

Once there, Alexander ordered that he be immediately informed of the courier's condition as soon as there was any news. Shortly after midnight, Tarasov arrived at Orekhov and went straight to the emperor's quarters. Baron Diebich announced the physician's arrival and Tarasov hurried into the tsar's room. He found the monarch seated by the fire, dressed in a robe, studying the newly arrived dispatches. Alexander jumped up and demanded, "How is Maskov?" The physician replied that the officer was dead: he had suffered a massive concussion; in fact, the fall had split his skull, and he had died within minutes.

Alexander was visibly moved and distressed. With tears in his eyes, he remarked, "What a tragedy! I so pity the poor man." After a few silent moments, he turned away and the physician left. "I couldn't help noticing," Tarasov noted cryptically, "the extraordinary expression that fell on the emperor's face, a face I knew well from many years of observing it. I'm not certain what it reflected."

The next day, November 4, Alexander was in Mariupol. That evening he summoned Wylie to his room; the doctor reports that he found him in the throes of serious malarial seizures. "Wylie was highly disturbed by the emperor's condition," records Tarasov, "and he seemed temporarily to lose his usual practical good sense. What he gave the emperor was a strong rum punch, then tucked him into bed, covering him warmly. This seemed to make the emperor all the more restless, although by early morning he did fall asleep. When he woke up, Alexander was advised to remain in Mariupol for a day or two, but he rejected the idea, arguing that the town was less than sixty miles from home. He was anxious to return to Taganrog and be with the empress, who, according to the planned itinerary, was expecting him back on the fifth.

"At ten o'clock the carriages finally pulled out of town. Alexander, who was still feverish and appeared exhausted, was bundled up in a greatcoat and bearskins."

11

The Fatal Illness

THE EMPEROR ARRIVED BACK in Taganrog on schedule on November 5, at six in the evening. Entering his quarters, he met Volkonsky and complained of feeling ill — he thought that he had managed to catch a touch of malaria. Alexander reported that his sickness had begun some seven days ago at Bachtchysar. He then briefly related details of his visits, particularly mentioning the malaria wing at Perekop.

"At this point," wrote Volkonsky in his diary, "I dared to suggest to His Majesty, that he might very well have hastened the development of his sickness by making such an imprudent visit — of all places, to a ward full of malaria cases." The prince went on to remind Alexander that a person pushing fifty has less stamina than someone in his twenties.

"My dear friend," replied the tsar, "I understand what you are saying all too clearly and I frequently reflect on that. Ultimately, however, one must trust that all will be well." With this the emperor repaired to his wife's quarters, where he spent the rest of the evening.

As he was preparing for bed late that night, Alexander chatted with his valet, Anisimov. He recalled the incident of the burning midday candles and said to his trusted servant, "I'm very sick." And then he went on to remark, "The candles that I ordered removed never seem to leave my mind. This means that I am to die — then they'll be placed before me for good reason." The horrified Anisimov threw up his arms and protested: "What are you saying? God save us from such a calamity!" Alexander retired for the night.

And here, the Taganrog drama begins to unfold with startling rapidity. The historian's task in tracing the exact sequence of events of the next thirteen days is Herculean. Equally difficult is reconstructing precisely what took place in Taganrog immediately following the tsar's death. The information we have concerning that period comes to us primarily through the diaries, letters, and memoirs of those who were present: Empress Elizaveta, Prince Volkonsky, General Diebich, and Drs. Wylie and Tarasov. Important but perhaps less significant are the accounts of others who were on the spot — people such as ladies-in-waiting, valets, and attendants.

The problem with the diaries and memoirs is that they are inconsistent and frequently contradictory. In addition, so-called daily reports were composed *post factum*. Dr. Tarasov's journal, for example, was certainly compiled some time after the tsar's death. And the surviving letters do not offer the historian much satisfaction, for they too contain contradictory information and, frequently, innuendo, particularly the letters of Empress Elizaveta.

The imperial archive contains a document written in French entitled *L'Histoire de la maladie et des derniers moments de l'empereur Alexandre* (The History of the Illness and Final Days of Alexander I), which for nearly a century was viewed as the official, authoritative account of the tsar's death. The subtitle of the work, however, is *fondée sur les informations les plus authentique* ("based on the most authentic information"), which makes it clear that the report is a reconstruction, not the day-by-day log of events it claims to be. The basic problem with this manuscript is that its author is unknown. It is highly unlikely that any of the attending physicians wrote it, inasmuch as the work is frequently at odds with their individual writings. Whoever penned the report was doubtless present in Taganrog at the time, or, if not, he certainly had direct access to those who were.

The contradictions in the reports of those who were on the spot are disconcerting. For example, one day Elizaveta notes that Alexander took a purgative and that "the medication bore results." But on that same day, Volkonsky informs us that "unfortunately despite all sorts of persuasion, he refused to drink the mixture." Wylie gives a third version, in which he claims that no medication whatsoever was even *offered* that day. On another occasion, Wylie writes, "His Majesty had a bad night and refused medication," while the empress reports, "Alexander told me that he had had a good night." Again, Wylie reports, "His Majesty continues with a blocked stomach, and when I offered him a purge he became quite angry and refused to speak to me." But Elizaveta tells us that on that day her husband was in good shape, and free from discomfort. Volkonsky reports that after dinner on November 6, he and Wylie together went to the monarch's sickbed and sat with him alone. Elizaveta, however, writes that she was already there and that Wylie entered alone, with Volkonsky appearing only much later. In his own journal, Wylie claims to have been alone with the emperor; no mention is made of either Volkonsky or Elizaveta, despite that, on the other occasions when she was present, Wylie inevitably makes note of it.

In dealing with the Legend, the historian's task is made all the more difficult because of Nicholas I's lamentable decision to destroy much of the documentation related to his brother's twenty-four-year reign. One presumes that the new emperor wished to eradicate all record of his brother's liberal views, which were diametrically opposed to his own. At any rate, by his express orders files of documentation related to Taganrog were burned, as was virtually the entire collection of letters that the dowager empress had accumulated over the years. Nicholas's assiduous effort to suppress this critical archival material has been viewed by many as an attempted cover-up. In any event, it certainly strengthens the Legend's credibility. Generations of historians have been frustrated both by the countless contradictions of contemporary witnesses and by the willful destruction of invaluable archives.

The basis of the narrative that follows is largely taken from N. K. Shilder's massive work *Imperator Alexandr pervy,* which in turn was largely culled from the official court account of Alexander's death, *The History of the Illness.* It must be borne in mind that, although Shilder's book appeared in print in 1898, after censorship had been lifted in Russia, it was composed in the years immediately preceding, at a time when the censor's influence prevailed. No publication was permitted to see print if it ran contrary to the sanctioned account of the tsar's death. All scholars and historians were stymied in their attempts to ferret out the truth, if the government did not wish to have it revealed. The fact is, much of what has come down to us about Alexander's death is shrouded in contradictions and inexplicable testimony. In addition to Shilder, I have consulted several other sources, so that what follows is, I believe, as full and authentic a chronicle as one can reconstruct.

November 6: Wylie reports that the night passed badly for the sovereign and he writes with alarm, "Refuses medication. He brings me to despair. Am concerned that such stubbornness might have unfortunate consequences." On the previous night, the emperor had complained merely of "a bit of a fever." Could the night have brought such a rapid downturn that the doctor foresees "unfortunate consequences"?

At eight in the morning, Volkonsky comes to the emperor and inquires how he has slept. Alexander replies that he slept soundly and feels nothing of malaria. "But," Volkonsky observes, "it seemed to me that His Majesty appeared weak and his eyes looked slightly clouded over." Alexander lunches in his bedroom with Elizaveta. Midway through the meal, he breaks into a hot sweat and excuses himself from the table. At three o'clock the valet Feodorov summons Wylie, who appears in Alexander's bedroom with Volkonsky. They find Alexander seated on the sofa, bundled up in a heavy robe with his legs wrapped in a blanket. Wylie urges the tsar to accept a laxative, to which Alexander agrees after some persuasion. The emperor then informs them that he wishes to work on the documents recently delivered from St. Petersburg. The prince and Wylie, however, convince him to put work aside and get some rest. Toward the end of the afternoon, Alexander seems in better shape, and the empress comes to join him. She remains with him until ten o'clock.

November 8: Volkonsky reports that the emperor "passed a restless night and had a fever." And Wylie notes in distressed tones, "This fever appears to be *Febris gastrica biliosa,*" and observes that the intestines are blocked. Tarasov, on the other hand, tells us that Wylie, "finding the emperor in satisfactory condition, returned from his patient not only calmed but even in a happy mood, and told me that he was entirely pleased with the emperor's condition." Elizaveta, bearing out Tarasov's testimony, writes that after visiting the tsar Wylie was in a jovial mood and "told me that, although the emperor did have a fever, he was certainly in better shape today." In the early afternoon, in any case, Alexander feels well enough to dictate several letters, including one to his mother. In them he does not even mention his illness.

November 9: Elizaveta reports that, although the emperor does not look particularly well, he is in a jovial mood and talkative. She is pleased to have persuaded her husband to take a purgative. He eats with gusto, moves about the room, and engages in animated conversation. "He was in a good humor," she writes, "happy as of old . . . he laughed." Wylie reports, "The emperor is a bit better today, but he relies exclusively on God for the relief of his symptoms." The doctor concludes that the patient is suffering from diarrhea, a condition he imputes to the fish Alexander ate at Bachtchysar. "What a senseless stop that was," laments Wylie.

In the evening, the empress spends some time with her husband at his bedside and continues to fret over his state. She sends her own physician, Dr. Stoffregen, to consult with Wylie. Before retiring, Alexander dictates another letter to the dowager empress, but this time he takes pains to inform her of the illness. He signs the missive, then issues an inexplicable order: the letter is to be post-dated the eleventh. Volkonsky is puzzled by this irregularity — Alexander has invariably been meticulously correct in his correspondence.

November 10: Wylie reports that "he is better today." Alexander rises from his bed at eleven o'clock and works at a pile of documents at his desk. The afternoon, however, brings on a fever and the sovereign appears weakened: he is not his usual buoyant self and he spends the rest of the day alone, in contemplation. "The fever persisted all day," reports Volkonsky, "and toward evening heavy perspiration developed, together with forgetfulness." In his diary, Wylie makes the cryptic remark, "Since the eighth, I've noticed that he is preoccupied with thoughts other than recovery and that he is disturbed."

The apathy and moroseness that Alexander had displayed prior to his departure from St. Petersburg now appeared as clearly as before. He had again become self-centered and inward-looking, seemingly indifferent to much around him. One cannot help but recall his response to Golitsen when questioned about a possible succession: "Let's rely on the Almighty. He will arrange matters far better than we poor mortals can." Then there was his passively indifferent response to de Witte's report on subversive activities. Or recall his reaction to Volkonsky on the matter of punishing the plotters: "It's not for me to be harsh with them." Not to mention his firm statement of 1825 to William of Orange that he wishes to retire, and the same statement to Volkonsky: "I'll soon move to the Crimea, and you will retire with me." Finally, bear in mind the heavy circumstances of Alexander's departure from St. Petersburg.

Over and over the haunting memory of that fateful night in March 1801 came back to him: his guilt about his father's death, more burdensome than ever. As Adam Czartoryski noted in his memoirs, Alexander's "grief and remorse, which he was continually reviving in his heart, were inexpressibly deep and touching . . . I am certain that toward the end of his life it was the same terrible thought that so depressed him. It filled him with a disgust for life and a piety which was perhaps exaggerated, but which is the sole possible and real support in the most poignant grief."

Wylie's observation that the emperor seemed preoccupied with distant thoughts may not be altogether surprising; neither was his cry for solitude and quiet. A number of developments in the empire that were unfolding were increasingly worrisome, and, it is safe to say, the tranquillity of the country was at risk. The peace and quiet that the ailing monarch so devoutly desired was not to be.

A courier arrived at Taganrog bearing a fresh letter from the distraught Arakcheyev, this one dated October 27. Full of gloom and despair, Alexander's friend again bewailed the tragic turn of events in Gruzino and complained of his miserable solitude. Arakcheyev's health and state of mind had deteriorated badly. "I try each day to be upbeat but at night, heart palpitations, fever, and cold sweats weaken me tremendously." What Arakcheyev now wished above all was to leave Georgia and move to Novgorod, to distance himself from the burdens of responsibility. General Kleinmikel had kindly taken over the running of his office. Should his health really fail, he then, and only then, would move to St. Petersburg, where medical attention was readily available. For the moment, however, he wished to avoid the capital, "where, I confess, I am afraid to live, and where our modern-day dissidents will give me little peace." The count apologized that he was unable to accept Alexander's invitation to join him in Taganrog, much as he might like to. His chest pains were too great, and he simply could not face the prospect of the poor roads and a lengthy trip in bad weather. "Farewell, my father," the letter concludes, "be assured that should I live I will be forever yours. Should I die, my soul will remember Your Majesty's kindness to me." Alexander's deep upset with the assassination of Arakcheyev's mistress was made all the more poignant by the realization that not only had he lost the services of his most valued councillor but that the person he knew so well, trusted, and loved was now a broken man.

Further, dispatches from St. Petersburg from the head of the secret police, General Benckendorff, continued to arrive in Taganrog, reiterating how serious the subversive activities had become. Four weeks earlier General de Witte had apprised the tsar of one such group. Some of the finest names in Russia were associated with these movements, including well-known ranking army officers. Now, it seemed, the secret societies were not only growing numerically but were becoming increasingly bold. But no matter how much people tried to ignite Alexander's interest in these increasingly worrisome developments, it was to no avail. He appeared apathetic, as though refusing to acknowledge the insidious threats. Perhaps he recognized in these malcontents his own youthful self — in the unrealized ideals that were now being espoused by them. For the most part, they sought the same goals that he and the Committee of Friends had so ardently espoused years before. In response to the threat posed by these conspirators, Alexander adopted an ostrich-like posture.

Unfortunately, we do not have details on Benckendorff's dispatches, since the files were among those destroyed by Nicholas I. It is certain, however, that the situation was never fully out of Alexander's mind, for he frequently referred to it. Conspiracy was never far from his mind. Finally, the sovereign directed Diebich to dispatch an officer to Kharkov to arrange for the arrest of the members of a particularly active group of plotters. This was the emperor's last formal order.

The bright days of tranquillity that Alexander had come to enjoy in his early days in Taganrog had become overcast. Dark clouds of disappointment billowed. First came Arakcheyev's tragedy, resignation, and grief; then, at a time of his own weakened physical condition, the treachery of some of the land's foremost citizens in plotting to overthrow the government. For a quarter of a century Alexander's life had been given over to the care of his people, but still they were dissatisfied, always demanding more. He had devoted himself to the empire and to the affairs of Europe and he was bone-weary. Too many problems remained unsolved. For Russia, he desired constitutional reform and relief for the serfs and peasants — yet resistance to that remained high. To the Poles he had given representative government, but what had been his reward? Not gratitude but dissatisfaction. In fact, the Polish experience served only to foster unrest in his own country — his own people viewed themselves as less favored by their tsar than the Poles. As for the Orthodox Greeks, he had failed them miserably; at this stage he was an impediment to a resolution of their problems. The Hellenic conundrum could only be broken by his complete withdrawal from the situation. And then came the death of his beloved daughter, cruelly taken from him at such a young age, in addition to the terrible flood that had devastated his capital, a catastrophe wrought by God, surely as punishment for his sins.

Yes, he had given a quarter century of service to the throne. The crown had been thrust upon him; he had never coveted it. But it was a crown dipped in his father's blood. The world was closing in on him, and there appeared little possibility of respite. Alexander wished only to be left alone and to give himself over to a spiritual life of prayer and meditation. Mikhailovsky Castle obsessed him. However the murder had occurred, whatever the circumstances, he could not escape having been part of it. He had sinned, grievously, and he had yet to atone. To serve the empire was one thing; to save one's soul from eternal damnation was another. All Alexander desired was peace.

November 11: "At about five o'clock," Elizaveta writes that morning, "I sent for Wylie and asked him a number of questions. He was very cheerful and informed me that despite his high fever, the emperor was decidedly better than yesterday and that I might go visit him."

On the surface, the day passes quietly, everyone continuing patiently to await some improvement of the emperor's condition. In many ways, however, it is a very unusual day. For starters, during the night the emperor receives Colonel Nikolaev, commander of the Don Cossack troop that guards his residence, and Baron Frederiks, military commander of Taganrog. He gives to them "important secret orders and commanded them immediately to leave Taganrog in such a way that nobody would notice them. The meeting and these orders were unknown even to Chief of Staff Baron Diebich." What the nature of these "important secret orders" is and the surreptitious circumstances in which they are issued are confounding, to say the least. Could they somehow relate to what history will later term the Imperial Legend?

At ten in the morning, Alexander receives Elizaveta, and the two are closeted for an inordinately long time, an unprecedented occurrence. At four o'clock, the empress emerges from her husband's bedroom looking distraught. For six uninterrupted hours they have been together in deep discussion. What went on?

Immediately after leaving her husband, Elizaveta goes directly to her quarters and pens a despairing letter to her mother: "Where does one find peace in life? Just as you think that all is settled for the better and that you can enjoy life, there suddenly appears an unexpected trial that steals away the ability to enjoy the blessings around you . . . it's so unfair." Strange words from one who that day has received an encouraging report from Wylie and who makes an upbeat entry in her diary. The meeting between husband and wife was extraordinarily long. Could it be that during that intense session Alexander unveiled his plan to flee the world in favor of a monastic or solitary existence? And could Elizaveta's "unexpected trial" have been the rude realization that the happiness of her marital reconciliation was a sham and that her husband was leaving her forever? Again, this is speculation. But between the time that Elizaveta makes her cheerful diary entry in the morning and writes the despairing letter to her mother, something dramatic has certainly taken place.

There is one further unusual element to the day: the entry Elizaveta makes in her diary that morning is her last. Since her arrival in Taganrog she has carefully recorded the events of each day. Her journal now terminates abruptly, and we hear no more from the empress, not even during the momentous days that follow, which are surely worthy of note. Why did she abruptly stop writing? Could it be that she wished no one to know what had transpired between the two on November 11?

After Elizaveta leaves his room, Alexander summons Volkonsky and instructs him to write Grand Duke Constantine in Warsaw, informing him of his illness. One recalls the tsar's promise to his brother: "When the time comes to abdicate, I shall inform you." He orders that this letter be dispatched immediately, and he further instructs that the postdated letter he had dictated a couple of days earlier to the dowager empress now also be sent.

November 12: Wylie begins his daily journal entry with the curious words, "If I recall correctly," and then goes on to report that the emperor steadfastly refuses to take a laxative. "There is no human power that can talk sense into this person. I am miserable," he cries. Volkonsky: "In the morning the fever continues . . . he asked for the orange drink that Wylie and I had prepared and that stood at the ready. He thanked me for it. In the evening his condition improved." (Tarasov confirms that the tsar did accept medication, but he informs us that the preparation was concocted by Wylie and Stoffregen — there is no mention of Volkonsky.)

November 13: Tarasov records that the emperor worked all morning at his desk. "Suddenly," he writes, "a thick cloud passing so darkened the sky that he ordered his valet, Anisimov, to bring two candles." The physician then goes on to recount the same details of the episode of the flaming candles that Shilder wrote as having taken place on October 20.

By the thirteenth, things have failed to improve; indeed, the tsar's condition appears to have deteriorated significantly. Wylie's diary entry for that day: "All is going badly because he does not listen to advice and does not permit treatment. Such a course does not bode well. His pulse is irregular."

"I know exactly what's good for me," Alexander informs Wylie. "I require solitude and quiet. I am relying exclusively on the Almighty and on my constitution. I want you to pay attention only to my nerves, which are becoming frayed." The physician suggests that monarchs are more prone to frayed nerves than ordinary people — hazards of the job, so to speak. "At this particular time," Alexander assures his secretary, "I've got the best of reasons to be nervous." Sick, yes. Depressed, yes. But why *nervous*?

November 14: As usual, Alexander orders hot water for his morning shave. He lathers his face and has begun to work with the razor when his hand starts to shake uncontrollably. The blade nicks his chin, and, letting the razor drop into the washbasin, Alexander begins to lose consciousness. The attending valet isn't quick enough to catch the monarch as he collapses to the floor. The alarmed servant rushes from the room, crying for help. People arrive from all directions, and general consternation follows. The physicians arrive on the scene and, Tarasov subsequently reports, Wylie quite simply loses his head, becoming totally ineffectual, while Stoffregen begins to rub eau de cologne on the forehead and temples of the prone figure. At this point the empress hurries into the room, and together the company lift the unconscious figure onto the bed. (The tsar's loss of consciousness during the morning shave is in contradiction with Volkonsky's account. He claims that Alexander fell unconscious at eight o'clock in the evening, while rising from the couch upon which he was resting; he does not mention the morning shave.)

The frantic ministrations on the inert Alexander eventually bring him around. He opens his eyes and says a few words but continues to lie on the bed. Toward lunch hour, his temperature rises and his face and neck visibly redden. Wylie and Stoffregen attempt without success to persuade the tsar to accept leeches behind his ears. He adamantly refuses and "sent the doctors to the devil," complaining that his nerves are in a poor enough state without having physicians irritate them further with useless demands for more treatment. Wylie notes in his diary, "Things can only become worse, although at this point he is not hallucinating. I wished to give him muriatic acid in some water, but there was no way. I received the usual, 'Get out!' I burst into tears and when he saw me he said, 'Forgive me, my dear friend. I hope you are not angry with me. I have my reasons.'" Volkonsky becomes so exasperated with the emperor's refusal of treatment that, in the presence of the empress, he announces to the doctors that there is only one means left to persuade the patient to accept medication and leeches: get him to receive Holy Communion, following which Father Theodotov would exercise his well-known powers of persuasion and talk sense into the tsar. The priest might just prevail. The empress agrees and takes it upon herself to make the arrangements. At midnight Elizaveta visits the sickbed and announces to Alexander that she has a cure for him. "Very well, what is it?" he asks wearily.

"I know more than anyone else," she replies, "what a strong Christian you are and how firmly you follow the rules of our Orthodox Church. My advice to you is that you turn to a spiritual physician. He invariably proves helpful and will undoubtedly bring about a positive turn to the burdens of our spiritual ills."

"Who told you that I was in such bad shape as to require this sort of such 'medicine'?" Alexander asks.

"Your chief physician, Dr. Wylie," the empress responds. Wylie is promptly summoned, and the emperor demands to know exactly how bad things really are. After some hesitation, Wylie replies candidly that, in his opinion, His Majesty's condition is very grave. Alexander pauses for a moment, then, turning to his wife, he says very calmly, "Thank you, my dear friend, order this to be done. I am ready." At this point, however, he dozes off, and it is decided to hold off bringing the priest until morning.

November 15: The emperor sleeps listlessly, awakening a number of times. Tarasov keeps watch by the bedside throughout the night. Off and on, Alexander, his eyes closed, murmurs prayers and psalms. Shortly after five in the morning, he opens his eyes and asks Tarasov whether the priest has arrived yet. "I immediately carried the news to Baron Diebich, Prince Volkonsky, and Baron Wylie, all of whom had spent the night in the reception room outside the bedroom," writes Tarasov. "They, in turn, summoned the empress, and everyone gathered in the sickroom. Father Theodotov was ushered in. The emperor rose on his left elbow, greeted the pastor, and asked him for a blessing. After receiving the blessing, the tsar kissed the priest's hand. 'I wish to confess and take Holy Communion. I would ask you to hear my confession, not as of an emperor but as of an ordinary citizen. Please begin — I am prepared to receive the Holy Sacraments.'"

Following the prayer before confession, Alexander orders everyone out of the room — he wishes to be left alone with the priest. The rites take the better portion of an hour and a quarter, following which the empress is asked back into the bedroom. Diebich, Wylie, Stoffregen, Tarasov, and the valets follow her in. Elizaveta kneels at the bedside and kisses Alexander on the forehead and also his hand. In return, the emperor kisses her hand and remarks, "I've never experienced such great joy, and I thank you for it."

At this point, taking advantage of Alexander's wakefulness and peaceful mood, the empress and the priest begin pleading with him not to refuse medical attention. Father Theodotov, "crucifix in hand and on his knees," argues that by not accepting medicine, the emperor is in essence precipitating suicide. It is a palpable argument and, with little further hesitation, Alexander turns to Tarasov and sighs. "Very well, gentlemen, now it's up to you. Apply your treatment — whatever you feel I require." The doctors promptly bring cold compresses for his forehead. Medication is administered and thirty leeches are applied to the back of his neck and behind his ears. By evening things seem better, with little sign of fever.

November 16: Wylie writes, "It all seems too late. Only because of a weakened physical and moral condition were we able to administer some medication following [yesterday's] administration of the Sacraments." Alexander has a bad night and falls into a coma for a brief period. At two in the morning he asks for some lemon sorbet, which he takes with some tea. The entire day goes poorly. Toward evening, reports Volkonsky, "we applied mustard plasters to his thighs but the fever did not subside." Tarasov writes, "The emperor passed a restless night without sleep but in somnolence. High temperature, dry skin. In midday the emperor spoke with the empress, but in spurts and with a weak voice."

That night passes peacefully. According to *The History of the Illness,* "the temperature returned to him between 0300 and 0400, accompanied by all the signs of death."

November 17: The day breaks into a splendid, bright morning. The sun shines in all its brilliance and the warm rays fall through the emperor's windows. When Alexander awakes in midmorning he orders the shutters fully opened and, basking in the fullness of the autumnal light, he exclaims, "How utterly beautiful it all is!" Hope seems in the air, and Elizaveta, who hasn't left her husband's bedside since daylight, is in a joyful mood. She dashes off a note to her mother:

Dearest Mother,

I have been in no condition to write you since yesterday night. Today — thanks a thousand and thousand times to the Almighty — there has been an evident amelioration in the condition of the emperor, this kind angel who suffers so. For whom and on whom does the Lord lavish more his boundless mercy than on him? O, my God, what terrible moments I have passed through! I can imagine your own worries, dearest mother. You'll receive the official bulletin, from which you'll understand the cause of our yesterday's despair and even that of last night. But today Wylie himself says that the condition of our dear sufferer is more satisfactory. He continues exceedingly weak. I must confess, dear mother, that I am not myself. Beyond this I cannot add much. Pray with us, with five million people, that the Lord will see fit to make whole our dear ailing one.

"But death already hovered over the poor sufferer," writes Shilder. "He was fading fast. What the empress and others took for a turn for the better, was in fact the final flicker of life." By nightfall the situation again deteriorates. The feverish attacks become stronger and Alexander is unconscious much of the time. "From bad to worse," writes Wylie.

November 18: "There is no hope to save my beloved lord," Wylie enters in his diary. Tarasov reports:

> The emperor passed the night unconscious or in a daze. His eyes remained closed most of the time — only when the empress sat by him and spoke to him did he open them, and then he gazed either at her face or at the crucifix. Despite the mental wandering and unconsciousness, which stemmed from developing brain damage, the emperor unfailingly sensed the presence of the empress whenever she neared him, and then he reached out for her hand and placed it to his heart. By night the emperor grew still weaker. When I offered him drink from a spoon, I noticed that he swallowed with increasing slowness and unease. I didn't hesitate to report this. Prince Volkonsky immediately informed the empress, who at ten o'clock at night came to the sickroom and sat down by the sufferer, frequently holding, with her left hand, his right hand. At times she cried. I remained with the empress for the entire night, standing at the foot of the emperor's bed. He swallowed drink with profound difficulty. At four in the morning the breathing became noticeably shorter, but more tranquil and without hardship.

The whole suite was present in the room throughout the night, and quietly awaited the curtain to drop on the final scene, which rapidly approached.

November 19: "It was a gloomy and misty morning," Tarasov tells us. "The square in front of the palace was jammed with people, who after church service and prayers for the tsar's deliverance, arrived in droves to stand quietly before the building, in expectation of fresh news. The emperor grew even weaker, and only rarely opened his eyes, which invariably focused on either the empress or the crucifix. His final glance was touching and expressed such a tranquil and heavenly hope that all of us found ourselves sobbing uncontrollably, overcome by a sense of indescribable piety . . . no suffering at all."

"At 10 hours and 50 minutes the great monarch stepped into eternity," Wylie notes succinctly.

12

A Time for Mourning

ELIZAVETA HAD SAT BY ALEXANDER'S BEDSIDE throughout the final hours, and when he took his last breath she fell to her knees and plunged into prayer. She then made the sign of the cross over the emperor's still body and, crossing herself, closed his eyelids. With her kerchief she tied up her husband's chin and again spent a few moments on her knees by the deathbed. She arose, made a deep bow, and quietly left the room. That evening, Elizaveta wrote her mother:

> O Mother! I am the most miserable being on earth! I wish simply to tell you that I continue among the living, after having lost this angel who suffered so through his illness and who, despite all, invariably found a smile for me or a tender glance, even though he recognized nobody. O mother, mother, how miserable I am. How you will suffer with me! O Lord, what a fate! I am profoundly depressed and I don't understand myself. I don't understand my fate. In short, I am very miserable.

And to her mother-in-law, the Dowager Empress Maria Feodorovna, Elizaveta wrote:

> Our angel is in the heavens, and I remain on earth. I am the most miserable creature of all who mourn; if I could

only join him soon. I am sending you a locket of his hair, dear mother. Why did he have to suffer so? Now, however, his face reflects satisfaction and benevolence to everyone who is around him. He appears to be approving all that is going on about him . . . for the time being he will remain here, and I with him; when he is moved from here, I will accompany him — provided I have the strength. I still don't know what will become of me.

"Our angel is in the heavens." Eventually these words spread through the country, and soon they came to be engraved on every sort of commemorative memorabilia — medals, plaques, posters, and other souvenirs. As word of the emperor's death spread, eulogies by statesmen, poets, and the common person poured into the capital. "Behold that splendid genius who was so joyously acclaimed in 1801," wrote one emotional mourner, "and behold that glorious tsar to whom Russia was so indebted in 1813 and 1814. Behold the one who spread calm following last year's floods. Behold the good and helping person who was kindness itself." The historian Shilder wrote, "Deep down inside there was great idealistic beauty. He sincerely wished well and he was a man of goodness, something he forever sought." Austrian chancellor Metternich, on receiving news of Alexander's death, voiced with a tint of sarcasm a less prosaic opinion: "If I'm not wrong, the history of Russia will begin — where the romance has now finished."

As the pall of mourning slowly drew across the country, nobody was more deeply affected than the small circle gathered in Taganrog. The barely cold body lay before them; the imperial family and the seat of government were 1,400 miles away. Isolated, at the edge of the empire, they were in a quandary about what to do next. Who would mount the throne? Who would now give the orders for the disposition of the body?

And what about that body? Were these the authentic remains of the Autocrat of All Russia? The members of that small circle —

Volkonsky, Diebich, Wylie, Tarasov, the empress, and others — were they in genuine mourning for their beloved, immersed in grief? Or were they at the eye of a terrible storm that was fast unfolding, a surreal hoax that would touch every corner of the country and have serious repercussions, both political and personal?

If indeed Alexander had made up his mind to stage an escape from Taganrog and shed the crown, the body soon to repose in the imperial coffin could not have been his. Whose then was it, and by what means did it come to be there? This certainly is one of the most critical pieces in the Legend's puzzle.

Nothing further could be done until instructions were received from the new tsar. Who was that to be? Alexander had no legitimate children. Presumably, therefore, the throne would pass to Constantine, his younger brother, and logically next in line for the throne. Insofar as anyone knew, however, the late emperor had left no clear instructions to that effect; if provision had been made, the country certainly was ignorant of it. Even in his final hours, when it was perfectly clear to him that the end was near, Alexander made no mention of succession. "In fact," Shilder observes, "in his last days, the emperor seemed deliberately to have distanced himself from every matter of state. He died the death of a private citizen, satisfied that he had squared away his earthly accounts." Alexander's intentions for the passing on of the throne, if any, were seemingly carried to the grave.

Earlier, when it had become evident that the ailing emperor might not survive, Diebich determined to establish to whom he, as chief of staff, must report upon the death of the tsar. Together with Volkonsky he approached the empress and asked what information she had on the matter.

"Is he so ill that there isn't further hope?" she asked.

"God alone can help and save the emperor," replied Volkonsky. "However, for the good order and safety of Russia we must provide for any contingency."

"It seems to me then," replied Elizaveta, "that in the event of tragedy you should report to Constantine Pavlovich." The two officers thus satisfied themselves that the empress was ignorant of any possible arrangements for the succession.

Diebich continues in his diary, "Prince Volkonsky and I supposed that the deceased Alexander Pavlovich had a will, otherwise he would not have consistently carried on his person an envelope containing certain papers." It was a well-known fact that the emperor wore a peculiar leather pouch on a cord about his neck, which, except when he bathed, he never removed. After his death, the envelope was opened and, to everyone's disappointment, all that was found in it was a paper with some scribbled prayers. It was not a last testament — it contained no clue to the succession. At first, the empress wanted to keep this envelope, but later she ordered it placed on the body within the coffin.

The three people closest to the tsar — his wife, Elizaveta; his chief of staff, Diebich; his secretary and confidant, Volkonsky — were ignorant of any plans for the naming of the new emperor. There was a secretive side to this complex, enigmatic man. Napoleon once called Alexander "the Northern Sphinx." Pushkin later elaborated: "A sphinx who carried his riddle with him to the grave." Part of the riddle appeared to be the secret of his succession. But, unknown to anyone in Taganrog — and the world — the emperor had in fact two years earlier duly provided for his successor. By 1823, Alexander had seemed more determined than ever to divest himself of the crown, and in anticipation of that possibility he had made clear provisions.

If he were to step down, the throne should logically pass to the next-younger brother. Technically, however, Constantine had excluded himself from the succession by a morganatic union with Jeanne Groudzinska, a Polish commoner, which followed the annulment of his first marriage to Grand Duchess Anna Feodorovna. But the final decision on such a matter rested with the emperor. The two brothers had met to discuss the situation. The crown simply could not pass to a divorcé who was remarried to someone not of the blood. Constantine readily agreed, and in fact requested to renounce his right to the throne in favor of Nicholas, the third brother. Besides, he liked Poland and was content to remain on as the country's viceroy, living with his Polish wife in Warsaw's Belvedere Palace.

On August 16, 1823, Alexander signed the manifesto that confirmed Constantine's renunciation of the throne and formalized the appointment of Nicholas as his successor. Count Arakcheyev knew of these arrangements, as did Philaret, the metropolitan of Moscow, who penned the formal document. Alexander insisted on the absolute secrecy of these arrangements, doubtless to try and avoid any unnecessary controversy. In his own hand, he wrote on the document, "To repose in the Cathedral of the Assumption until further orders from me. In the event of my death without my having issued further instructions, this envelope should be opened by the archbishop of Moscow and the governor-general of Moscow within the Cathedral of the Assumption." To assure no error, copies of the manifesto were deposited with the Council of State and the Senate. Alexander's desire for secrecy on the matter was honored and the empire remained ignorant of the arrangements. An autographed copy of the document today lies in the State Archive of the Russian Federation in Moscow.[†]

Nicholas, of all people, was not consulted on any of these arrangements and remained in complete ignorance of the secret succession plans. Alexander, however, had shared his intentions with the Prince of Orange, not only in discussion but by letter. "I shall forsake the throne when I reach fifty," he wrote. "I know myself well enough to feel that by then I shall no longer have the physical and the mental strength to govern my vast empire . . . Nicholas is a reasonable and comprehending person, just the right man to guide the destiny of Russia down the right path. On the day of his coronation I shall be among the crowd at the foot of the great stairs of honor in the Kremlin, and I shall be among the first to shout 'hurrah!'"

In Taganrog, a confused General Diebich dispatched the first of the couriers bearing news of Alexander's death to Constantine in Warsaw. "With sadness in my soul," he wrote, "I have the

---

[†]See Appendix A for the full text.

sacred duty of reporting to Your Majesty that the Almighty has cut short the precious days of our august sovereign, Emperor Alexander Pavlovich . . . I attach hereto the death certificate, signed by the attending aides-de-camp and physicians." Another courier was sent to the dowager empress in St. Petersburg, bearing a letter by Diebich: "I now await with impatience orders from our new and rightful Emperor Constantine Pavlovich."

Protocol and government records demanded that an autopsy be carried out. On the day following the tsar's death, a medical team assembled at seven in the evening to carry out the work. It was a lengthy, carefully executed procedure. Few parts of the body escaped scrutiny, internally or externally. The autopsy report details the exterior condition of the body and the findings within the skull, pectoral region, and abdominal cavity. Completing the operation, the medical team considered the evidence and concluded, "The august monarch was taken by extreme illness, which at first affected the liver and other organs serving the secretion of bile. The illness in its progression developed into a fierce fever, coupled with the rush of blood through vessels of the brain and secretion and accumulation of ichor in the cavities of the brain. The disease was the cause of the death of His Imperial Majesty."[†]

Nine doctors signed the final report: Dr. Yakolev, a junior surgeon from a local hospital; Dr. Vasiliev, the staff surgeon of the Cossack Guards Regiment; Dr. Laquier, the chief physician of the Taganrog Quarantine Station; Dr. Alexandrovich, staff physician assigned to the court; Dr. Rheingold, a state medical councillor; and Drs. Wylie, Dobbert, Stoffregen, and Tarasov. In addition to the medical team, the protocol also bore the signature of the overseeing authority, General Chernichev.

The work of the autopsy completed, the body then had to be embalmed. Earlier, Prince Volkonsky had asked Tarasov to take charge of both procedures; he was, after all, the court surgeon. But because of "filial feelings and respect for the emperor," the

---

[†]See Appendix B for the full text.

doctor writes in his memoirs, "I could not take upon myself such a responsibility," and he refused. The task was given over to a team of physicians, including Drs. Rheingold, Dobbert, Laquier, and Vasiliev, plus a certain Mr. Prott, a local pharmacist.

General Diebich's adjutant, N. I. Schoenig, who was ordered to attend the procedure as an official witness, provides a vivid account of the procedure:

> At nine in the morning, on orders of Dr. Diebich, I, as seniormost among my colleagues, attended the embalming of the late emperor's body. Entering the study, I found him already undressed on the table. Four surgeons from the garrison were cutting out fleshy parts. They stuffed the cavities with some sort of grass that had been boiled in spirit and then they bandaged up the area with cotton dressings. Drs. Dobbert and Rheingold, cigars in their mouths, were busy boiling these grasses in a large casserole in the fireplace. They had been at this task all night, ever since Wylie completed the autopsy and the official report had been signed. The skull had already been dealt with, and in my presence they stretched the skin with all its hair back into place, which in no small way changed the expression of the facial features. The brain, heart, and entrails were deposited into a silver container that resembled a huge sugarbowl with a top, and the thing was locked.
>
> Nobody was in the room, or, in fact, in the palace other than those mentioned, plus a duty officer of the Cossack Guards Regiment. The empress had on the previous evening moved for a few days into the Shikhmatov house. The doctors complained that during the night everyone had abandoned the palace and they were unable even to obtain clean sheets. This greatly saddened me. Just recently these same scoundrels trembled at his very glance, and now they forgot their fears and all they owed! I immediately went to Volkonsky, whom I found in bed, and described to him the state of the emperor's body. He jumped out of bed

and ordered the valet to summon the maids to fetch fresh linen. Within a quarter hour clean sheets had been provided to the doctors.

All the while the surgeons did their work, occasionally turning the body over as though it were a piece of wood, and I with trepidation and curiosity had an opportunity to examine the corpse of our sovereign. I had never seen a better-built person. The arms, legs and all parts of the body might well have served as an ideal model for a sculptor; the tenderness of the skin was extraordinary. Only one spot that Tarasov handled clumsily was a darkish color.

After the embalming had been completed, the doctors dressed the emperor in the uniform of a general, complete with a star and decorations. White gloves were placed on his hands and then the corpse was transferred onto a metal cot. The whole was then covered with a light muslin cloth. At the foot of the bed was set a lectern, on which was placed a Bible, and from it priests took turns reading the Scriptures. In addition to the clergy, both servants and Cossack officers also took turns at watch, each lasting two hours. Every hour, one of the doctors passed by to sponge the deceased's face with alcohol. With all the doors and windows closed and the three large church candles burning brightly, the temperature in the room rose to an uncomfortable level. "The pungent odor of spirit, together with some sort of aromatic smell, drove us to faintness," reports Schoenig, "and our uniforms became so impregnated with the smells that for at least three weeks thereafter the odors lingered."

"The doctors," continues Diebich's servant, "admitted that they were unable properly to attend to the embalming or fully to follow the prescribed procedures, for lack of sufficient quantities of alcohol. Under normal circumstances, the entire body should have been deposited into a bath of spirits for a few days. In addition, I think, the doctors were unused to such work."

Tarasov examined the results and declared himself well pleased. Fifteen weeks later, when the coffin finally arrived at

St. Petersburg, he found "the body and form of the face were perfectly preserved." This declaration, as will be seen, was in direct
contradiction with the notes of others.

That same day, the walls of the study were covered in black
linen and additional candles were brought in. The room was
transformed into a chamber of mourning. Dr. Robert Lee, an English physician on Count I. Vorontsov-Dashkov's staff, came to pay
his last respects. He describes the scene thus:

> I went to see His Imperial Majesty lying in state in the
> house where he had lived and died. I did not see the face of
> the emperor, but I was informed that it was already com-
> pletely changed and had become quite black. The coffin
> was placed upon a slightly elevated platform and covered
> by a canopy. The room was hung with black and the coffin
> covered with a cloth of gold. There were numerous wax
> lights burning in the apartment and each individual pres-
> ent held a lighted wax taper. A priest was standing at the
> head of the coffin reading the Evangelists. I was told that
> this was carried on day and night. On each side of the
> body a sentinel was placed with a drawn sword. In the
> anteroom were a number of priests putting on their robes
> and preparing for the services and masses, which were cel-
> ebrated twice a day. There were no symptoms of melan-
> choly in this crowded room and some young military
> officers even displayed a degree of levity altogether unsui-
> table to the solemnity of the scene. The empress, I was
> informed, remained constantly in an apartment, the door
> of which opened into that where the body of the emperor
> was lying and where the services were performed. Guards
> were stationed around the house, at the door, as also on
> the stairs and in the anteroom.

Schoenig picks up the narrative:

> On the second day, as I raised the muslin in order to
> sponge the face, I informed Diebich that a corner of the

necktie was sticking out improperly above the collar. He gently tugged at it and to his horror he found that it was loosened flesh. The face had begun to darken considerably. The heat of the room and the evaporation of the alcohol from the open dish standing in the warm atmosphere weakened the liquid to such an extent that rather than acting as a preservative, it became in fact an agent for spoilage. Wylie was summoned and he determined that the only means of preserving the corpse was with cold. We opened all the windows, placed a container of ice under the bed and hung a thermometer nearby in order to assure ourselves that the cold would never rise above 10°C (50°F). By that time the cold and the winds had become forceful, and standing watch dressed only in uniform was highly uncomfortable. Only during the morning and evening requiem services, always attended by the empress, were the windows closed. Those who stood watch were permitted to wear heavy greatcoats.

At the conclusion of each service, everyone was ordered out of the room except the clergy, who continued with their prayers and Scripture readings. The empress then appeared, unattended, and spent some ten minutes by the coffin in silent prayer and meditation. This ritual over, she exited the room and the sentinels and valets resumed their posts. The Greek archbishop, attended by six priests, led the first requiem services. Not knowing Russian, the clergyman read the responses in Greek. By December 7, a Russian archbishop had arrived at the port town and the services came to be read in the familiar Slavonic and Russian. The body now awaited its final disposition. In St. Petersburg, the Romanov ancestral crypt within the spired cathedral would soon receive the earthly remains of Alexander, known as "the Blessed."

13

From Taganrog to
St. Petersburg

THE COURIER SENT BY GENERAL DIEBICH bearing the news to
Constantine of the emperor's death made all haste. Despite the
poor roads and early snows, he arrived at the Belvedere Palace in
Warsaw within six days. For over a week Grand Duke Constantine had been receiving daily reports on the state of his brother's
deteriorating condition. Despite the forewarning he had of possible death, the latest dispatch with the tragic news came as a
shock.

Constantine had kept secret the contents of the daily mes-
sages, even from his wife and his youngest brother, Grand Duke
Michael, who was visiting Warsaw at the time. They had no idea
of Alexander's illness. But now, with the arrival of the latest
courier, he finally broke the news to his family of Alexander's sickness and death. Subsequently he told Michael, "My resolve is as
strong as it ever was . . . nothing has changed, I am more determined now than ever before to refuse the throne."

On November 27, news of the emperor's death reached
St. Petersburg. Everyone hastened to take the oath of allegiance to
Constantine — the imperial guard, the civil service, and the higher

officers of state, including Grand Duke Nicholas himself. Within a few days, Moscow received the shocking tidings, and there too, the oaths of allegiance to Constantine were administered. Black bunting of mourning was draped throughout the two cities, and the public streamed to the churches for the singing of the requiem services. At the same time, shop windows displayed banners with pictures of the new ruler, Constantine I, Emperor and Autocrat of All Russia. Now the two capital cities anxiously awaited the return of their sovereign from Poland.

In Warsaw, however, Constantine steadfastly maintained his renunciation of the throne, and declared his loyalty to Nicholas. For three anxious weeks, couriers raced back and forth between St. Petersburg and Warsaw, as Nicholas tried in vain to persuade his brother to return to the capital and make a formal declaration of abdication. Meanwhile, the empire was without a sovereign, or, as the *Times* of London neatly put it, Russia was "in the strange predicament of having two self-denying emperors, and no active ruler."

As noted, a number of subversive groups had by now taken root, all sharing the same goal — the overthrow of the established order. Alexander's secret police had kept him informed of the plans and plots of several of these societies, one of which had been stopped in its tracks with the recent arrests of its leaders. The most notable underground group was the Northern Society, whose members were particularly active in their revolutionary aspirations. These young idealists were noblemen, mostly officers of the guards regiments, who sought to establish a new social and political order by means of a coup d'état. The intransigence of the existing order, its absolutism, was confounding. In the conspirators' view, what Russia needed was a constitutional monarchy, with a constituent assembly and a federal form of government, as in the United States. Many of these enthusiasts were veterans of the Napoleonic Wars, and in France they had sipped from the cup of the Rights of Man and wished to carry it back home. But in most cases their idealism was matched by naiveté.

The unexpected confusion concerning succession that enveloped Russia in December offered the group a sudden window of opportunity — more correctly, perhaps, forced its hand — and their members decided to act regardless of the consequences. It was expeditiously decided to try to prevent the Senate from publishing a proclamation of succession, and instead force the members to issue a revolutionary manifesto. To lead them, the conspirators looked to Prince Sergey Trubetskoi,[†] whom they elected "provisional dictator" in the new order. Trubetskoi came from one of Russia's oldest and most noble families, whose members over the centuries had played prominent roles in its history. After the failed revolution, Tsar Nicholas was shocked to discover Prince Sergey among the arrested rebels. "What was in that head of yours, when you, with your name and family, got involved in such an affair?" demanded the infuriated emperor. Then, tapping his forefinger against the young officer's forehead, he added, "Colonel of the Guard, Prince Trubetskoi! Have you no shame for having joined with such rabble!"

In the first two weeks of December, members of the Northern Society met in almost continuous sessions at the home of Prince Evgeny Obolensky, plotting strategy and fine-tuning their plan of action. On the thirteenth, the conspirators held their final meeting. Word had been received of two developments: first, the oath of allegiance to Nicholas was to be administered to the army on the following day: and second, a traitor from among them had informed the police of their activities. Nicholas had been warned of their plans. The game was up; the dreadful choice that now confronted the frantic conspirators was either to abandon forthwith the enterprise and disperse or gallantly rise up — on the very next day — in order "to awaken Russia." By this time most everyone had become physically and emotionally drained — strung tight. As the meeting unfolded, initial doom-and-gloom comments were drowned out by patriotic outcries, and soon one inspirational speech flowed after another. A romantic frenzy took hold of the meeting. "We've gone too far; we're committed," someone cried out. "We are destined to die!" exclaimed another. "Better to be

---

[†]Prince Trubetskoi is a legendary member of the author's family.

seized on the street than in bed," concluded a third. And finally, the poet Alexander Odoevsky gushed, "We shall die. O, how gloriously we shall die!"

In the early hours of December 14 the revolt was launched, and by eleven o'clock the Moscow Regiment had taken up its station on Senate Square. At this point, everything that could go wrong did. Those who should have been at a specific spot simply failed to appear. Assigned tasks were either botched or went unfulfilled. Support for the Moscow Regiment never showed. The Grenadier Life Guards failed in their attempt to seize the imperial family. Action soon came to a grinding halt, long enough for Nicholas to take the initiative. By four o'clock, thirty-two artillery pieces had been placed along the perimeter of the square. Seven rounds of gunshot were fired at the mass of rebels, and the Decembrists' forces scattered. The revolt was over. Nicholas accepted the throne and the nation pledged its allegiance.

The "first Russian revolution" was precipitate and amateurish. The young men behind it understood the risks and the awesome price that failure would extract. They were, however, dogged in their determination, and they went ahead, almost as though they recognized from the start that they were doomed. On the eve of the revolt, Trubetskoi openly admitted that "this is a hopeless undertaking from which nothing but ruin will result." That same evening, the poet Ryleev declared, "I am certain that we shall be ruined, but our example will live. We shall be sacrificing ourselves for the future freedom of our motherland." More than anything else, the Decembrist revolt was a pathetic yet noble expression of revolutionary fervor. In the six months that followed, arrests were carried out and scores were sentenced to hard labor in Siberia, Trubetskoi included, while others were sent off to the Caucasus to serve as privates in the army. On July 13, 1826, five of the ringleaders were executed. Two months later, Nicholas was crowned emperor.

In Taganrog, throughout the uncertain period of the interregnum, Alexander's body awaited a decision as to its disposition.

Constantine referred the matter to St. Petersburg, but St. Petersburg expected Constantine to take charge — he would either travel to Taganrog or shortly appear in the capital. On December 11, the body was transferred to Alexandrovsky Monastery. Feodor Romanovich Martos, chairman of the Taganrog commercial court, tells of the transfer. Martos, incidentally, had developed a friendship with Wylie, to whom he rented rooms in his ample home. In a letter to his brother, he wrote:

> The ceremonial began at nine o'clock and it went on until 1:30 P.M. Except for the adjutant generals and the court, all of whom had on overcoats and fur hats, everybody was dressed merely in uniform and with bared heads. In our left hands we held our caps and in the right, candles. I'm certain many will fall sick as the frost and winds were fierce. The empress, in her extreme grief and in her ill condition . . . remained in the residence's chapel.

Dr. Lee was also in attendance, and he depicts the event thus:

> The streets were lined with troops. At half past nine the procession set out. A small party of gendarmes commanded by the Master of Police, under his direction, led the way. Then followed the valets, cook, and others employed about His Majesty. Next, the persons employed about the quarantine and others of the town. Then came a number of priests with flags, torches, and crosses, usually carried in processions. Then came a band of singers. After these a number of generals bearing the orders, crosses, etc. of His Majesty. Six horses covered with black cloth drew the car. The coffin was exposed at the head. The feet covered with the same yellow gold cloth that I noticed in the chamber in his house. Over the coffin was a canopy with yellow silk. Attached to the car were a number of cords, which were held by some of the most distinguished officers of His Majesty. After these followed a body of

Cossacks with their pikes reversed; guns were fired at short intervals from the time the procession set out.

Each morning a memorial liturgy was held at the monastery, with the archbishop officiating, and every evening a requiem service took place. At long last, instructions arrived from Nicholas ordering the transfer of his brother's remains to the capital. On December 29, the sad funeral cortege set out from Taganrog on its long journey to St. Petersburg and its final destination, the Fortress of St. Peter and St. Paul. In a letter to Grand Duke Constantine, Volkonsky reported,

> At ten o'clock, following the Liturgy and requiem service, the carriage left here with the same pomp as with the transfer of the remains from the palace to the monastery. The public escorted the carriage to the town limits and beyond, into the countryside. The widowed Empress Elizaveta Alexeyevna attended the final requiem and made her last farewell to her beloved husband. This eternal separating could not have but have exacerbated her weakened condition, suffered by grief and illness.

Shortly after the coffin's departure from Taganrog, Elizaveta wrote to her mother:

> All earthly ties are severed between ourselves! Those which originate in eternity will be different and even more wonderful, but in the meanwhile I still bear my grief. It pains me to realize that he will no longer be a part of my existence here on Earth . . . Naturally, I deserved this, for I did not sufficiently appreciate the kindness of God . . . When I think of my fate, at every turn I recognize the hand of the Creator.

Within six months, the empress herself would meet her Creator.

The funeral procession moved out of Taganrog and headed for Moscow, via Kursk, Orel, and Tula. The military escort and the entourage were under the command of Count Orlov-Denisov, who maintained the strictest discipline and order not only in the business of travel but also in the ceremonial occasions en route. Curiously, among the files Alexander had carried to Taganrog with him was the record of the funeral ceremonial used at the death of Catherine II. In sorting through the late tsar's effects, Volkonsky and Diebich came across these papers; they found them useful guidelines for the next steps. Of all the files Alexander had packed, this singular document, a seemingly redundant historical record nearly thirty years old, appeared the least necessary. Perhaps he desired to have it available in the event of his ailing wife's death. On the other hand, is it possible that as he left St. Petersburg he anticipated needing it for the precise use to which it was put after November 19?

Baykov, Alexander's coachman, drove the carriage bearing the emperor's remains. Each night, the procession stopped in some town or city, and the heavy coffin was lovingly borne into the principal church. Requiem services were held in full ceremony, and the populace turned out in droves to pay last respects. The stops were rarely more than thirty miles apart, and as the cortege passed from diocese to diocese, the presiding bishop, accompanied by attending clergymen, waited at the border to greet the party and to pay his respects. When the procession passed out of a given province, it again halted at the border, to permit the governor accompanying the cortege ceremoniously to pass the responsibility to the next governor. In settlements where army units were garrisoned, an honor guard greeted the procession, and wherever artillery was stationed, a gun salute was fired. Frequently the citizens met the entourage on the outskirts of their town, detached the horses from the coffin's carriage, and themselves pulled the vehicle into the settlement. Everywhere, even in the steppes, masses of people gathered.

From time to time, word would reach Orlov-Denisov of some possible hostile demonstration that might be awaiting the cortege in a neighboring town. Nearing Tula, for example, it was learned that factory workers were intending to intercept the procession and force open the coffin. Rumors were already circulating that the body within was not that of their sovereign, and they were demanding reassurances. This was not surprising, for the people had become used to the sudden deaths of their sovereigns. But when the workers met the cortege three miles from the city, it was not to challenge but rather to honor. They unharnessed the heavy carriage bearing the imperial remains and, heaving on long ropes, laboriously pulled it to the city's cathedral.

In his memoirs Tarasov writes:

> In addition to the personal instructions of the empress given me in Taganrog, I also had specific orders from Count Orlov-Denisov to attend to the state of the body through its entire voyage. With this in mind, I informed the count that in order to verify the state of the emperor's corpse, it would be necessary from time to time to open the coffin and actually examine the remains. Such examinations were carried out five times during the trip, always in the middle of the night and in the presence of the count. On each occasion I rendered him a full report . . . when the temperature rose a few degrees above freezing, boxes of ice were placed under the casket.

On February 3, the procession approached the outskirts of Moscow, where for miles on end the road was lined on both sides by troops from infantry and cavalry regiments. Outside the city gates, the coffin was transferred to a ceremonial hearse, and the weary horses were replaced by a team of finely groomed fresh mounts, each covered in bunting of black mourning and resplendent in their finest harness. Fresh personnel from the court, all splendidly dressed in smart uniforms, replaced the cortege's attendants who had traveled the long route from Taganrog.

Then the harmony and understanding that prevailed in the change of the personnel of the cortege was suddenly shattered. Tarasov writes:

> As the horses were being changed, the court coachman of the deceased emperor, Ilya Baykov, hurried to take his place

on the newly provided hearse. At this point, the officially appointed coachman of the hearse, resplendent in ceremonial mourning dress, approached him and asked him to step down. Baykov, in no uncertain terms, refused the demand. The Deputy Master of the Horse happened by and ordered Baykov off the carriage. Baykov steadfastly disregarded the order. This stubborn intransigence was reported to Prince Golitsen, the governor-general of Moscow, who immediately ordered that Baykov should be forthwith removed by force from the carriage. There was no way that the bearded fellow could possibly participate in the ceremonial entry into Moscow. At this, Baykov, in faithful solidarity to the emperor, answered, "I drove His Majesty for thirty years and I wish to serve him to his grave. If only my beard stands in the way, order me immediately to shave it." Prince Golitsen, deeply touched by such fidelity, ordered to have Baykov remain at his post, beard and all.

The parade cortege entered Moscow and made its way to the Kremlin, where the coffin was placed on a catafalque within the Arkhangelsky Cathedral. The doors were flung open to the citizenry to pay their respects, and queues rapidly formed, although they moved along reasonably expeditiously. Rumors had circulated in Moscow that an attempt of some sort would be made to disrupt the proceedings. The police, therefore, were in evidence everywhere, and security was stricter than might normally have been expected on such an occasion. Every evening at nine o'clock the Kremlin gates were locked, and armed sentries stood guard at the entrances. Infantry troops were stationed within the walls of the Kremlin and the cavalry patrolled the outside perimeter. Everything, however, remained quiet and there were no incidents. Alexander's remains reposed for three days in Russia's former capital.

On February 6, Metropolitan Philaret, accompanied by all the high clergy of Moscow, celebrated the last of the services held in the city. Immediately following, the procession reformed and the cortege set out of Moscow, bound for Tsarskoye Selo, outside St. Petersburg. In the ensuing days, it would pass through Tver and Novgorod.

Outside the walled city of Novgorod, a distraught Count Arakcheyev met the cortege. In Tarasov's words, the aged count "with his crying and tears expressed the full extent of his grief at the immense personal loss." Arakcheyev commanded the troops standing by to escort the sovereign's body into the city, and there he provided the magnificent catafalque upon which the coffin was placed at the center of the Cathedral of St. Sophia.

After three days, the procession moved out of Novgorod. Progress was slow, for the snows were deep and the winter winds billowed hazardously. On February 26, Alexander's body arrived at Tosno, not far from Tsarskoye Selo, and there his mother, Maria Feodorovna, joined the cortege. The grieving empress accompanied the procession to its destination. Before the actual entry into Tsarskoye Selo, on orders of Emperor Nicholas, Dr. Wylie made a thorough examination of the body. He found it in good shape; "the muscles were strong and hard and substantially maintained their original form. The body was in a perfectly preserved state . . . there was nothing which had to be done for it."

Two days later, the cortege approached Tsarskoye Selo. Emperor Nicholas, accompanied by Grand Duke Michael, Prince William of Orange, and the principal persons of the court, drove out to meet the party, which was followed by large numbers of servants and inhabitants of Tsarskoye Selo. It was a sunny and unusually warm day, so that much of the snow on the road had turned into slush and mud. Nicholas alighted from his carriage and bowed deeply toward the hearse. He then climbed onto it and, prostrate on the coffin, burst into deep tears. On the other side of the carriage, Grand Duke Michael did the same. In time, the procession continued and the two brothers, dressed in mourning with their hats under their arms, took positions immediately behind the coffin's carriage, tramping through the mud the remaining distance. Once they had arrived at the palace church, the casket was taken in and placed on a handsome catafalque.

On March 1, Dr. Tarasov was asked by Prince Golitsen whether the coffin might be opened so that the imperial family might make its final farewells. "I replied in the affirmative," writes the doctor,

> and I assured him that the body was whole and in good shape and that the casket certainly could be opened for them and for everyone else. He then informed me that on the emperor's orders, at twelve o'clock midnight I, with himself and Orlov-Denisov present, should open the coffin with every possible care and put everything in order for the visit of the imperial family. With the exception of the reigning empress who was pregnant, everyone would be present to bid a familial farewell to the deceased.
>
> At 11:30 P.M., the priests and those on duty were dismissed from the church and guards were stationed at the doors. There remained only Prince Golitsen, Count Orlov-Denisov and me, together with Zavetayev, the deceased emperor's valet. On opening the coffin, I removed the light mattress of aromatic herbs which covered the body, brushed off the tunic onto which a few herbal leaves had fallen, changed the white gloves on the hands (the previous ones had discolored), replaced on the head a crown and washed off the face. The body appeared entirely whole and there wasn't the least evidence of decay. Prince Golitsen ordered that we remain in the church behind the screen and then he hurried off to report to the emperor. Within a few minutes the entire imperial family, including children but not the reigning empress, entered the church in respectful silence. In turn they each approached the body and kissed the face and hands of the deceased. The entire scene was so touching that I was in no shape to express my personal grief.

Tarasov writes as though everything was quite normal, both as to the preserved state of the body and the circumstances of the reported visit by the grieving family. Indeed, throughout his narrative, the physician stresses that there was nothing unusual in any aspect of the situation. Yet a great deal was amiss. Up to that point, the coffin had, throughout its long journey from Taganrog, remained closed to virtually everyone. Apart from the doctors, the remains had been exposed only to the most exclusive of the sovereign's closest associates, and then always well after dark. And now the imperial family appeared to pay its last respects, almost clandestinely. It was midnight — extraordinary timing for such a visit, particularly with children in attendance. Superfluous personnel, including priests, were dismissed and guards posted at the door. Why such unusual arrangements? Why was the viewing limited to the immediate family?

As the dowager empress approached the coffin she made a startling pronouncement. Having bent over the remains and kissed the gloved hands, Shilder tells us, she declared in a loud voice, "Yes, this is my son, my dear Alexander. Ah, how he has thinned." In view of the unique conditions of the visit and the familial company in which she found herself, the remark seems almost studied, if not redundant. Was Maria Feodorovna's exclamation merely the *cri de coeur* of a distraught mother? Or was the empress deliberately helping to tack down a confirmation of the sovereign's reported death?

Prince William was also in attendance and, according to Shilder, was much shaken by the appearance of the deceased. From the earliest postmortem days of Taganrog we have repeated testimony that the face of the deceased was virtually unrecognizable, and since then much time had passed. What was it precisely that disturbed Prince William? There can be no doubt that, despite Tarasov's assurances to the contrary, the body reposing in the imperial coffin could not have escaped deterioration. First, there was the autopsy; then the body was embalmed by inadequately trained physicians; and, finally, more than a hundred days passed before it was buried. Could it be that the coffin was kept closed precisely because the body was in such bad shape — or, in the words of St. John, because the "body stinketh, for he hath been dead for four [months]." It may also be that the remains were being jealously shielded for fear that they might be recognized as not being those of the emperor. Insofar as members of the family are concerned, apart from the one unusual midnight visitation, there is no record of any of them having again passed before the open coffin. It seems that even the dowager empress viewed the remains of her beloved son but once. Witnesses to the event were family members — uncharacteristically, all others were dismissed, including the priests.

Following the family's visit after everyone had left the chapel, Tarasov removed the crown from the body, again covered it with the aromatic mattress, and shut the coffin. The sentries and priests were recalled into the church and the readings from the Scriptures began anew.

The emperor's remains were then transferred from Tsarskoye Selo to the chapel of nearby Tchesma Palace. "At twelve o'clock midnight," writes Tarasov,

> in the presence of Prince Kurakin and Prince Golitsen, the body of the emperor under my direction was removed from its wooden coffin with its lead interior and was placed into a large and magnificent bronze casket. The silver container with the entrails was placed within the casket at the feet and the vase with the heart was put alongside the body on the left side of the chest. The former casket was then and there taken apart, sawed up and, with all its accoutrements, also placed into the new casket.

On the morning of March 6, a formidable procession moved out of Tchesma Palace and proceeded to St. Petersburg. The weather was impossible, freezing cold, with a biting wind and billowing snow. The order of the cortege had been drawn up at the time of Peter the Great, from a ceremonial borrowed from the Prussian court. Following the various military units innumerable clergymen proceeded, dressed in vestments and bearing religious banners. Then came the diplomatic corps, representatives of various organizations and societies, courtiers, and other suites, each person wearing various decorations, orders, insignias, or coats of arms. Everyone in the procession, from Emperor Nicholas on down, was dressed alike in long, broad black cloaks and black hats — a somber picture indeed. Finally came the magnificent hearse bearing the casket, and immediately behind it walked the emperor, Grand Duke Michael, and foreign princes, including the Duke of Wellington. Following the imperial family came the cavalry with lances at the slope, and more military personnel.

By one-thirty the grand procession had arrived at the Kazan Cathedral, where the casket was deposited. For seven days it remained there, receiving the public. Thousands from every walk of life came to pay their respects, and it was said that by the end of the period virtually every citizen of St. Petersburg had passed through the cathedral. The coffin remained closed, which upset people greatly. Again, Nicholas was asked permission to have the casket opened, and again he refused. Tarasov explains that Nicholas's decision was based on the fact that "the face of the deceased emperor had become somewhat altered; it had turned a light-chestnut color as a result of the vinegar-spirit treatment it had received in Taganrog."

At eleven in the morning of March 13, the final funeral procession left the Kazan Cathedral in a swirling snowstorm. It wended its way through the whitened streets, along the Nevsky Prospect, across the Trinity Bridge, to the formidable Fortress of St. Peter and St. Paul. To muffled drums and the cadence of marching troops, the lengthy parade approached the cathedral whose distinctive golden spire dominated the skyline. Since the time of Peter the Great, this sanctuary had served as the burial place for all of Russia's rulers but one. The only post-Petrine ruler not buried in the fortress was the fifteen-year-old Peter II, who, having died in Moscow, was laid to rest in the Kremlin's Arkhangelsky Cathedral, the burial site of Russian rulers up until 1689.

The deceased emperor's coffin was now ready to be deposited into its final resting place. The priest intoned the closing prayers: "O Lord, give rest to the soul of Thy servant Alexander in a place of brightness, a place of refreshment, a place of repose, where all sickness, sighing, and sorrow have fled away." The choir sang for the last time the haunting hymn — "With the soul of the righteous departed give rest to the soul of Thy servant, O Lord, preserving him in the Blessed life which is Thee, who lovest mankind. Memory eternal! Memory eternal! Memory eternal!" At two o'clock the sovereign was lowered into the earth.

Within arm's length of the fresh tomb reposed the remains of Alexander's mentor, Catherine the Great. Grandmother and grandson, side by side — both had come to their thrones through murder. And in nearby tombs lay those whose blood had been shed — on the one side, Catherine's husband, Peter III, and on the other, her son Paul. And now, in a fresh casket, lay Paul's firstborn son, who in his lifetime had seemed unable to cleanse his hands of his father's blood. Within the penetrating cold of the cathedral's massive walls, the monarchs now lay at peace with one another in the still silence of their eternal repose. Or certainly it so appeared.

14

The Life and Death
of Feodor Kuzmich

ONE CHILLY SEPTEMBER DAY in 1836, a stranger astride an impressive white horse rode into the Siberian town of Krasnoufimsk, in Perm province. A tall, balding figure, with a full gray beard, he was a man in his fifties or early sixties and modestly dressed in a peasant's black tunic and trousers. He made his way to the blacksmith's shop and asked to have his steed reshod. Then as now, strangers in provincial Russian towns invariably aroused curiosity, and the blacksmith made little attempt to disguise his interest in the distinguished-looking visitor standing before him. The bearing and manner of speech of this solitary horseman were those of a refined gentleman, yet his ordinary dress was that of a common peasant. As he set about his work, the blacksmith engaged the visitor in idle banter. Where had he come from? Where was he headed? What was his business?

The stranger responded evasively and volunteered little helpful information, obviously not anxious to talk. The blacksmith pressed more aggressively but received little satisfaction; he continued at his forge. Before long, a small crowd had filtered into the shop, as much to enjoy the warmth of the furnaces as to satisfy their curiosity about the new arrival. They listened attentively to the exchange and, perceiving that the stranger seemed to be deliberately hiding something, they grew suspicious. Perhaps the fellow was on the run. Perhaps he was wanted by the law. After some dispute among themselves, they forcefully hustled him off to the police station for questioning. Try as they might, however, the authorities were no less successful in finding out anything meaningful about the man, who volunteered nothing. He told the police that he had no recollection of his past, but he knew his name to be Feodor Kuzmich. It was not that he was really suffering from amnesia, but that he was unwilling to reveal his true identity to the police. He also informed them that he was homeless and that the horse belonged to him. The irritated officials persisted in their questioning and even threatened him with the whip. In those days the laws governing vagabondage were inordinately harsh. Kuzmich nevertheless steadfastly maintained his silence.

When all else had failed, the exasperated police stripped Kuzmich of his tunic and, according to the law, beat him soundly with a birch rod. He received twenty strokes and was sentenced to exile near Tomsk, a few hundred miles deeper into Siberia.

On April 8, 1837, Feodor Kuzmich arrived from Perm to join the 43rd Exile Settlement at Bogotolsk, near Tomsk. This time he came by cart and foot; his horse had been sold to settle his account with the Perm innkeeper, with whom he had lodged before being sent into exile. The long and arduous passage was shared with prisoners of every sort, including thieves and murderers. But the elderly man endured the trip patiently without complaint, even offering encouragement to the weaker prisoners. When they arrived, Kuzmich was assigned to work in a vodka distillery, to which he assented without complaint. From the outset, a warm relationship developed between the newly arrived exile and the plant's administration. The distillery's director treated him especially well, with considerable deference; this workman, he had decided, was no ordinary person. After the first few weeks of hard toil, no further demands were made of him and he was excused from compulsory labor. Factory staff and colleagues showed equal consideration. Everybody liked the reclusive gentleman, who got along readily with one and all. Within the distillery's precincts, Kuzmich spent nearly five years, living in relative solitude.

In 1842, for reasons unrecorded, Feodor Kuzmich was moved to another exile settlement at Beloyarsk, where he eventually took up residence in a small hut, generously constructed for him by a Cossack named Simeon Siderov. Within a few months, Kuzmich had developed a local following. Attracted by his ascetic mode of life and good education, people gravitated to him for every conceivable reason, mostly to ask questions and to seek advice and spiritual comfort. On the one hand, he enjoyed receiving visitors — but in small doses and mostly when it suited him. On the other hand, his burgeoning popularity denied him the privacy and seclusion he so desired. Eventually it became such a problem that he left Siderov's cabin and Beloyarsk and moved on.

For the next fifteen years, Kuzmich moved from one place to another. From Beloyarsk he traveled to Zertsali, thence to the gold-mining center at Enyisei, and eventually to the secluded banks of the Tchulvin River. Later he relocated into the deep taiga near the village of Korobeinikov, where he spent a few months, following which he moved on to Krasnaya Rechka.

In all, Feodor Kuzmich spent almost three decades in the greater Tomsk area. They were searching years, during which he seemed never fully satisfied. His constant moves suggested that he was in quest of an elusive something, or perhaps escaping from some invisible force.

Wherever he traveled or settled, the local populace invariably took to him. Peasant children in particular were attracted to him, and he freely instructed them in grammar, history, geography, and religious knowledge. With adults, he held religious discussions and recounted colorful events of national history — the old man was well versed in the details of various battles. His followers were especially captivated by his vivid accounts of life in St. Petersburg. By his piety and simplicity and through the sympathetic counsel he freely offered, Kuzmich earned the warm affection of those around him. As in his earlier years in Beloyarsk, visitors of every sort sought spiritual counsel from him or simply asked for practical advice. At first he appeared genuinely to welcome his callers, but as time went on it became increasingly clear to the people that the starets required privacy and seclusion. A tacit understanding was eventually reached, and before long people ceased imposing on the old man's hospitality.

The longest time Kuzmich spent in any one place was in Krasnaya Rechka. There a wealthy peasant named Ivan Latyshov took an exceptional liking to him and generously erected a small cabin for him. As in his previous places of domicile, the poor, the lonely, and those in need of advice or moral support came to him, initially out of curiosity, but before long out of affection and a sense of deference. The starets received everyone equally warmly, and shared whatever food happened to be at hand. He was especially fond of children, whom he continued to teach, and who frequently brought him flowers.

When visitors did call, the starets was invariably polite, although on rare occasions he showed flashes of irritation. Once, for example, a couple of workmen were sent to repair a broken window frame in his cabin. The carpenters set about their work noisily while Kuzmich remained at his table inside the hut. Twice he asked them to be less noisy, to no avail. Finally, he raised his voice and ordered them to do as he bid, adding threateningly, "If only you knew who I am, you would not dare aggravate me this way!"

Among the regular visitors whom Kuzmich received were two elderly sisters living nearby, who noted that the old man was particularly attached to St. Alexander Nevsky, the patron saint of Tsar Alexander. An icon of St. Alexander hung in Kuzmich's cell, and each year on August 30 the starets made a point of marking the saint's feast day. One year on that day the sisters baked sweet cakes, which they took to him. The starets seemed pleased to receive the women and was openly moved by their attentions. He sat them down at the little table to share the cakes, and in the course of conversation he enthusiastically told of the massive celebrations that took place in St. Petersburg on St. Alexander Nevsky's Day. The women listened attentively, enthralled by the colorful details of the large crowds massing the streets, the spectacular fireworks, and nighttime illuminations decorating the city. Kuzmich assured them that such festivities gave much pleasure and happiness to the tsar.

One incident that provoked comment related to the visit paid by Count General Pyotr Kleinmikel to Krasnaya Rechka. From earliest days, the count had been one of Alexander's closer friends and advisers. By 1825, he had risen to become one of the most influential officials in the country, serving as Arakcheyev's chief of staff. During an extensive inspection tour of Siberia, the general stopped off at Krasnaya Rechka and visited the local hospital. As coincidence would have it, Feodor Kuzmich, whose health had always been sturdy, was at the time suffering an illness that required hospitalization. He therefore happened to be in the hospital during Kleinmikel's visit, which was something of a state occasion for the staff and patients. When the inspecting party entered the ward where Kuzmich was lying, the physicians were upset to see the starets turn his face to the wall and cover himself with a blanket, as though trying to avoid eye contact with the honored guest. Until then, Kleinmikel had been greeted by one and all with the warmest Siberian hospitality. Now, it seemed, he was ignored, if not insulted. Why had Kuzmich acted so churlishly? It was so uncharacteristic of him. One can only surmise that he might have feared the general would recognize him. Given the more than thirty years that had elapsed since Alexander's death, it was highly unlikely that Kleinmikel would have known the patient, but Kuzmich was doubtless taking no chances.

On another occasion in Krasnaya Rechka, three peasants called on Kuzmich and, no doubt having been taken by rumors concerning the possible imperial origin of the starets, bluntly asked him, "Little father, is it true that you are the Grand Duke Constantine Pavlovich [Alexander's younger brother]?" The starets crossed himself and blurted out without thinking, "Thank God, I'm not. He's shorter than me, not very handsome, and has a pug nose."

At the end of October 1858, Kuzmich made his final move. From Krasnaya Rechka he relocated to the outskirts of Tomsk itself. Earlier in his wanderings, he had met and was befriended by a merchant named Khromov. The kindly businessman offered to settle the starets on his country property just outside the city, where he proposed to build him a cabin, or rather a cell. Kuzmich gratefully accepted the generous proposal and soon found himself in his new quarters, where he lived out his final years.

During those years, Khromov's guest aged rapidly. When they had first met, Kuzmich was still tall and broad-shouldered, a handsome man with delicate features, his deep blue eyes sparkling with kindness. Now he was nearly bald and sported a graying beard. The merchant was taken by the man's gentle, reserved manner and by his thoughtfulness and generosity. A considerate person, but oh so secretive — never speaking of his past or of himself. The old man soon captured a place not only in Khromov's heart but in those of his family as well. But why so guarded? Who was he really? The "vagabond" was obviously a cultured person who possessed the sort of tact one could hardly expect to find in an ordinary peasant. Might there be something dark in his past? Surely such a man should have the initiative and wit to secure honest work, and make something of himself. Perhaps, thought Khromov, he had sometime in the past committed a crime or serious transgression and now, in his declining years, was destined to wander the vast country, knocking on monastery doors for food and shelter.

From the start, the relationship between Kuzmich and the

Khromovs was familial, and soon the starets became something of a fixture in the household. An especially close friendship blossomed with the merchant's young daughter, Anna, and she was always welcome at the old man's cabin, where the two spent hours in discussion. Over time, Anna recorded many anecdotes and incidents concerning the family's enigmatic guest, which, if we take them at face value — and there is no reason we shouldn't — comprise a valuable record of the starets during that period.

The mode of Kuzmich's life was simplicity itself. His dress invariably consisted of a peasant's full-length chemise of crude linen, loose trousers of the same cloth, thick white stockings — which he changed daily — and hard leather shoes. His hut was a single room with a tiny vestibule leading outdoors, a sort of mud-room, in which hung a heavy winter overcoat. The cell itself measured eleven and a half by fourteen and a half feet and was sparsely furnished, containing only a rough wooden table with two or three chairs and a cot with wooden slats that served as a mattress, together with a pillow and a heavy quilt. In addition, there was a small stove, a couple of benches, and a shelf. On the table lay a Bible and prayer book, and a wall shelf contained a collection of religious books. On another wall hung a crucifix and a display of icons with a votive lamp that burned day and night. The two small windows provided little light; in freezing winter, however, the room was warm and cozy. Visitors invariably remarked on the tidiness and cleanliness of these spartan quarters.

Among Kuzmich's belongings was a chest containing writing materials and packets of papers that he scrupulously concealed from all but his most trusted visitors, such as the Khromovs. He wrote many letters, but always behind a locked door. Few people were aware of the extent of his contact with the world at large, an aspect of his life Kuzmich guarded jealously. Letters were received and sent; unfamiliar visitors came and went, often bearing a parcel or an envelope. Khromov tells us that on one occasion he and members of his family overheard Kuzmich speak with his visitors in a foreign tongue, which he presumed to be French.

The starets arose early in the morning but did not emerge from his cell until well into the day. Weather permitting, he spent as much time as possible outdoors, usually working the garden or tending his bees. At night he slept fitfully, with long hours given over to prayer. The old man dined sparingly and simply — mostly hard biscuits, vegetables, and water. Occasionally he ate some fish or meat that was offered to him, which he consumed with indifference. "You see," he declared to one visitor, "I'm not a rabid vegetarian!"

Even by the time of Kuzmich's move onto the Khromov property, the staret's notoriety had already spread throughout the region. The inhabitants were now drawn to him in ever greater numbers. An aura of sanctity seemed to envelop him. "The saintly old man of Tomsk," they called him. One longtime resident of Tomsk, V. Dolgoruky, recounts the following prophetic story that circulated in Siberia at the time. On an especially cold midwinter day, Kuzmich asked one of Khromov's workmen to report to his master in Tomsk and request additional firewood. Without hesitation, the obliging merchant dispatched his servant back to the starets with the message that firewood would be arriving shortly. Khromov then ordered another employee to load up a cart and make the delivery. The delegated servant, enjoying the warmth of his own hut, was displeased with the order but grudgingly carried out the task, all the time cursing his lot, his master, the starets, and the two-and-a-half mile journey ahead of him. But when he arrived at Kuzmich's cell, the old man informed him that the wood was no longer required.

"What do you mean, you don't need the wood?" protested the exasperated workman.

"From you, I won't accept the wood," replied the starets. "You bring the logs with resentment and anger. As you loaded your cart, you swore and cursed me." And the old man repeated to the dismayed deliveryman every word that he had uttered in Tomsk before departure. The awestruck workman fell to his knees and pleaded for forgiveness, which was readily given and the wood accepted. Real or apocryphal, the story reflects the way the people regarded their starets.

Anna Khromov relates how she and her father once called on Kuzmich, who, on seeing them approach, exited his cell and asked if they would kindly wait for a few moments until his guests left. The two distanced themselves from the cabin and patiently bided their time. The "few moments" turned into an hour, then two, before they finally saw Feodor Kuzmich emerge from the cabin together with a young woman and an officer in a hussar's uniform. The starets escorted the couple for some distance and, as "they were leaving," recalled Anna, "it appeared to me that the hussar kissed the old man's hand, something he never permitted anybody to do." It is surmised that the mysterious hussar whom the Khromovs observed that afternoon was none other than the tsarevich, Alexander II. In his work on Alexander I, Prince Vladimir Bariatinsky provides solid evidence that the heir at one time did visit Feodor Kuzmich, who, if the Legend is true, would have been the young man's blood uncle.

Another extremely intriguing incident was related in Anna's diary. As Kuzmich awaited the construction of his cell, he was provided a room in the Khromov house for a brief period. One evening, as was their wont, the family was gathered around the dining room table, listening to the younger daughter read aloud. Kuzmich's room was adjacent, its door ajar. The girl had chosen to read from a newly published work on the reign of Alexander I. She came to a passage that read, "Emperor Alexander turned to Napoleon and said to him . . . ," and she quoted a statement Alexander was alleged to have made when the two emperors met. Suddenly an angry voice was heard to cry out, "I never said that!" At first nobody understood where the voice had come from, but then they all rushed into the starets's room, where they found him "on his knees in submissive prayer."

The historian Grigory Vasilich tells of Kuzmich's attachment to a young orphan girl called Alexandra, who often visited him, frequently bearing fresh berries, mushrooms, or other little presents.

At an early age she was adopted into the large family of a priest, a certain Father Polikarp, who lived not far from Kuzmich's cabin. While on a walk with her brothers, Alexandra, then twelve years of age, first saw the starets and immediately wanted to run up to him. The boys held her back, arguing that it wasn't for her to bother the stranger, and that at any rate the old man would never speak to her. A few days later, as Alexandra emerged from the forest where she had been alone picking bilberries, she again spotted the starets. Without hesitation, she ran up to him, held out her basket, and said, "Grandfather, would you like some berries?"

Kuzmich smiled tenderly, clasped her head in his hands, and kissed her forehead. Tears welled in his eyes — perhaps he was touched by the child's impetuosity and purity, or possibly from some memory that the unexpected encounter dredged up from the past. It didn't take long for the old man and the girl to bond, and before long they were spending many days together. Alexandra helped Kuzmich work the garden and delighted in helping him clean his cell. The old man taught her reading and writing and gave her lessons in history, geography, and religion. The girl was enchanted by the stories her friend told of far-off countries and places, of the monasteries he had visited and of holy sites and pilgrims.

Alexandra was a religious girl, which no doubt helped cement the incongruous relationship. Over the years, the girl's admiration for the starets developed into a profound affection, obviously reciprocated by the old man. At age twenty, Alexandra announced her intention to make a pilgrimage to the holy places of Russia. Her brothers did all they could to dissuade her from such an uncertain and possibly perilous undertaking, urging her instead to seek a husband. Kuzmich, however, encouraged her. "Wait," the starets advised, "there's plenty of time to marry; none of these people is worthy of you. When you marry, it will be to a fine officer."

Plans for the trip went ahead, and Kuzmich worked out a detailed itinerary for the girl. He counseled her on which monasteries to visit, what people she might turn to for hospitality, and gave her all sorts of practical advice on the do's and don'ts of travel. Years later, Alexandra recalled an exchange that took place during those planning sessions. At one point, in her exuberance, she asked the starets how she might arrange to see the tsar when she was in Russia. "You really want to see the tsar?" asked Kuzmich. "Of course, father," Alexandra exclaimed, "how can one possibly miss seeing the tsar? Everyone speaks of the tsar, the tsar, the tsar . . . but what sort of person is he really like?"

"Wait," replied the starets. "Perhaps in the course of your life you'll have a chance to meet more than one tsar. God willing, you will speak with him and then you'll see that tsars are human like everyone else!"

Alexandra bade farewell to her family and to her beloved starets and set off on her lengthy pilgrimage. In Kiev, she visited the sacred Kievo-Pechersky Monastery, which since 1051 had been Russia's foremost monastic and religious center. While in that ancient capital city, Alexandra also called on Countess Osten-Sacken, to whom she bore a letter of introduction from the starets. The countess was much taken by the new arrival and hustled her off to their country home at Kremenchuk, to introduce her to her husband, Count Dimitry Erofeyevich, a much-decorated general who later became one of the heroes of the Crimean War. It is reported that he and Feodor Kuzmich exchanged letters, although no hard evidence of any such correspondence has been found. After the count died, his wife returned to Kremenchuk and opened the secret box in which her husband had locked his most valued papers; presumably, Kuzmich's letters might have been there. However, she discovered the box empty; evidently someone had already opened it and managed to remove the contents. Nothing else in the house was reported missing. It is also possible, of course, that the count himself had removed the contents. But it is equally feasible that the same forces responsible for the destruction of material related to the Taganrog death were at work here, in Kremenchuk. The apparent connection between Alexander I,

Osten-Sacken, and Kuzmich is tantalizing. A further interesting aside: for decades, Count Osten-Sacken steadfastly refused to attend memorial services for the emperor.

Both the count and countess were delighted to receive the Siberian girl and persuaded her to stay on with them for a while; Alexandra dallied for several months. During her stay at Kremenchuk, Emperor Nicholas I happened to be touring the region and was a guest of the Osten-Sackens. The couple informed him of Alexandra's presence in the house and he asked to see her. The young pilgrim was brought before him, and in the company of their hosts a leisurely conversation took place between the tsar of Russia and the Siberian peasant girl. The emperor queried her on her life there, on her family, and on Feodor Kuzmich. Alexandra answered the sovereign's questions enthusiastically and with childlike naiveté, often causing him and the Osten-Sackens to chuckle with delight. "Well," said the tsar at one point, turning to his hosts, "you've certainly got a daring young girl in your house." To this, Alexandra shot back, "What's there to be afraid of? I've got God on my side . . . and also, the powerful prayers of Feodor Kuzmich are with me. Besides, you're all very kind people." At this spontaneous *cri de coeur,* Nicholas became pensive and softly commented, "Feodor Kuzmich is indeed a holy man."

As he left, Nicholas asked Osten-Sacken to give Alexandra a pass — a laissez-passer — and told the girl that if ever she got to St. Petersburg, she should come to the palace. "Present the pass and nobody will stop you."

Alexandra never did get to St. Petersburg, but sometime later she returned to Siberia, to the relief and embrace of her anxious family. She lost little time in calling on Feodor Kuzmich, who received her enthusiastically. Over the next few days, the girl related to him the details of her adventures. During one of the sessions, Alexandra records, "I observed him with intense care and blurted out, 'Father Feodor Kuzmich, how greatly you resemble the Emperor Alexander Pavlovich!' No sooner had I said this than his face changed. He rose out of his chair, his eyebrows contracted menacingly, and he looked sternly upon me. 'And how do you know? Who prompted you to say that to me?' I became frightened.

"'Nobody prompted me. In Count Osten-Sacken's study I saw a full-length portrait of Alexander Pavlovich. The thought then, as now, came to me that not only do you look like him but you even hold your hands as he did.' The starets made no reply but simply moved away into the entry hall, apparently overcome by emotion."

Five years later, the Russian historian Lev D. Lubimov tells us, Alexandra made a second pilgrimage to Russia, and again Kuzmich gave her letters of introduction. One of the people upon whom the girl called directed her to the monastery of Valaam on Lake Ladoga, north of St. Petersburg, an enormous lake navigated by capital vessels. By chance Alexandra found herself on the same ship as the Empress Maria Alexeyevna, wife of Alexander II, who was also traveling on a pilgrimage to the island monastery. The empress learned of the Siberian girl's presence on board and invited her to her cabin; the two were closeted together for a long time in conversation. If one does not question the authenticity of this report, then it might well be asked why a reigning empress would not only deign to receive a simple Siberian girl in her state-room but would also engage her in extended conversation. Maria Alexeyevna must have been aware of some connection between the girl and Feodor Kuzmich.

Years later, again in Russia, Alexandra met a dashing officer, Major Fedorov. The two fell in love, married, and raised several children. The prophecy of the starets was thus realized, and Alexandra never returned to her Siberian roots.

The substance of what we have on Feodor Kuzmich, particularly his various movements from place to place, comes from civic records studied by historians such as Grand Duke Nikolai Mikhailovich, Vladimir Bariatinsky, Lev Lubimov, Anatol Kulomzin, and others. Fleshing out the starets's life is possible only through memoirs and anecdotes of his contemporaries — what they themselves recorded or related to others, who in turn set it down.

We come now to where we began with Kuzmich. By late January 1864 the starets was nearing his end. His breathing grew increasingly labored; it was evident that he was suffering great pain, and he appeared totally wasted. By January 31, his eyes remained closed, but his lips occasionally moved in silent prayer. Late that afternoon, a small crowd of people filtered into the cell to be with their beloved recluse. Just before eight o'clock, it became evident that the end was truly at hand. In the silence of the darkened cell, the weeping assembly held candles and prayed. Kuzmich awoke.

Standing at his side was his kindly benefactor, Simeon Khromov. As the old man steadily weakened, the merchant gently persisted in the matter of his true identity. Kuzmich determinedly deflected the questions, steadfastly refusing to divulge anything. And then at last, pointing to his chest, he murmured, "Here lies my secret." And with those enigmatic, intriguing words, he died.

As the body was being washed in preparation for burial, Khromov removed from around the neck a small, stained cloth sachet, which was attached to a leather cord. It was evident that, whatever it was, Kuzmich had carried it on his person for years, wearing it much as one might one's baptismal cross. On prying open the packet, Khromov discovered a yellowed scrap of paper on which was written a message in numbered cipher. A few recognizable words appeared on it, as well as the initials A and P. The puzzled Khromov retained the relic but made no secret of its existence. Some years later the scrap of paper was given to the authorities in St. Petersburg and was eventually photographed and examined by a succession of experts, including Grand Duke Nikolai Mikhailovich. But try as anyone might, for over sixty years the message defied decoding. Finally, in 1927, two cryptographers, one in Riga and the other in Belgrade, working independently of one another, almost simultaneously broke the code and uncovered the secret. The message read:

> Anna Vasilievna:[†] we have discovered an incredible flaw in our son. Count Pahlen informs me of Alexander's participation in a conspiracy. We must hide tonight, wherever it is possible.
>
> PAUL
> St. Petersburg. March 11, 1801

[†]The note appears to be addressed to Paul's mistress, Anna Vasilievna Gagarina. Her apartment was in Mikhailovsky Castle.

15

The Core of the Mystery

"A SPHINX WHO CARRIED HIS RIDDLE to the grave." But here we have two graves: one in Tomsk, that of Feodor Kuzmich "the Great and Blessed," and the other in St. Petersburg, that of Alexander "the Blessed." The solution to the Legend's haunting — and tantalizing — enigma lies in these two burial places. Is the casket in St. Petersburg empty? And if it contains human remains, are they truly those of the emperor? And what of the remains of Feodor Kuzmich?

We are at the core of the mystery. It is almost certain that the tomb in St. Peter and St. Paul Fortress has been uncovered, probably on more than one occasion. At least three unofficial accounts speak of the grave being opened. On the orders of Alexander II, the tomb was apparently first unsealed in 1866, and then once more in the 1880s, during the reign of Alexander III. Finally, it is said, the Soviets reopened the grave in the 1920s. No archival record has yet been found to substantiate any of these claims. It is true, however, that each of the four tsars who followed Alexander not only carefully avoided discussing the matter but also appeared actively to obstruct any investigation. Grand Duke Nikolai Mikhailovich, for example, in the course of his research of the Legend, requested permission from his nephew Nicholas II to open Alexander's tomb. The tsar denied it without explanation. As mentioned, Nicholas's sister, Grand Duchess Olga, told me in 1958 that "in our family Alexander's death was not a subject for discussion." The tsars studiously avoided the subject, and over the years a pall of secrecy increasingly shrouded the Legend. Just as Nicholas I destroyed much of the written documentation relating to Alexander's last months, so it is possible that Alexander II and Alexander III did likewise and for the same motive. That nothing has been found concerning the alleged Soviet exploration is less readily explained. Soviet record-keeping was always meticulous, and it is hardly likely that a singular venture such as the digging up of a tsar's remains would go unrecorded. Besides, the Soviet authorities would have had little reason to maintain secrecy.

Decades after Alexander's tomb was sealed, an elderly soldier by the name of Igor Lavrentiev lay dying in his home not far from the Fortress of St. Peter and St. Paul. He had once been the chief porter at a then newly constructed hospital in St. Petersburg. Shortly after the hospital opened, Alexander II had visited it and was taken on a tour by the director, a well-known psychiatrist named Ivan Balinsky. At the conclusion of the visit, the tsar remarked to the doctor that the hall porter who had taken his cloak when he arrived seemed to him too old and frail for his job. He would see to it, he said, that the hospital was assigned someone more able. Within days a strapping new porter, Lavrentriev, arrived to fill the post. As the years passed, this soldier's ties to the Balinsky family grew closer, and eventually he became a fixture in the household. In particular, he helped look after the director's children, who became very fond of him. One of these children, Ignace Balinsky, who later became a general, recalled the porter with warm affection and related the strange circumstances of his death.

Realizing he was dying, Lavrentiev had asked that his daughter be summoned, so he could bid her a final farewell. When she appeared, he informed her that he was leaving the family 10,000 rubles. He then went on to say that since he was a poor man, "such a significant sum will create suspicion and I will inevitably be accused of coming into the money dishonestly. At the time I received it, I swore that I wouldn't disclose to anyone how it came to me. Now, however, I greatly fear that my name will be dragged through the mud."

The dying man then told the girl that in 1866 — two years after Kuzmich's death — he was a sentinel at the Cathedral at the Fortress of St. Peter and St. Paul. One spring day, several members of the cathedral guard were summoned to the sanctuary. They were joined by some marble workers and artisans of bronze. Shortly, the minister of the imperial court, Count d'Adlerberg arrived, and in a businesslike manner demanded that all the guardsmen and workmen take an oath never to divulge the least detail of what they were about to witness. A priest administered the oath to each person, all of whom placed their hand on the Holy Bible and kissed a crucifix.

Lavrentiev went on to explain that the marble workers were then ordered to remove the heavy cover from the tomb of Alexander I. The casket was drawn up from the bottom, and when it was pried open by the bronze workers, it was found to be empty. At this point, the guardsmen were directed to a wagon outside the cathedral, from which they removed a wooden coffin, which they placed in the emperor's casket. The tomb was then resealed — no further comment was offered. Before it disbanded, the little group was again reminded of the solemn oath everyone had just taken. Before they were dismissed, Count d'Adlerberg announced that each soldier and worker present would receive the munificent sum of 10,000 silver rubles for the singular services just performed.

Two days after making this revelation to his daughter, the old soldier died. It was General Balinsky who related his testimony to his friend, Grand Duke Andre Vladimirovich — nephew of Alexander III and uncle to Nicholas II. Before the revolution, Balinsky researched the archives of the Ministry of the Imperial Court and found that their family friend and servant had indeed served as a chief porter in the hospital and that in 1866 he was a guardsman at the fortress. As an exile in France, the grand duke recorded the story, and in a letter from Cannes to Prince Bariatinsky dated April 12, 1926, he passed it on.

Grand Duke Andre had the reputation of being scrupulously accurate in historical detail. Nor is there any reason to question the general's integrity. Little is known of the porter's daughter, except that she remained close to the Balinskys. The general attests to the grand inheritance received by her. The soldier's story is made all the more curious by the recorded personal involvement of the tsar. It was Alexander II who personally assigned this soldier to what certainly must have been in those days a plum of a job. Russian emperors did not normally involve themselves in such mundane personal details. Could the tsar have been aware of the secret to which the soldier was privy? Did he perhaps feel uniquely indebted to the fellow?

The account of the soldier-porter that Balinsky gave to Grand Duke Andre was also related seven years later to Alexandra Dubasova, daughter-in-law of Nicholas Tatichev, governor of Tavrich. As she tells it, however, there is a twist. "After the coffin was uncovered, the remains were transferred to a simple casket which was then transported to the cemetery and there they were buried."

Balinsky's and Dubasov's accounts of the tomb's uncovering are but two of several; all, however, come to us at second or third hand. The contemporary Russian historian A. N. Saharov, for example, writes of this same event but adds a further, tantalizing detail. Quoting a witness who was allegedly present, he writes that within the wooden coffin that was placed into the bronze casket there "lay a long-bearded starets."

Another tale of the disinterment comes to us as having taken place twenty years later, during the reign of Alexander III. Countess A. Shuvalova, daughter of Count I. Vorontsov-Dashkov, the former viceroy of the Caucasus, maintained a thoughtful diary. In it she relates how one day in the late 1880s her father returned home in the early hours of the morning in a state of great agitation. He told his wife and daughter that he had just been to the

Cathedral at the Fortress of St. Peter and St. Paul with the tsar, because the emperor had decided to open the tomb of Alexander I. The count's presence was required, he related, because as minister of the court he was the sole layman who held copies of the keys to the cathedral doors. After the preliminary work had been completed, the attending laborers were ordered out, leaving only himself, the emperor, and four soldiers of the imperial guard at the site. Together they removed the coffin's cover and, much to their astonishment, found it empty. The count instructed his wife and daughter that under no circumstances might this confidence be revealed to anyone. Shuvalova makes no further comment.

The final reported disinterment of Alexander is said to have taken place by the Bolsheviks. In 1921, rumors were rife throughout Leningrad that the authorities had opened the imperial tombs in the Fortress of St. Peter and St. Paul to search for valuables, ostensibly for the relief of the poor. When the grave of Alexander I was opened, it was purportedly found to be empty. Eventually these rumors trickled to the West, and soon European newspapers and journals were reporting this startling development. Soviet authorities were apparently disappointed to discover no valuables, but were even more chagrined to find the coffin empty. It was also rumored that they discovered signs that the casket and coffin therein had been previously unsealed. As noted, however, no record of such an unsealing has been found.

Sergei Mironenko, archivist of the Russian Federation, is a historian specializing in early-nineteenth-century Russia. In my discussions with him, he pointed out that opening any of the tombs in the Cathedral of St. Peter and St. Paul is extremely difficult. A handful of laborers without modern equipment, he argues, could hardly have been expected to remove the heavy marble slabs of the tombs. In addition, there is the arduous task of extracting a large casket from its eight-foot depth and then undoing the elaborate metalwork that seals it. In 1994, Mironenko was present when the tomb of Grand Duke Georgi Alexandrovich, brother of Nicholas II, was opened. A body sample was required by the scientific community for a DNA investigation of the remains of Nicholas II and his family.[†] It was a Herculean task, and Mironenko was impressed by the effort required to carry it out. Mironenko rejects the stories of Alexander's tomb having been opened; in short, he is not a supporter of the Legend.

The Bogoroditsko-Alexeyevsk Monastery in Tomsk where Feodor Kuzmich was interred had in his day some fifty monks. Today there are but seven, and Father Siluan is the abbot. The grave of Feodor Kuzmich in the monastery's cemetery, he informed me, was preserved over the decades, although the chapel erected in 1912 was dismantled in the early 1920s. The Soviet authorities needed its bricks for the construction of a nearby school. "In 1995, the grave of Feodor Kuzmich was uncovered by our monastery's personnel and the remains were transferred into the church," reports Father Siluan. "When we opened the casket, we discovered that over a third of the body was missing, including the skull. The grave had obviously been opened on at least one previous occasion." There is no doubt that at the time of Kuzmich's death in 1864 the entire body had been placed in the coffin that had been lowered into the grave. If almost a century and a half later, a third of the body was missing, the tantalizing question then arises: who opened the grave and for what purpose? To verify the authentic body or perhaps to remove a part of the remains in order to confound identification? Maybe even to substitute a body?

The riddle of the graves is but one unresolved question regarding the Legend. Alexander's sudden illness and death is a minefield of curious circumstances and inexplicable contradictions. And the autopsy and treatment of the body pose even more

---

†The result was instrumental in positively identifying the remains as those of Nicholas II and his family. On July 17, 1998, the remains were laid to rest in the cathedral, alongside the other Romanovs. Certain circles continue to deny the evidence and do not acknowledge the remains as being authentic. At the moment of writing, the Russian Orthodox Church and the émigré Russian Orthodox Church in Exile are among them.

difficult questions. Together, the material cannot escape fueling the cause of the Legend.

Whenever a sovereign dies, protocol demands that every detail be recorded with meticulous accuracy by a designated authority. The document is then signed by witnesses, sealed, and deposited in the official state archives. The time of death is recorded, a list of those attending is appended, and every pertinent word, gesture, and movement of the dying is documented. In the case of Alexander's death, none of this strict protocol was followed; all we have are a brief death certificate and the suspect official history. In addition, there are the memoirs and letters of those present, but, as noted, these are frequently contradictory. Who was actually in the room when Alexander died? The fact is, there is no clear undisputed record of the emperor's death.

To begin with, the precise time of death is uncertain. Volkonsky: "He took his last breath at 10 hours 50 minutes." Wylie concurs. *The History of the Illness and Final Days of Alexander I* has it, "At ten forty-five, the emperor breathed his last." Was it 10:50 or 10:45? Normally a five-minute disparity would appear unimportant. In the case of a sovereign, particularly of a Russian autocrat, this is indefensible. To further confuse the issue: in Tarasov's notes we read that that same evening an extraordinary commission was assembled to formulate a death certificate. Members included Tarasov himself, Volkonsky, Wylie, Diebich, Father Theodotov, Adjutant Chernischev, and Secretary Longinov. The certificate records the time of death as 10:47, and everyone signs off on that, including Wylie.

The autopsy — its circumstances and report, together with the secretiveness surrounding the body — poses further, even more difficult questions. *The History of the Illness:* "Just prior to death, the paroxysm terminated with moaning and hiccoughs. The breathing became increasingly jerky. On five occasions it stopped and restarted only with difficulty." Dr. Dobbert wrote, "He died in the most horrible suffering. His agony continued some eleven hours." The valet Feodorov testified, "He couldn't speak but he maintained his spirit; he gestured for his august wife to approach." Schoenig: "Before his end, he suffered and at the last moment he asked the empress for her forgiveness and then died, holding her hand in his." And yet Tarasov tells us that "his final glance expressed such a tranquil and heavenly hope . . . no suffering at all."

Each of the extant diaries describing the hours leading up to the moment of death are frequently contradictory. Some of the diaries pick up the story again later that evening and describe what happened after the emperor's demise. The eight-hour span between the time of death, in the morning, and seven that night, however, is mysteriously unaccounted for. One would have surmised that those hours must have been frantic, filled with emotion and bustling activity. But nothing worthy of note appears to have occurred — almost as though on purpose.

And we have other anomalous situations. On November 15, as we have seen, Alexander agreed to receive a priest. He was now apparently prepared to confess and receive communion, which until then he had steadfastly refused, despite his wife's pleas. Father Theodotov was summoned and the last rites administered. In the four days that followed, however, the dying man received no further ministrations of the church, although the priest was apparently present at the reported moment of death. This is passing strange. It is difficult to believe that the pious, spiritually sensitive Alexander, knowing that he was dying, did not request the comfort of a priest to ease him through his final days. It is equally strange that those who were literally standing around the monarch, suffering through the hours of his agony, would not have done everything to ease the passage of death. Surely someone — Elizaveta, first and foremost — would have recalled Theodotov earlier, if for no other reason than to recite the comforting prayers traditionally read to the dying:

The night of death, dark and moonless, has overtaken me who am unready, sending me unprepared on that long and

dreadful journey . . . mercifully accept now the visitation
which has come on me, that looking on Thee, with rejoic-
ing I may depart from the body.

The Orthodox among the group were familiar with church ritual
and fully aware of the comfort that such prayers could bring to the
dying. Yet Theodotov was not called, and no other clergy attended
the tsar in his final hour. Very strange indeed. One possible explanation, of course, is that Alexander was not really dying.

Following the "death," an inordinate thirty-three hours
passed before the start of the autopsy. In Russian Orthodox practice, a person's remains are quickly prepared and brought into
church, where family and friends join in prayers and memorial
services. One would have expected that Elizaveta and the others
would have pressed for an immediate start to the funerary rites.
Why then the inexplicable delay in attending to the autopsy and
embalming? There might well have been a perfectly legitimate
explanation — the immediate unavailability of the required materials, for example. The supporters of the Legend, however, generally believe the long delay was caused by the need to bring in a
substitute body for autopsy and embalming. Surely such a challenging maneuver could not be effected without complication.

As for the autopsy itself, it is insufficient, irregular, and contradictory. The report, for example, speaks of a discoloration of one
leg. A horse had once kicked Alexander on his left leg, and for years
he suffered discomfort from the blow. In 1824 the wound became
infected and fever set in. Drs. Tarasov and Wylie satisfactorily
attended to the leg, but not before it was affected by a permanent
discoloration. In his memoirs, Tarasov speaks of the wound as
being on the *left* leg. The autopsy report, however, notes it as being
on the *right*.

Then we have Tarasov's own questionable role in the proceedings. The doctor claims that he absented himself from the
autopsy — because of "filial feelings and respect for the emperor."
In Schoenig's account, however, the doctor *was* in attendance.

Tarasov, however, admitted that he authored the final report, although he refrained from signing it since he was not present. But his signature appears on the final protocol. What are we to believe? Is Schoenig mistaken? If Tarasov was in attendance, why did he take pains to deny it? If the doctor really did not sign the document, is his signature a forgery?

Ultimately, the autopsy fails in its purpose — to define the actual cause of death. It concludes with such words as "taken by an extreme illness," "fierce fever," a "rush of blood," "secretion and accumulation of serus exidate," and ends with these words: "This disease was the cause of the death of His Imperial Majesty." *What* disease? Precisely of what did Alexander die?

In his research, Prince Bariantinsky carried out an interesting experiment. He submitted copies of the autopsy report to four medical experts, without identifying the subject's name. He requested their professional opinion regarding the cause of death, mentioning only that it might have been from typhoid or malaria. A Dr. N. Tchigaeff replied that it could not have been typhoid and that it was unlikely to have been malaria. Certain symptoms made him believe that the deceased might have suffered from syphilis or alcoholism. He could offer no conclusions, "because the account is far from being a scientific report and it is too succinct." A Dr. Manasseine wrote that the "report is done so unscientifically that it is impossible to establish the cause of death." He too concluded that in his opinion it was neither from typhoid or malaria, then added: "One might suppose that this individual died of syphilis." Dr. Dombrowsky, a surgeon, wrote, "The autopsy report was insufficient to conclude the cause of death." He too was virtually sure that neither typhoid nor malaria was the cause of death. Finally, another surgeon, Dr. Hubbenet, reported that "it is impossible to admit that typhoid fever or malaria (*fièvre paludéenne*) was the cause of death." Syphilis, he felt, was certainly present. Based on these independent opinions, malaria and typhoid, it might appear, can be discounted as the cause of death. It is interesting to note, however, that three of the doctors noted the symptoms of syphilis. So far as we know, however, Alexander never contracted that disease — unless it was very late in life. But from what we know of his various liaisons in those later years, this is highly unlikely.

A British physician, Dr. Robert Lee, who happened to be in the Crimea during Alexander's tour, supported the typhoid theory. At the time, Dr. Lee was serving on the personal staff of the governor of South Russia. Invited to join the imperial party for a portion of the Crimean tour, he attended one particular dinner when oysters were served. Dr. Lee wrote of a marine worm being found on one of the shells. "Wylie was consulted and pronounced it innocuous, so the oyster was eaten by the emperor. I mention the incident of the oyster because we are inclined in this country to associate oysters with typhoid and the symptoms of Alexander's twenty-one-day illness were compatible with this diagnosis."

Upon his return from the Crimea, Alexander informed his wife that he had caught a touch of malaria. A few days earlier he had visited the malaria wing of the Perekop Hospital and while there had displayed singular curiosity over the symptoms of the illness. As we have seen, at one point he queried Dr. Wylie at some length about quinine. Quite probably he was more familiar with malaria than he was with typhoid or other such serious illnesses. At any rate, in Alexander's opinion, what he had was "a touch of malaria."

Malaria and typhoid differ significantly, and their symptoms are readily distinguishable. Each calls for a distinctly different treatment. The medical team in Taganrog was experienced and competent. It is indeed strange that not only did the doctors not pinpoint the condition but the autopsy report was inconclusive.

In my own research, I sought to repeat Bariatinsky's 1910 experiment by submitting the autopsy report to three forensic pathologists, requesting their opinion on the matter — Dr. David Chaisson, chief forensic pathologist for the province of Ontario; Dr. Leslie Lukash, chief medical examiner for Nassau County, New York; and Dr. Yasmine Ayroud of McGill University. The specialists all concurred that the report is so deficient that meaningful conclusions cannot be drawn. An examination of the clinical records, they suggested, would serve better than a review of the autopsy report. Dr. Chaisson does, however, observe that there is nothing in the report to indicate death from malaria or typhoid.

Typhoid and malaria are the two illnesses most commonly mentioned as being the probable cause of Alexander's death. Typhoid usually comes from the ingestion of contaminated food or water. The average incubation period is from one to three weeks and the symptoms are frontal headache, fever, and at times diarrhea or constipation. Over the following several weeks, the condition develops further and the fever rises sharply, as high as up to 40°C (103–104°F). Frequently there is a vague anorexia as well as joint and back pains. Alexander suffered from fever, fitful sleep, and occasional delirium. He did not complain of any of the other symptoms, except for diarrhea on November 9. On the contrary, he is reported to have suffered from a blocked stomach; the doctors frequently fretted over purgatives, and on at least one occasion an enema was prescribed. Under no circumstance does his condition fit typhoid.

Malaria is contracted by the bite of infected mosquitoes, and the first symptoms manifest themselves in one to three weeks, generally in three stages: (a) chills and shaking, (b) high fever of 40°C and higher, accompanied by severe headaches; (c) profuse sweating and a return to normal temperature. The spleen and liver increase in size, and frequently there is renal failure. Although Alexander suffered from varying fevers, he did not complain of headaches and his doctors' notations regarding chills or undue sweating are few and far between. Moreover, the autopsy report clearly states that the "pancreas, spleen, kidneys and bladder did not deviate from the normal." The case for malaria is also very weak indeed.

Dr. Ayroud adds that food poisoning was an unlikely culprit. Had either the suspicious fish or oyster that Alexander had eaten during his Crimean tour been tainted, he would have been violently ill within twenty-four hours. Such was not the case.

Among the various rumors that circulated shortly after the emperor's death was that he had been assassinated by poisoning. In London, the *Times* of March 3, 1825, carried an article on this. A curious manuscript of anonymous authorship reposes in the rare manuscript collection of the Bodleian Library, Oxford, to which some historians make reference. *Unpublished Details Relative to the Death of Emperor Alexander* consists of extracts from the diary of "a Russian nobleman." The author details Alexander's sojourn in Taganrog, describes his tour of the Crimea, and tells of the illness that felled him — "a slight attack of ague [malarial fever]." He suggests that the illness might have resulted from "the unwholesome or ill-cooked" food served during the inspection tour of the Crimea. The author pointedly argues against any possible poisoning, vague rumor of which first surfaced in Taganrog immediately after the tsar's demise.

And then we have the condition of the body. During the thirty-two-hour hiatus between the demise and the autopsy, the body had so deteriorated that when the physicians were opening it they smoked strong cigars to offset the overpowering odors that arose from within. In the nineteenth century, a cigar was not an uncommon accoutrement among doctors performing an autopsy, particularly if some time had elapsed between death and the procedure. The rapidity with which a body decomposes depends first and foremost on the temperature at which it is found or kept. Assuming a room of approximately 17°C (64°F; this seems to have been the common indoor temperature in those days), the experts with whom I consulted agree that it is unlikely that after thirty-two hours the remains could have so decomposed that cigar smoke would have been required to help overcome the odors of decay. It must be allowed, however, that those working over the body were probably unused to the work, in which case the slightest odor might have been offensive.

There can be no question that the remains were badly decomposed almost from the start. A number of witnesses comment on the body's state, some immediately after the embalming, others a bit later. Schoenig's gruesome detail may be recalled: on the second day after the embalming, Diebich tugged at the corner of the emperor's necktie and "to his horror he found that it was loosened flesh." Five days after the embalming, Volkonsky notified State Secretary Vilyamov in St. Petersburg that "although the body was embalmed, the face has so blackened on account of the humidity that the features are virtually unrecognizable. They are certain to get worse with the further lapse of time. It therefore seems to me far better that the coffin not be opened upon its arrival in St. Petersburg."

Princess Volkonsky's account is more vivid. On November 26, she wrote, "The chemicals used for the preservation of the body totally darkened it. The eyes had considerably sunk but it was the form of the nose that changed most — it had become almost aquiline!" On receiving news in the capital of the tsar's death, Countess Edling, a lady-in-waiting and companion to Elizaveta, hurried to Taganrog to be with her mistress. She arrived on December 15 and noted in her diary, "I could not bring myself to unveil his face. I knew it was disfigured. Those who were sufficiently curious assured me that he was unrecognizable." The empress herself wrote as early as November 29, "I am under the same roof with the dear mortal remains, but one doesn't see them. He is covered and I don't wish to behold that dear face so badly decomposed . . . on the first day, he appeared as though he would arise and resume his habitual vivacity and movements. And now, what a cruel change! Where did it come from? How can you explain this virtual transfiguration?"

Is it possible for an embalmed body, within four days of death, to have become so decomposed as to have someone mistakenly tug "loosened flesh" from the neck? The pathologists I consulted agree that this is highly unlikely, possible only if the room in which the body was kept was greatly overheated. Volkonsky's observations on the state of the body also cause concern for the experts. Certain disfiguration was bound to occur within five days of embalming, but hardly to the extent reported by Volkonsky and subsequently by others. Was this the body of someone who died on November 19? How is it possible that decomposition set in so rapidly? Is it not too wild or illogical to speculate that the remains being embalmed could well have been those of someone who had died earlier?

In St. Petersburg, as soon as the dowager empress received news of her son's death, she asked General Diebich for a detailed report on the illness and the passing. On December 7, the general composed a lengthy reply, beginning with a thorough account of the tsar's Crimean trip during which he had contracted the fatal illness. His letter betrays his military and bureaucratic background. In detailed diary form he describes, step by step, the progress of the tour. Nearly every day has a comment on Alexander's overall appearance and state of health. Notations are made on the weather and on the suitability of the tsar's dress for the day. The report clearly reflects the respect and affection Diebich had for his master. At times he writes as a fretting nanny: "He covered 30 versts [twenty miles] on horseback . . . didn't seem to bother him"; "it was very hot, but he appeared unaffected"; "the bad weather and the long ride seemed not to bother him"; "despite the darkness and the strong wind, he insisted on pressing forward"; "it was excellent weather and he was dressed only in his tunic"; "he seemed full of pep and happiness."

When Diebich's narrative arrives at the illness and subsequent death, it abruptly terminates. The general pleads that he saw little of the tsar after their return to Taganrog — "only twice daily, at noon and at nine in the evening, but merely to exchange state papers. I therefore did not have the frequent occasion to be with His Majesty during the illness, as did Pyotr Mikhailovich Volkonsky . . . and I can add little to what Your Majesty might read in the letters of Prince Volkonsky." In short, Diebich carefully refrains from commenting on the tsar's illness and death, basing his reticence on his lack of contact with his beloved emperor. In fact, he spent more time with Alexander than he admits. For example, Volkonsky reports that on November 10 Diebich spent over an hour closeted alone with the tsar.

As chief of staff to the emperor and a critical member of that select palace community, there is no way that Diebich was not witness to what was going on, hour by hour. He could easily have provided the dowager empress with the full information she specifically requested. Why the prevarication? Is it possible that, as a good civil servant, he wished to avoid appending his signature to a written record that he knew would have been fraudulent? Incidentally, Baron Diebich concluded his report with a cryptic and intriguing aside: "On the 10th," he wrote, the emperor "called me out at night and gave me a series of orders on highly important matters. On the 11th he received my detailed report on how I had executed his orders." If one takes the baron's statement at face value, one is led to wonder whether the tsar's summons might not have been related to the fateful day, the nineteenth. The imagination strains to explain what this secretive business was all about. Was there any connection between the baron's mission and the "important secret orders" the tsar gave that same day to Taganrog's military commander and the Cossack officer?

Alexander's body remained in Taganrog until December 29. Eighteen days earlier it had been moved from the catafalque in the imperial residence to Alexandrovsky Monastery, where the memorial services continued. The people of Taganrog flocked to the church to pay their last respects and offer prayers. Service after service was conducted over the body, and it was never left unattended. Soldiers from the Cossack Guards Regiment stood twenty-four-hour guard over it, and people came and went to kneel in prayer beside the coffin. In accordance with Orthodox tradition, the remains lay exposed in an open coffin. But contrary to established custom, the face was draped by a dark cloth and the mourners were denied the opportunity to gaze upon it, much to their resentment. Was the dark cloth covering a disfigured face? Or was it hiding a secret?

That the body reposed in Taganrog for a full six weeks — a month in the imperial residence and another two and a half weeks at the monastery — might well appear unusual. One must not forget, however, the exceptional circumstances of the period: a throne standing vacant, confusion about the succession, the short-

lived but serious Decembrist uprising. Not until the new emperor
Nicholas I had issued the orders could the body be moved north to
its final resting place.

Considering the inexplicable circumstances and irregularities
in the period of post-death, it might fairly be asked whether the
corpse that underwent embalming in Taganrog, and was later displayed in an open coffin, was truly that of the tsar. At one point in
the autopsy procedure, the flesh covering the skull was pulled forward over the face. Apart from those brief moments, the deceased's
face was always covered by cloth, never exposed, not even in the
open coffin. Viewing the body under those circumstances, who
could positively identify it as being that of the emperor?

Let us for the sake of argument assume for a moment that
the body sent to St. Petersburg was *not* Alexander's. Whose then
was it? One possibility emerging from the literature of the Legend
is that it was the corpse of a soldier from the Semeonovsky Regiment who died on November 18 at the local military hospital.
Dr. Alexandrovich, who was part of the autopsy team, happened
also to have been the hospital's chief physician. Might the good
doctor have been conscripted into the conspiracy and persuaded
to supply a body? Grand Duke Nikolai Mikhailovich scoffs at this
suggestion: "It is impossible to play around with corpses this
way." Certain things, however, are never impossible, particularly
if the emperor and Autocrat of All Russia so desires. The burial of
the Semeonovsky soldier has not been documented, and we have
no record of his grave.

The other candidate is the unfortunate courier Maskov, who,
it will be recalled, suffered a fatal accident some sixteen days before
the emperor's death. Maskov happened to be approximately the
same height and build as Alexander.

Maskov was buried almost immediately, on the day following
his death on November 3, in a cemetery near the spot where he had
fallen at Orehov. A surgeon-intern named Pavel Velch was specifically detailed by General Diebich to attend the funeral and, apart
from the priest and cemetery workers, it appears he was the sole

witness. That the burial took place so precipitously is, as we have seen, contrary to traditional Orthodox practice. Normally there would be at least a day or two of services and prayers beforehand. In this instance, Maskov was interred hurriedly, almost indecently, and the burial was officially witnessed by a single person only, one detailed for the duty by the tsar's chief of staff.[†]

Given General Diebich's personal involvement in the courier's funeral arrangements, it is difficult to comprehend why Maskov was not provided with a more solemn, befitting funeral. Surely the tsar, who had so solicitously attended the courier upon his arrival and who shed tears on learning of his death, might have done better for his loyal servant. In any event, there are other questions: did Maskov's coffin really contain a body when it was lowered into the ground? If so, and assuming Maskov was the substitute, how could his body have been surreptitiously disinterred for transport elsewhere without anyone knowing? If the coffin was empty, how could the body have been spirited away before the funeral, later to be transported some thirty miles to Taganrog?

In the Maskov family, a tradition has long held that it was the body of their ancestor who was laid to rest in the Fortress of St. Peter and St. Paul in place of Alexander I. In 1902, Grand Duke Nikolai Mikhailovich researched the family and found that all five Maskov children had died long before. He did, however, make contact with a grandson, Apollon Kourbatov, a professor of chemistry at a technological institute. Kourbatov confirmed that his mother and her entire family firmly believed the story. His grandfather's grave, unfortunately, had long disappeared.

Maskov's widow and children were well looked after by Nicholas I. The family was given a pension and the imperial treasury rarely refused requests for additional sums. Kourbatov's mother was enrolled in and graduated from the Smolney Institute, an exclusive school in St. Petersburg for the daughters of the nobility.

[†]Grand Duke Nikolai Mikhailovich, however, cites a certificate he found in the state archives, attesting to Maskov's burial on November 6. If the certificate records the truth, then the credibility of Tarasov and Shilder is called into question and suspicion over Maskov's hasty interment is removed.

The appointment of an outsider such as she was an exceptional privilege. For whatever reasons, the family of this obscure, low-ranking officer received deferential treatment from on high.

Let us now assume for the moment that the body that was autopsied, embalmed, and interred in St. Petersburg was Maskov's. The courier suffered his accident on November 3. Is it possible that the officer's remains, sixteen days after death, were in sufficiently good shape to be processed by the Taganrog physicians? Each of the pathologists whom I consulted again argued that it would have depended on the temperature. If the body was kept in heated quarters, no. If, however, it had been at outdoor temperature, which we know to have been cold — by no means freezing but sufficiently cold to warrant heavy overcoats — it could have been in satisfactory shape for treatment by the doctors. Dr. Chaisson, alone, suggests caution in quickly jumping to such a conclusion.

Substituting one body for another is, under any circumstance, a difficult and dangerous procedure. If such a maneuver did take place in Taganrog, it obviously had to have been executed in the strictest secrecy, with as few people involved as possible. One way or another, however, the tsar's intimates could not have arranged for the exchange without the assistance and cooperation of at least a handful of others, in which case it would have been extraordinary if such a feat had been kept secret. This may explain why persistent rumors of a false death began to circulate in Taganrog almost immediately, even while the coffin was still open. It didn't take long for the rumors to reach St. Petersburg and then spread throughout Russia. So widespread were they, in fact, that at one point the authorities in Taganrog had to employ force to keep the clamoring curious from approaching the coffin. The same thing occurred at various points along the route of the funeral cortege as it slowly wended its way north to St. Petersburg.

After the funeral procession began its passage north, the makeshift Taganrog court began to disband. As his brother's heir, Tsar Nicholas took pains to reward Alexander's trusted entourage, which had so faithfully tended him in life and after his death. Prince Volkonsky was given new titles — Field Marshal, Court

Minister, and Chancellor of All the Imperial Orders. Diebich became the army's chief of staff. Chernischev, who signed Alexander's death certificate, was made a count and subsequently elevated to prince. Nor did the new tsar neglect Tarasov and Wylie, the two chief physicians in the Taganrog drama. During his long years of retirement, Tarasov lived comfortably "in grace and bounty" at Tsarskoye Selo. Like Count Osten-Sacken, he refused for many years to attend the annual memorial services that were held in the palace chapel each November 19, the anniversary of Alexander's death. He seemed always to have an excuse for not appearing. In 1865, Tarasov's close personal friend, Vassily Sergeyevich Arseniev, a ranking official in the court of Alexander II, informed him of Feodor Kuzmich's death. The following November 19, attired in full-dress uniform, Tarasov, after forty years, went for the first time to a memorial service for his beloved emperor. In his memoir, he wrote that in all this lay a profound secret that would die with him.

Dr. Wylie's career was as unique as were the circumstances of his retirement. At age twenty-two he had quit his modest home in the Scottish highlands to join the Russian military medical services. Early in his career, he acquired a reputation for compassion, loyalty, bravery — and miserliness. Some have said that what Florence Nightingale was to nursing, Wylie was to medicine. For him, the welfare of the common soldier was paramount, and through his efforts attitudes toward the lower ranks of the military improved measurably. His courage became legendary, as he seemed always to be in the thick of battle, attending to the wounded, not only Russians but also the enemy. Thrice wounded, he won dozens of decorations, from Russian emperors as well as from other grateful, often enemy, sovereigns.

In the sixty-four years Wylie spent in his adopted country, he saw service under four emperors. Early in his career, he was appointed to the court of Paul, and subsequently he became chief physician to Alexander, with whom, as we have seen, he developed an especially strong professional and personal relationship.

If the tsar successfully effected an "escape" from Taganrog, it is hardly likely that the trusted Wylie was not a vital player. But apart from the Scotsman's terse Taganrog diary entries, we have no comment from him. On his death in 1854, Wylie left behind an extraordinary fortune, one far beyond any sum that a court physician could reasonably have been expected to amass, however parsimonious, however favored by the sovereign he might be. When Wylie's will was read, Scottish relatives successfully contested 70,000 pounds sterling, a most handsome sum for those days. The bulk of his estate was bequeathed to the tsar of Russia. The funds that thus tumbled into the state coffers were used to establish a military hospital in St. Petersburg, which still stands today. How is it possible that such a large fortune was amassed by a civil servant? Could it have come from a grateful monarch to one whose services to him had been far beyond any normal or reasonable expectations?

In Wylie's diary, we hark back to that enigmatic comment by him, made on September 13, the day Alexander's party arrived south from St. Petersburg. That day the physician ended his entry with the words, "We've arrived in Taganrog and here ends the first part of our journey." Why the *first* part of the journey? Apart from brief tours in to the region, Alexander, so far as we know, had no plans to continue his travels. Could Wylie already have been privy to the extraordinary new "journey" the emperor was planning to make in November?

16

Elizaveta and Alexander

ALEXANDER'S JOURNEY TO TAGANROG was, as we have seen, made in the interest of his wife's health. Elizaveta was the reason they were there, and as the days passed into November all eyes were turned on her — particularly the gaze of the emperor. In fully exploring the Legend, one has to focus especially on Elizaveta. Indeed, if the tsar successfully staged his death, it could not have been without her knowledge, and presumably, her understanding. Within months of November 19, she too was dead.

However surprising it may seem that, given her fragile health, the tsar opted to take Elizaveta south, she not only survived the 1,400-mile journey, but, as we have seen, arrived in surprisingly good shape, alighting unaided from her carriage and walking briskly into the church on the emperor's arm. From the outset, her husband gave himself over to her well-being and happiness, attending to her with remarkable warmth and tenderness. Alexander seemed to anticipate her every wish, and no detail was too trivial to escape his attention. Both tsar and tsarina appeared relaxed and at ease, especially in one another's company; the tranquil existence they shared brought them closer together. Elizaveta flourished, and her condition improved dramatically, both physically and psychologically. Within a few days color had returned to her face and she became more animated. "The entire suite rejoices at the state of affairs," recorded Tarasov. "Behind their backs, their majesties are referred to as 'the newly-weds.'"

"It gives me such pleasure," wrote Elizaveta to her mother about her husband, "to have him so firmly convinced that I am his everything." The empress took up a quiet and regular life and saw more of her husband than she had for months before back home. From time to time the couple strolled in the garden, hand in hand. When he was "in residence" and before he fell ill, Alexander took daily walks about town either with his wife or alone and unattended. Taganrog's inhabitants seemed unconcerned by their monarch's presence, and paid him scant attention. During one of the couple's frequent walks along the waterfront, the empress expressed a special delight with a particular shoreline not far from the quarantine station. Alexander promptly ordered that a park be constructed on the spot. He himself sketched the preliminary plans and commanded Volkonsky to summon from St. Petersburg the court gardener, a Scotsman named Duncan Grey, to put the plan into effect. "In the solitude of Taganrog, the bond between them grew stronger, having been weakened first by the frivolity of youth and then by the demands of state," observes Prince Bariatinsky.

Alexander became so encouraged by his wife's improved health that he felt secure enough to leave her for five days. He undertook the brief inspection of surrounding territories and, shortly thereafter, set out on another, longer tour.

In their thirty-two years of marriage Elizaveta and Alexander had lived mostly apart, leading substantially separate existences. The celebrated "marriage of Psyche and Cupid" over which Catherine the Great had gushed had proved to be a bit of a bubble. From the outset, the fifteen-year-old Elizaveta complained to her mother of her husband's lack of attention, which sometimes bordered on the rude. She craved his attention, but Alexander turned away; the tsarevich delighted in the company of women, but Elizaveta was not one of them. Despite her suffering, however, she always gave him whatever support and encouragement she could, both before the coronation and after. But this basic fidelity did not prevent her from seeking solace in the arms of certain courtiers. Elizaveta developed a particularly strong attachment to a dark and handsome Polish nobleman, Adam Czartoryski, who had served Emperor Paul. That he happened at the time to be Alexander's closest friend in no way hindered the liaison. The tsarevich was not only aware of the situation but encouraged it. Six years into her marriage, Elizaveta gave birth to a swarthy, dark-haired girl, baptized Maria Alexandrovna, who unfortunately died in her fourteenth month. There was no doubt as to the infant's paternity: the baby was the antithesis of the blond, blue-eyed lineage of either parent. The infidelities of the imperial couple were well-known not only to the court but also to each other, and both seemed comfortable with their mutual independence. Nor did passing decades bestow a life of marital bliss upon Elizaveta and Alexander.

For well over a year, from mid-1823 on, Alexander had found himself increasingly alone and isolated, even from the warmth of family and friends. And during the summer months of 1825, as he became more introspective, his mind filled with dark thoughts, Elizaveta, despite her weakened condition, stood by him. An appreciative Alexander slowly drew closer to her, and their relationship seemed to be acquiring a new glow, a reconciliation of sorts. In Taganrog they spent a great deal of time together, often dining in the privacy of his apartment. For Elizaveta, it was a dream come true, what she had hoped for over the past three decades of unfulfilled marriage.

Newfound glow, reconciliation, walking hand in hand — but when the time came to journey south, the two traveled the exhausting distance in separate carriages, one leaving St. Petersburg two days after the first. Granted, Alexander was anxious to arrive beforehand in order to oversee the preparation of their new quarters. Nevertheless, it was not unreasonable to expect that a frail and ailing wife, undertaking a tiring and lonely journey, might have gladly shared the same carriage with her husband. But it was not to be.

From the time of Elizaveta's arrival at Taganrog and her husband's death, fifty-seven days passed. During twelve of these days Alexander was laid low by the illness that presumably killed him. His inspections of the surrounding regions took up another twenty-one days. Thus, the idyllic period of their second honeymoon was a brief twenty-four days.

During those Taganrog days, Alexander lavished attention on his wife, and in various accounts we read of the tenderness between them. One report of the deathbed scene says that "he suffered and at the last moment he asked the empress for her forgiveness and then died, holding her hand in his." The letters Elizaveta wrote as her husband lay dying, and in the days immediately following his death, are expressions of love and unmitigated grief. "Our angel is in the heavens . . . I am the most miserable creature of all who mourn." The sort of marital harmony and happiness Elizaveta enjoyed in Taganrog was exactly what she had been yearning for throughout her married life. On the surface, it appears that a real reconciliation did take place, certainly from Elizaveta's perspective: "I am his everything," she wrote to her mother.

There is little reason to doubt that Elizaveta was indeed happy in Taganrog. She was feeling better, her energy had returned, her husband was often at her side, and they were both far from the complexities and intrigues of St. Petersburg court life. She liked the seaside town; life had taken on fresh perspectives.

Alexander also appeared pleased with Taganrog and all that surrounded him — certainly at the beginning. Since his arrival, he too felt reinvigorated. The cares of state seemed to press less forcefully, and he found the simplicity of Taganrog court life refreshing. Here his insatiable thirst for travel was also quenched: both tours he took were gratifying; wherever he went he was warmly received. What was more, he was able to make amends to the wife whom he had so long neglected. The gloomy open coffin in the darkened cell of that prophetic monk in Nevsky Monastery on St. Petersburg's outskirts seemed but a distant vision.

Was Elizaveta's obvious pleasure over their reconciliation felt as strongly by Alexander? Might he in his turn ever have written to his mother, "She is my everything"? It is true that at a time when Alexander felt deprived of familial warmth, he most assuredly found comfort in the faithful Elizaveta. Supporters of the Legend would argue, however, that the tsar's rediscovery of his wife was disingenuous, that if he was especially attentive to her it was for his own selfish reasons, not to mention his assuaging of his guilty conscience. From the earliest days of their marriage, he had callously neglected her. Isn't it strange that, all of a sudden, he became the faithful, doting husband? Indeed, if he was preparing an escape he had little time to make up for thirty years of neglect. And if his plan was to stage his death, he was in essence leaving her forever, even if he was alive in a whole new identity.

The various accounts of the emperor's illness note the presence of Elizaveta at the sickbed, or of her request to visit. With one exception, there is no record of Alexander specifically asking for Elizaveta's presence. That exception was on November 11, when he spent those six long hours alone with her. It was immediately after that meeting that Elizaveta cried out, "Where does one find peace in life? Just as you think that all is settled for the better and that you can enjoy life, there suddenly appears an unexpected trial."

In Orianda, when Alexander informed Volkonsky that he would retire to the Crimea and "you will retire with me," no mention was made of Elizaveta. In fact, with one very early exception, in the numerous recorded references made by Alexander to retirement, all were in the first-person singular. As far back as 1796, he did include her in his declared intention, "to settle with my wife on the banks of the Rhine."

The emperor lay on his sickbed for ten days as his illness passed through its various stages. On November 17, Volkonsky urged Elizaveta to move out of the imperial residence, away from the depressing sickroom. He had already made arrangements with a neighboring family, the Shikhmatovs, to take the empress into their home. At first Elizaveta refused, saying that she should stay where she was "so long as he is here. When he goes, so shall I too, but I don't know when . . . if I dared, I would follow the one who has been my very life." Later, however, the empress did accept Volkonsky's urgings, moving to the Shikhmatovs' on either November 19 or 20. Tarasov says on the nineteenth, but *The History* claims the twentieth.

It is understandable that Volkonsky might have wanted the empress out of the house in case the emperor were to die. The postmortem requirements, such as autopsy and preparation of the body, would be awkward and uncomfortable for her. But why did he ask her to move on November 17, when Alexander's death was far from certain? To be sure, if and when he was actually dying, she would expect — and be expected — to be at his side. Still, Volkonsky's suggestion that the empress move out appears strange, unless he wished Elizaveta out of the house because he and whoever else was involved were entering the crucial and ultimate stage of their clandestine activity.

For a quarter century, Elizaveta had shared Alexander's reign in name only. In matters of state, the tsar generally turned to the dowager empress rather than to his wife. The bond that had developed between mother and son at the time of Paul's death never slackened. Thus Elizaveta found herself shut out not only as a spouse but virtually as an imperial presence. Her determined mother-in-law took center stage, effectively commandeering the role of empress; it was her influence, not Elizaveta's, that dominated in court. As for the rest of the imperial family, Elizaveta was never fully accepted, and she responded by distancing herself from it. In Taganrog it was no secret that after her husband's death, instead of returning to St. Petersburg, she would much rather have gone home to Baden. But that could never be. So it was that, following the departure of the funeral cortege for the capital, she remained in Taganrog, where she stayed on for over four months.

Kind and solicitous letters flowed from the capital urging the empress to return. The coronation of Nicholas would soon take place and she really should be in attendance. The new tsar and her mother-in-law extended the widow every courtesy and consideration. She was offered two attractive residences near St. Petersburg, both of which she refused. Nicholas also granted her a handsome pension, which she turned down. Elizaveta wished to have nothing from her brother-in-law. Instead, she spoke of acquiring a residence in Moscow where she proposed to settle, presumably at a distance from the St. Petersburg court. Meanwhile, according to the French historian Henri Pirenne, she had purchased the Taganrog residence where the couple had lived, and plans were being drawn up for a church to be built on the site.

Following the death of her husband, Elizaveta's health fluctuated wildly — sometimes she grew stronger, at other times she seemed alarmingly frail. On December 7, Volkonsky reported to the dowager empress that Elizaveta was weak, sleeping poorly, and experiencing chest pains. A fortnight later later, he asserted that overall she appeared better, despite continued sleepless nights. On April 12, he wrote that Elizaveta was again in poor condition. "She suffers from a tightening in the chest that sometimes even affects her speech . . . She herself supposes that this is due to water in the lungs . . . I am concerned for the empress's weakness, and Stoffregen also begins to be afraid." A week later, however, things seemed to have improved, and plans were now made for her departure on April 21. She had to be in Moscow in advance of the coronation, which was now scheduled for mid-June — the country would expect that of her. Volkonsky expressed concern over the road conditions, which despite generally favorable weather were reported to be poor. In Russia, then as now, unpaved roads in the spring thaws are difficult at best, impassible at worst.

At this stage it might be asked: of the dramatis personae in the Taganrog mystery, how deeply was Elizaveta involved? To what extent was she aware of what was going on? If Alexander staged his death and did effect an escape, practically speaking there was no way he could have done so without his wife's knowledge and cooperation. Elizaveta had to be part of the plot, if for no other reason than to lend credibility to the death. Furthermore, if her husband was shedding the crown it was to expiate a sin. It would seem strange for him now to impose such an unfair burden — really, a sinful one — on his innocent wife. If the Legend is true, then Elizaveta had to be involved, perhaps not as an active participant but definitely aware.

That she did not accompany her husband's body to St. Petersburg is very strange. He was, after all, her "everything," and it is only reasonable to expect that she would have been anxious to be present during the final rituals and interment in the imperial crypt. But when the coffin was finally lowered into the tomb, Elizaveta was 1,400 miles away. Why did the empress refuse to travel north that December? It is of course possible that her state of health simply did not permit such an exhausting journey, but on the whole, she was in better shape at the time of her husband's death than she was in April of the following year, when she finally set off.

It is also possible that Elizaveta was simply in no mental condition to return home, especially if she were privy to the plot. Imagine her state of mind in late November: after years of neglect, a newfound relationship is established with her husband and she delights in it. Then, suddenly, the poor woman is shattered to discover that the whole reconciliation is illusory; that she is pressured not only to accept but to support an unholy deception of incredible magnitude. Suppose that, in the course of their six-hour session together on November 11, the emperor laid bare his plan to Elizaveta, swearing her to secrecy but explaining to her how essential it was to him to carry it out — for which he required her help and allegiance. She could feel deceived, betrayed, yet her husband's taking her into his confidence this way could also be construed by her as a declaration of love. Then came the death itself, real or staged. If the latter, she was then thrust into the unwelcome role of grieving widow. And all this at a time when her health was precarious. Her husband was disappearing into the unknown with the likelihood she would never see him again. Into the coffin prepared for her husband, the body of a complete stranger was placed that she must venerate. Finally, both St. Petersburg and the court in Taganrog expected her to be at the side of the catafalque as it slowly wended its way north. For whom was she living this lie? A man who neglected her for most of their marital life, and his family, for whom she bore no great love. Little wonder that Elizaveta elected to stay on in the seclusion and tranquillity of Taganrog.

Eventually, however, Elizaveta's party did leave the city, as scheduled, and headed north in short stages. Each day of the journey her condition worsened, and before long she was so weak that she had great trouble speaking. On April 26 she wrote her mother, "I suffer and am broken physically and spiritually." The dowager empress ordered that she be kept informed of her daughter-in-law's progress, as she wished to meet her at Kaluga, a hundred miles from Moscow. From there she planned to accompany the widowed empress during the journey's final segment. On May 2, Volkonsky reported to the dowager empress that Elizaveta "was in such bad shape that Your Majesty will find her terribly changed . . . I cannot describe to you how deeply concerned I have been about the health of Her Imperial Highness during our trip, and I unceasingly pray to God that He will grant her a safe passage to Kaluga."

On May 13, at the provincial town of Belaev, one stop before Kaluga, Elizaveta halted and traveled no farther. In the evening she wrote her mother-in-law that she planned to stay there for a day or two, in order to rest. All along the way, she had pushed herself. "I don't know how Her Majesty bore the fatigue of the journey," Stoffregen subsequently wrote to Wylie. "In each town I proposed a rest of a day or two. But this she vehemently refused, saying that she wished to get to Kaluga as quickly as possible in order not to cause worry to Her Majesty the Empress Mother." On the morning after her arrival in Belaev, Elizaveta's maid entered the empress's bedroom and found her dead.

"We have been witness to the suffering of our angel who has just been released from her prison," wrote Stoffregen to Wylie; "we are now both orphans!" The dowager empress was informed of the tragic news and hastened to Belaev that same evening. The following day, Nicholas signed the court announcement of Elizaveta's death, the cause of which was noted as "a result of prolonged illness of body and spirit." The coronation was now postponed to September, to permit a proper period of mourning. On June 21, the empress's coffin was paraded to St. Peter and St. Paul Fortress and interred next to that of her husband.

In the weeks that followed, rumors of every sort circulated concerning her death. As with Alexander, so with his wife: the people did not readily accept that Elizaveta had died a natural death. Both had died so far away from the center of things, and in peculiar circumstances. In time, such talk faded away, as did the memory of this long-suffering woman.

17

The Mystery That
Will Not Die

ALEXANDER'S BODY WAS FINALLY laid to rest in March 1826. But
in the decades that followed, the world did not leave the account of
his death at rest. Within days of the monarch's passing every imaginable rumor circulated — first in Taganrog, then in St. Petersburg,
and finally throughout the country. The emperor lived. The coffin
did not contain the imperial remains. The crypt in the Fortress of
St. Peter and St. Paul was empty. And, much later, in 1836, the
Siberian appearance of Feodor Kuzmich captured the popular
imagination. Was it possible the emperor and the starets were one
and the same?

Alexander III — the grandnephew of Alexander I — who
reigned from 1881 to 1894, was sufficiently intrigued by the Legend, it is said, that he appointed a secret three-man commission in
1884 to investigate it thoroughly. One of his closest advisers, his
former tutor Constantine Pobedonostsev, was named to head the
group. The commission's other two members were also confidants
of the tsar — Adjutant-General Andrei Cherniva and General N. M.
Baranov.[†] The commission, it is reported, met regularly over a

---

[†]An intriguing historical anecdote: General Baranov married into the Troubetzkoy
family. As I write these lines, my father stands beside me and recalls his boyhood
memories of this aged officer.

two-year period and examined in detail all the extant documents and testimony relating to Alexander's death and the life of the starets. Investigators were dispatched to Siberia to interview those who had come in contact with Feodor Kuzmich. The commission finally concluded that the starets was in fact Emperor Alexander. Pobedonostsev then categorically forbade the publication of the commission's findings; no trace of its work exists. The report, it is claimed, was read by Alexander III and subsequently by Nicholas II. Knowledge of this secret commission comes to us from the historian, Lev D. Lubimov, who learned of it firsthand from Squadron Leader A. N. Baranov, son of the general.

Although Pobedonostsev began his career as tutor to Alexander III — later, also to Nicholas II — he acquired over the years other court responsibilities, eventually ending up as the procurator of the Russian Orthodox Church — in effect, its lay head. The man was a determined reactionary, who stood squarely for patriotism, Orthodoxy, and political conservatism, and these views he helped inculcate in both of Russia's last tsars.

Not only did the procurator forbid making public the commission's findings, he actively sought to discourage any further investigation or speculation on the matter. The historian K. N. Mikhailov offers the following, in a document published during the brief period when Russia was free of censorship, from 1905 to 1918. "On July 18, 1901, one of my highly placed correspondents, expert in matters concerning the epoch of Alexander I, wrote me from his estate that for unknown reasons C. P. Pobedonostsev was taking all possible measures to cover up the matter of Feodor Kuzmich, although he is obviously interested in it. He has therefore 'liberated' from the archives of the Third Section [secret police] all the documentation related to Feodor Kuzmich and has secreted them elsewhere. My correspondent was informed of all this by the previous director of the police department. This source, obviously, was entirely reliable."

In 1904, Mikhailov was introduced to Pobedonostsev, and before long they had struck up something of a friendship. The two met from time to time to discuss history. Mikhailov continues in his memoirs, "During one of my visits . . . Pobedonostsev, in comparing the reign of Emperor Paul to that of Ivan the Terrible, touched on Alexander I. Without thinking, I blurted out: 'What do you think of Feodor Kuzmich?' He instantly becaming guarded.

"'But what do *you* think of him, young man?' he retorted, staring at me. His skeletal face, large ears, and dark horn-rimmed glasses bore on me like a pistol . . . I froze.

"'I've no opinion on him,' I replied, 'but I've heard that the documentation on Feodor Kuzmich has been stolen. It will be difficult now to determine exactly who he was.'

"'Stolen . . . stolen . . .' repeated Pobedonostsev with anger and irritation.

"'But he *was* Alexander I?' I pursued, suddenly emboldened. 'Alexander I?'

"'I cannot . . .' he paused, 'say,' uttering the last word in a soft whisper, as if he didn't want to or as though they were frozen in his throat.

"'But to deny it: can you deny it categorically and absolutely?'

"'To deny . . . I don't know . . . one must study precisely the times, the events and the customs . . . perhaps . . . there are contradictions . . . some uncertainties . . . ambiguities. At any rate, stop busying yourself with this question,' he said, making no attempt to conceal his anger. 'Better that you should study more thoroughly Moscow historical and judicial antiquities . . .'

"'But Alexander I is also antiquities,' I persisted.

"'Yes,' he replied, rising out of his chair and sternly looking me in the eye. 'An antiquity, but one which is too early to study. It's not yet time . . . the time will come . . . then all will be clear. Meanwhile — goodbye.'"

"This conversation," Mikhailov continues, "took place in the Little Palace in Tsarskoye Selo, where the procurator was passing the summer. I stepped back. The very tone of the discussion and the words of Pobedonostsev are carved in my memory and to this day they make me shudder. In no way did this discussion dissuade me from my conviction as to the identity of Feodor Kuzmich. Furthermore, Pobedonostsev knew the secret.

"Subsequently I was informed by the same very highly placed person that Pobedonostsev had studied and sorted out the documents stolen from the Third Section and given them over to the personal custody of Alexander III. It is said that these papers detail the entire story of Feodor Kuzmich and of his life in the years from 1835 to 1864, the year of his death. Furthermore, Pobedonostsev, as indeed Arakcheyev, knew full well how Alexander I disappeared."

We hear of yet another commission, this one in 1911, formed to review once again the body of evidence related to the Legend. The two leading members of this body are said to have been Grand Duke Nikolai Mikhailovich and General Gregory Lvovich Miloradovich, a high-ranking official from the Ministry of Foreign Affairs. In its investigations, the commission allegedly uncovered that Nicholas I was in frequent correspondence with Feodor Kuzmich and that their exchanges were carried out through a secret code discovered in a hidden family safe. It was thus established that the starets was rarely unaware of the emperor's movements.

The commission, it is said, also concluded that the tsar had staged his own death in Taganrog and that Feodor Kuzmich and Alexander were one and the same. These findings were presented to Nicholas II, who then faced a twofold problem. First, should he make public the commission's findings? Second, should the body of the starets be exhumed from its grave in Tomsk and be reinterred in the imperial crypt of the Fortress of St. Peter and St. Paul in St. Petersburg? The alternative was to take no action and maintain the official historical version of Alexander's death in Taganrog in 1825. Nothing was done and silence was maintained.

Although much has been written of these two commissions, no archival evidence related to their work has been uncovered. We are reminded, however, not only of the sway of Russian censors, but of the deliberate efforts of persons such as Nicholas I and Pobedonostsev to suppress or even destroy pertinent documentation.

As noted earlier, Tolstoy took an interest in the Legend. Two years after his death in 1910, a manuscript by the author was published, *The Posthumous Notes of the Starets Feodor Kuzmich*. This work takes the curious form of a fictional diary written by Kuzmich himself. Despite the lack of the full body of circumstantial evidence favoring the Legend that we have today, Tolstoy believed in it and spoke of it as "credible." The author makes the interesting and salient point that Alexander's transformation into a Siberian starets was very much in keeping with the emperor's character. Tolstoy then lists five reasons for believing that the tsar did not die as recorded by history:

1. Alexander's death in Taganrog came on too suddenly and, prior to that, he had been in excellent health, never suffering any illness.
2. The death occurred in one of Russia's more remote outposts, thus making it easier to effect a disappearance.
3. The features of the corpse in the imperial casket were so distorted as to make them virtually unrecognizable.
4. On frequent occasions, especially toward the latter part of his life, Alexander declared his desire to shed his duties and retire quietly, out of the public eye.
5. The autopsy report noted that the body's back was bruised, as though from a lashing — an impossibility for an imperial person.

As for the starets, Tolstoy argues that physically he resembled Alexander, not only in height, build, and facial features, but also in bearing and deportment. Furthermore, they were the same age. He points out that although Kuzmich claimed to know little of his own background, he spoke foreign languages fluently. The starets received people of whatever station easily and confidently, as though "he had once stood above everyone." Tolstoy also points out that the old man never divulged his name, yet on more than one occasion he hinted at coming from a high station. Sometime before his death, the starets destroyed all his papers, save a few scraps of cryptic notes that included the letters *A* (Alexander) and *P* (Paul).

Finally, the novelist draws attention to the fact that, despite his extreme piety, the starets never once went to confession. In Tolstoy's fictional diary, the author has Kuzmich writing, "If at confession I did not declare the entire truth about myself, nobody would be the wiser; if I told the entire truth, the whole world would stand in wonder."

Nikolai K. Shilder was the official biographer of both Alexander I and Nicholas I, and the acknowledged authority on the two brothers. In his various publications, the historian either chronicles the known facts on the starets without making editorial comment on the Legend, or he avoids the subject altogether. From his writings, it is difficult to determine where he stood on the issue. It was, one must remember, an era of censorship in Russia. In private conversation, however, it is generally acknowledged that Shilder did not disguise his belief in the Legend. The historian is said to have become so convinced of the truth of the story that he wrote a treatise on it and submitted the manuscript to Alexander III. If he did, no record exists of the document's fate. Shilder, it would seem, was a firm believer.

Of all the researchers and scholarly authorities on the Legend, Grand Duke Nikolai Mikhailovich stands foremost. Not only was he an accomplished and highly respected historian but, as a nephew of both Tsar Alexander I and Nicholas I, and uncle to Nicholas II, he enjoyed a privileged position in court, with access to material not available to the public. As noted, the grand duke was preoccupied by the mystery and wrote a number of works on the subject. In his 1907 publication *The Legend of the Death of Alexander I,* he comes down against the Legend, but a number of knowledgeable people who have also explored the connection are convinced that in his heart of hearts, he was a believer, but was forced by his imperial position to maintain the façade. Again, the censors prevailed. And in 1918, the grand duke publicly reiterated his earlier view: as far as being on the pro side or the anti side of the Kuzmich controversy, he wrote, he "is of neither school."

Maurice Paleologue, France's last ambassador to imperial Russia and a member of the *Académie française,* was a leading biographer of Alexander I, and he too took a special interest in the Taganrog drama. He was a close friend of Grand Duke Nikolai Mikhailovich and the two frequently met to debate matters of history. Paleologue wrote that whenever discussions touched on Feodor Kuzmich, "I had the impression that his words, usually so trenchant and audacious, were not altogether frank."

In postrevolution Russia, the historian Lev Lubimov tells of an exchange he had with Grand Duke Dimitri Pavlovich, nephew of Alexander III. As fellow exiles in France in the 1930s, they met and the grand duke informed him that, immediately before the revolution, Nikolai Mikhailovich had declared that "on the basis of certain detailed evidence, he had become converted to the absolute conviction that Feodor Kuzmich was indeed Alexander I." Buttressing that, Russian historian Pyotr Kovalevsky of the Sorbonne informs us that the grand duke, shortly before his death, told Kovalevsky's father that "he had changed his mind and now accepts the authenticity of the legend of Feodor Kuzmich."

Finally, my maternal uncle, Dr. Alexander Obolensky, a retired professor of history at the State University of New York, recently informed me of the following: the families of our common forebear, Alexander Alexandrovich Polovtzev — his grandfather, my great-grandfather — and of Nikolai Mikhailovich were exceptionally close. (It was to the grand duke that grandfather Polovtzev gave over the chairmanship of the Imperial Historical Society when he retired from the post in 1909.) In the early 1900s, Polovtzev's son, also called Alexander, was visiting the Central Asian city of Tashkent when, much to his surprise and delight, he found that the grand duke was also in town on a visit. The duke explained that he was on an eastern tour, on his way to Tomsk to research the life of Feodor Kuzmich. A year later, young Polovtzev happened upon Nikolai Mikhailovich at the Imperial Yacht Club in St. Petersburg. My relative inquired about the grand duke's Siberian researches and conclusions. The imperial historian, after reporting on his explorations, finished by saying, "Strictly between us, in confidence, although I cannot write about it, there is now no doubt in my mind that Kuzmich was the tsar." It was Polovtzev himself who passed this startling news to my uncle, and from my uncle it came down to me. Its provenance is certain, and there is no reason to doubt its integrity. Considering Paleologue's observation, Lubimov's and Kovalevsky's testimonies, and my uncle's revelation, it is highly unlikely that Grand Duke Nikolai ultimately disbelieved the Legend. Whether he initially doubted and subsequently reversed his position is a matter of conjecture, but in the end a believer he was.

In addition to Shilder and the grand duke, such scholars as Bariatinsky, Lubimov, and Mikhailov wrestled with the problem of the Legend. Memoirs of those who were witness to Kuzmich's life have also survived, as have second- and third-hand accounts, some of which come to us on good authority. Much of what we read is hearsay and questionable. One author, for example, cites forty-nine instances of Feodor Kuzmich's recorded comments in which he hints at his imperial station — some quite far-fetched. What is real? What is to be discarded? The staggering problem in contemplating the overall picture is to sort through all the valid as well as questionable material available to us, and try to draw a meaningful conclusion.

As we have seen, Nicholas I ordered that much of the written documentation related to his brother's life and death, including family correspondence and diaries, be destroyed. Alexander II, Alexander III, and Nicholas II all interested themselves in the Legend, but not one of them openly declared himself on the subject. On the contrary, there seems to have been a shared anxiety to keep the matter quiet, even if the cover-up efforts were often clumsy. A leading culprit in this was the archconservative Pobedonostsev.

If Feodor Kuzmich was Alexander I, why the anxiety to conceal the fact? After all, the events in Taganrog occurred nearly three-quarters of a century before Nicholas II. The reason may be that the starets survived until 1864. If he was indeed the emperor, then — Siberian wanderer or not — he legally continued as the legitimate, unabdicated sovereign. The chrism of the coronation annointment, given by God, is not easily thrust aside. "There is no authority except from God and those that exist have been instituted by God" (Romans 13:1). The starets lived throughout the reign of Nicholas I and nine years into that of Alexander II. Hence, legal argument could be made that the reigns of the first sovereign and a good portion of the second were illegitimate. All the laws enacted from 1825 to 1864, therefore, might be null and void — a wildly unthinkable situation.

In judging the evidence of the Legend, we must constantly remind ourselves of the matter of censorship — Russia was free of it only for the briefest period. Anyone writing on issues as sensitive as the starets did so with circumspection and self-restraint. In postrevolutionary times, it was from the Russian émigré communities, Paris in particular, that we receive some of the most convincing material on the subject.

"A sphinx who carried his riddle to the grave." The answer to the riddle of the Legend lies precisely there — in the two graves, one in St. Petersburg and one in Tomsk. If the tomb of Alexander I were opened today, what would we discover? We would find either that the casket is empty or that it holds human remains. If it is empty, the wealth of circumstantial evidence regarding the Legend takes on significantly greater validity. If human remains are within, whose are they? Forensic testing could tell us whether the body in St. Petersburg is that of a forty-eight-year-old. DNA could tell us whether the remains are those of a Romanov. If the body is that of a forty-eight-year-old Romanov, the book on the Legend is closed and the question that has so intrigued people for more than 175 years will have found an answer.

Sooner or later, the tomb of Alexander I must be opened for a thorough investigation of its contents. It is felt that official authorization for an exploration by a qualified and approved team of scientific experts would not be withheld. Sergei Mironenko, archivist of the Russian Federation, cautions, however, that the cost of exhumation and testing will be high and that nongovernmental funding would have to be secured, probably from the West. Much of the impetus for this book lies in the hope that it will generate sufficiently strong interest in the Legend to precipitate an examination of Alexander I's tomb. It is the author's great hope that an adventurous sponsor with an historical bent will come forward to finance the exploration and help put this haunting mystery to rest.

And what of the grave of Feodor Kuzmich? It will be recalled that the starets was interred in the Bogoroditsko-Alexeyevsk Monastery in Tomsk. In 1902, on "orders from on high," a chapel was erected on the site. Details of the construction are lost, for the monastery's archive was carted away during the Soviet period. In its heyday, the monastery had some fifty monks and novices; today it has seven. Father Siluan is the abbot, and he is greatly interested in the Legend. Within the greater monastic community and in Tomsk itself, he told me, there is a wealth of oral tradition concerning the 1891 visit to the gravesite by Nicholas II while he was still tsarevich. As noted earlier, it is thought that the chapel was erected on his orders. The handsome little structure was torn down in the 1930s because the Soviets requisitioned the bricks for the construction of a nearby school. In 1997, through the generosity of a private benefactor, the chapel was restored on the gravesite to its original form.

Beneath that chapel, however, there are no human remains. It was not until 1995, after the last vestiges of Soviet authority had disappeared, that the body was exhumed and transferred into the monastery's sanctuary. As previously mentioned, over a third of the body was found to be missing, including the skull. Clearly, Kuzmich's grave had been opened on at least one occasion since 1864, although no documents or "corporate memory" exist of such an uncovering. Here, too, it would be critical to subject the remains to forensic and DNA testing. How old was the deceased? Is he a Romanov? If so, further credibility is given to the Legend.

If at the conclusion of all the investigations we satisfy ourselves that the Legend is without basis, the intriguing question arises: who then *was* Feodor Kuzmich? On this subject, there are a number of suppositions. One possibility advanced by Grand Duke Nikolai Mikhailovich is that the starets was Simeon, the illegitimate son of Paul I. It is known that among Paul's mistresses of his youth a certain Sophia Chertorzhskaya was prominent, a widow who bore him a son in 1794. The child attended elementary school in the Fortress of St. Peter and St. Paul, then went on to the naval academy. It seems that immediately thereafter he was dispatched to England, where he served in the Royal Navy, on board HMS *Vanguard*. One version of his death is that while sailing the Caribbean, the young man succumbed to a tropical disease. Another story has it that he drowned in the Baltic off the island-fortress of Kronshtadt. In his researches on this sad person, the grand duke was unable to find any record of his death, within the period 1794–1837 (the year after the first recorded appearance of the starets in Siberia). This in itself is interesting, for naval records of the time were meticulously kept and full dossiers on serving personnel could readily be accessed. Was the file on Simeon destroyed? The grand duke, however, did trace a family connection between the young naval officer and Count Osten-Sacken's wife. If Kuzmich was Paul's illegitimate son, herein perhaps lies the explanation for the correspondence that the count had with the starets.

A number of other people are listed as possible suspects, people who, having chosen exile in Siberia, adopted the identity of Feodor Kuzmich. Among them is a noble, Nikolai Andreyevsky, born in 1790, who served as a cavalry officer and later a chamberlain in the imperial court. Married and with children, he is said to have perished in the Neva River; his body was never recovered. Also up for consideration are at least two St. Petersburg cavalry officers, each of whom mysteriously disappeared in the 1820s.

One Soviet historian postulates cynically, "Probably this was a rich aristocrat who was guilty of one thing or another, and, bearing a likeness to Alexander I, he took on the role of Feodor Kuzmich's adventurism, hoaxing all those with whom he came in contact."

18

The Unknown Yacht

TWO CRITICAL ASPECTS of the Legend's mystery are particularly shrouded by uncertainty. If Alexander did indeed stage his death and steal away from Taganrog that November, how did he physically manage it? Secondly, the tsar's reported death was in 1825 and the first record we have of the starets is in 1836. If the two men were one and the same, where and how did he live during the eleven intervening years?

As a teenager, I spent, as I have noted, many captivating hours in the company of the historian and theologian Nicholas Arseniev, who related detail after detail of the Legend. Some of the material he recalled was from personal witness, albeit second-hand — the story, for example, of his sister, Princess Gagarina, finding the skullcap of the starets.

Arseniev dwelt on the matter of the escape. If Alexander did depart, what route did he take? An extended passage overland within Russia, solo and incognito, would have been virtually impossible, even in the cleverest disguise — the emperor was simply too well-known. The only alternative, and the simplest exit, would have been by sea; Taganrog, one recalls, was a port town. Ideally, such a departure would have best been executed on board a vessel flying a foreign flag, with non-Russian personnel. It was for this reason,

Arseniev surmised, that Alexander chose Taganrog as the place for his wife's recovery.

The professor told of an unknown yacht that lay at anchor in Taganrog for an indeterminate period during Alexander's sojourn in that port city. The vessel flew a British flag and, curiously, is said to have weighed anchor and sailed out to sea on the very day the tsar died. If this is true, certain questions arise. Whose yacht was it? What was it doing in Taganrog? After leaving the port, what was its destination?

As reported, Taganrog, despite certain shortcomings as a port, did manage to attract annually more than two hundred ships. November, however, was close to the end of the shipping season. Early-winter gales made the place impractical for the loading and unloading of goods, and ships' masters hurried to conclude their business as winter set in. One might suppose that at the time, therefore, the traffic of heavy vessels was minimal. As for private yachts, in the best of circumstances the place was hardly a tourist destination, certainly not at that time of year.

In pursuit of the truth, General Balinsky in the 1890s made contact with the Taganrog Port Authority to determine what records they held, if any, of the visits of foreign vessels in November 1825. The port master replied that all records of ship movements for the years 1823–26 had been requisitioned by special order by the Ministry of the Marine in St. Petersburg. How strange that the maritime records of this insignificant port were confiscated, as if the authorities were intent on erasing all trace of ship movements over that crucial period. In any case, Taganrog had no relevant documentation to offer. In his subsequent search of that ministry's archives, Balinsky found no trace of the missing dossiers there either.

If the emperor did escape by sea, it is not unreasonable to suppose that the vessel flew a British maritime flag. In those days, the Union Jack in its varied forms seemed to be everywhere, and it was universally viewed with awe; few ports would deny it a warm welcome. The average British sailor, furthermore, was unlikely to recognize the emperor, whatever his disguise, or take much notice of a solitary passenger.

It is well-known that Alexander had a number of close friends within St. Petersburg's English colony, particularly from among the succession of ambassadors from the Court of St. James's. At the emperor's invitation, several retired British envoys regularly revisited St. Petersburg. So close were certain of these relationships that Ambassador Whitworth, for example, is thought to have exerted a decisive influence on the young Alexander at the time his father's abdication was being plotted and the conspirators were courting the tsarevich. It is not impossible, therefore, to theorize that arrangements might have been concluded by one of Alexander's English friends for a vessel to stand by in Taganrog.

In his research on the yacht, General Balinsky came upon an unnamed British lord, a former envoy to Russia, whose descendants he traced and eventually approached. "They were not at all pleased and they replied that the documents relating to the yacht were a family secret that could not be communicated," Balinsky reported. "At any rate, the yacht's existence has been established, despite the refusal of the family to make available its log for 1825."

Professor Strakhovsky takes the case one step further. He names the vessel's owner and tells of its departure from Taganrog: "This vessel was a private yacht and she bore a British flag. Her owner was the Earl of Cathcart, former ambassador of His Britannic Majesty to the Court of St. Petersburg. When the sad news of the emperor's death ran through the town, hardly anyone paid attention to the belated stay of this yacht in Taganrog waters . . . [they] failed even to notice the day the lonely ship left the harbor."

In 1926, a certain Alexandra Dubasova, the mother-in-law of a onetime governor of the province of Taurida, wrote in some detail on the subject of the yacht. General Balinsky was a friend of the family and a regular visitor to their home in Simferopol. One evening, Dubasova says, the general confided to the family aspects of his researches into the Legend. First, he related details concerning the opening of the imperial tomb in St. Petersburg during the reign of Alexander III, then went on to speak of the yacht. In Dubasova's words, "He made an inquiry at Lloyd's and discovered that after November 25 [the thirteenth, O. S.], there was only one foreign ship in Taganrog. It was the yacht of the former British ambassador to Russia, the Earl of Cathcart. Officials of Lloyd's had noted a strange circumstance regarding this vessel. The yacht's log contained neither the date of her departure from Taganrog nor her destination. Only after a few weeks did an entry place her in the Mediterranean. This is most extraordinary, because according to naval custom and rules a ship's log is meticulously kept day by day. Thus, based on the yacht's presence in late November in Taganrog, the absence of entries in the ship's log, and the friendship between the emperor and the Earl of Cathcart, Balinsky concluded that Alexander I had indeed 'disappeared' on this yacht."

Lloyd's of London insured virtually every nineteenth-century British vessel. In my own researches on the subject, I discovered that the company's extensive archives predate 1825, but logs and documents related to private yachts are kept for no more than a hundred years, after which they are destroyed. In his day Balinsky might well have found all that he claims. In 1999, Lloyd's was unable to confirm anything for lack of records.

At the time of writing, the sixth Earl of Cathcart continues in retirement in Wiltshire, England. He succeeded his father in 1927 and has since taken a studious interest in the family archives. In my correspondence with him on the subject, he makes two telling points concerning the mysterious vessel. In the first place, he points out, the first earl was seventy years old in 1825, "a good age in those days," and by implication not the sort who would sail yachts, especially from British shores all the way to the remote and unfriendly Sea of Azov. Second, and more importantly, "there is no indication that he ever owned a yacht or traveled abroad in 1825." The earl appears adamant on both these points. Nonetheless, there is a reasonable possibility that, 175 years after the event, he is not in possession of all the pertinent documentation. It is also possible that the first earl, even if he did not own a yacht, might easily have chartered one, especially if he was in on the "plot." In those days, chartering was not uncommon. The sixth Earl of Cathcart generously extended every courtesy to me in my queries. The same cannot be said of his forebears, however, who were approached by Grand Duke Nikolai Mikhailovich in about 1904 and subsequently by Prince Bariatinsky in 1925. Both requests were summarily refused — which in itself raises questions. Seventy-five, and even a hundred, years after the tsar's death, maritime logs might still have been in the Cathcart archives. Why then refuse not unreasonable requests from two high-ranking members of the old Russian aristocracy? To have turned them down cold seems odd, even highly suspicious.

Two other former envoys of the Court of St. James's to St. Petersburg, Lord Lansdowne and Lord Augustus Loftus, have also been named as possible owners of the yacht in question. Research on these two names, however, has not uncovered any connection with the Taganrog yacht.

If this mysterious vessel was real, and assuming that Alexander was on it, there follows the tantalizing question of its destination. Thus we come to the second part of this aspect of the mystery: yacht or no yacht, where did the tsar travel, and how did he spend the unaccounted-for years?

Various accounts have it that the vessel made its way to Palestine, where the self-exiled monarch resided incognito in a monastery until 1836. Dubasova continues to write of Balinsky's account: the general "found traces of the presence of a mysterious traveler in Palestine and then established the arrival of this traveler at Kiev." She goes on to relate that Count Osten-Sacken received this stranger and provided him papers in the name of Feodor Kuzmich — both names being common to the Osten-Sacken family. What can be made of these speculations is uncertain. General Balinsky, we know, was a serious historian; we are less familiar with Dubasova. But virtually nothing remains of the general's written work; his entire archive was destroyed when he was shot by the Bolsheviks in 1920.

According to Lubimov, Balinsky determined that the yacht sailed for the Holy Land. The general cited E. C. Ozerova, a confidante and lady-in-waiting to Maria Alexeyevna, wife of Alexander II, as his authority. Ozerova is alleged to have examined in the imperial archive pages from the yacht's log, one entry of which read, "By order of our Envoy to the Russian Court, on the night of [here the month and date are cited] we boarded an unknown person dressed in peasant's clothing and we carried him to Palestine. We were forbidden to take on other passengers."

If the tsar did escape, it stands to reason that that he would have had to "disappear" beyond the borders of his empire. He could not have simply clothed himself in peasant dress and walked out into the night, into the countryside and a fresh identity and existence. He was too familiar a figure, particularly west of the Urals. For him immediately to have taken refuge within the realm was out of the question. If ultimately he determined to spend his final days in Russia, it could only be after a prolonged absence from his subjects — memory had to fade. Palestine would have been a logical interim destination.

Over the centuries, men moved by faith to touch and to kiss the spots "where Christ's holy feet have trod" have made their way to the Holy Land. By the early nineteenth century, religious communities of every ilk had sprung up throughout Palestine — Greeks, Russians, Georgians, Armenians, Copts, Roman Catholics, Lutherans, Anglicans, even American Congregationalists. There was no shortage of monasteries or hospices where an incognito penitent could find sanctuary and retreat into a life of solitude and prayer. In Jerusalem he could pray at the grave of the Savior and impose a self-inflicted penance. What could be more lofty? And what destination could be more attractive or practical?

In his study of Alexander, Paleologue argues that the tsar did escape in a private yacht belonging to an unnamed English aristocrat. "This Lord," he writes, "is not unknown, and he comes from a distinguished family from within the highest political levels." He agrees the yacht sailed to Palestine, but he believes that is where the emperor remained to live out the balance of his years. Prince Bariatinsky asked Paleologue to divulge the name of the British

aristocrat. "The testimony I have gathered concerning the departure of Alexander I from Taganrog," replied the member of the
Académie française, "is still too uncertain, for which reason I am
unable to share this information with you."

Scores of other stories concerning Alexander's death and
Kuzmich's life have come down to us, certain of which are recorded
in the chapter that follows. Ultimately, however, only a scientific
study of the St. Petersburg tomb, and the Tomsk remains, will prove
the case one way or the other.

A postscript: In 1984, the Synod of the Russian Orthodox
Church elevated eleven Siberians to sainthood, of whom Feodor
Kuzmich was one. In Orthodoxy, the process of canonization is
significantly less structured than in the Western tradition. While
the glorification of a saint may be initiated by miracles, they are
not an absolute requirement for canonization. Contrary to the
demands of the Roman Catholic Church, Orthodoxy does not
require three verified miracles.

According to Orthodox tradition, the church does not
"make" a saint; only God can do that. It merely recognizes in a public way that someone is so obviously already a saint in God's eyes
that it should corporately express devotion to that person and follow his or her example "on the path to the Heavenly Kingdom."
The person's holiness "is beyond a doubt." The criteria for canonization are fourfold: (a) holiness of life; (b) whatever teaching there
may have been by the person must be in full conformity with the
Orthodox faith; (c) popular veneration: a consistent, prevailing,
and profound reverence of the person by the church's clergy and
faithful; and (d) the need of the church to have the person as a saint,
"at present to strengthen and inspire Her." The citizenry of Tomsk,
Father Siluan reported, continue "to carry warmest feelings toward
Kuzmich and he enjoys popular veneration." The Russian Orthodox Church clearly felt satisfied that the criteria for sainthood had
been met by the mysterious starets, whoever he may have been.

In writing of the starets, Leo Tolstoy observed, "Whatever
was hidden behind the hermit Feodor, the drama of that life is

profoundly familial with deep and intimate connections to the national soul." And at the center of that impenetrable Russian soul, so fascinating to the Western mind, stands high moral judgment. Once a person has sinned, there is no easy redemption; one cannot expect to enter into the heavenly kingdom through self-deception. Salvation comes through total redemption, which might require a person to move off into a life of solitude and prayer. After nearly thirty years of such struggle, the troubled soul of the starets "entered into eternal rest." Might the heinous sin so long carried by Alexander have at last found redemption in that vast Siberian expanse? "So let historical evidence fail to connect Alexander with Kuzmich," Tolstoy concluded, "the legend lives in all its beauty and sincerity."

19

The Final Testimony

OVER THE YEARS, numerous stories and vignettes have been recorded by historians and diarists about the death of the tsar and the life of the starets. They are first- or second-hand testimonies by people who were actually on the scene or by the relatives of these witnesses. What follows is a selection of supplementary material that reflects on the story. Most of these vignettes appear authentic and there is little cause to dispute them. Others might seem less credible, but they are nonetheless of interest and add color to the tale.

1. The researches of Anatol Kulomzin

Anatol Kulomzin was the chairman of the Trans-Siberian Railroad, and it was largely through his efforts that this gigantic project was completed in 1903. Educated at the universities of Moscow, Heidelberg, and Oxford, Kulomzin was by training an engineer and by vocation an historian. In a 1923 memoir, he tells of an inspection tour he made to Siberia in the late 1880s. He stopped in a village near Tomsk where a colorful procession was issuing forth from the local church, bearing a large icon of the Virgin. Out of curiosity, he joined the parade as it wended its way to a small cabin in the garden of a large country property, which he subsequently discovered belonged to the widow Khromov. A prayer service was held at the cottage, following which the procession returned the icon to the village church. Later he learned that the procession he had serendipitously joined was by tradition held every Sunday morning.

Kulomzin did not return to the church with the parishioners but remained behind to inspect the cabin. There he found a scattering of simple wooden furniture, including a narrow, primitive bed, over which hung an admirable portrait of Emperor Alexander I. On one wall hung a photograph of "an old man of lofty stature with a long beard, clothed in coarse white shirt and trousers, white stockings, and simple slippers — this was Feodor Kuzmich, who had died thirty years earlier." Kulomzin asked the caretaker to open the chest in which was preserved the belongings of the old hermit. There he found some clothing, cutlery, and a wooden plate. On the underside of the plate was an inscription that read, "On this board ate the hermit Feodor Kuzmich, the great Emperor Alexander the Blessed." On a subsequent visit to Tomsk, Kulomzin learned that the plate had been stolen, and, he notes cryptically, the theft coincided with the visit to Tomsk and the cabin "of a well-known general."

Following that visit to Kuzmich's cell, Kulomzin devoted much of his life to a serious study of the mysterious starets. He records an interview he held with Archbishop Makary of Tomsk on the subject of Kuzmich. "When Feodor Kuzmich was alive," reported the churchman, "I, as a simple monk, was serving the archbishop of that time, who happened also to be called Makary . . . I know that while the hermit was alive, particularly during the last years, the archbishop often talked with him. The hermit was a highly educated man and knew French, German, and English . . . what they talked about I cannot tell, as I do not know foreign languages."

A scene witnessed and recorded by more than a single person is worthy of mention. While Feodor Kuzmich was living in Bogoyavlensk, Archbishop Afanasy of Irkutsk passed through town. He asked the locals for Feodor Kuzmich, and when he was directed to the old man's modest cabin, witnesses saw Kuzmich greet the churchman with the customary bow, low to the ground. The surprised villagers then saw the archbishop return an equally low bow. Then the two men went into the cabin, where they spent a long time conversing in a foreign language. At the conclusion of the visit, the pair emerged from the cabin and, in parting, they kissed each other's hands. For the townsfolk, that a high churchman would show interest in an obscure starets was puzzling enough. That the prelate would then bow down before him, and afterward kiss the old man's hand, was incredible.

Kulomzin also records that Grand Duke Alexei Alexandrovich, son of Alexander II, upon his completion of formal schooling was sent on a round-the-world tour. The young man's route home took him through Siberia, and local authorities recorded that the grand duke attended a memorial service that was held at Feodor Kuzmich's cell.

And finally, Kulomzin reports, "In 1912 I happened to make the acquaintance of a Tomsk official who, in a promotion, had been transferred out and had lately arrived back from Siberia. According to his story, before he left Tomsk he visited the grave of Feodor Kuzmich. Looking into the tomb, which at that time was being repaired by workmen, he saw that there was no coffin in it. When asked where was the coffin, the workmen told him: 'It was taken away long ago, soon after the hermit died, to St. Petersburg, to the Cathedral of St. Peter and St. Paul.'"

2. Kuzmich's icon

Among the icons Kuzmich kept on his shelf was one of Our Lady of Pochayev, on the backside of which were the letters *A. I.*, surmounted by the imperial crown.

3. A visit with Kuzmich that failed to impress

One who was not much taken by Feodor Kuzmich was a certain Smirnov, a long time resident of Tomsk, who in 1859 moved to St. Petersburg, where he died. Over the years, he had heard many stories of the starets and had developed considerable skepticism about the Legend. For one thing, it was reported that Kuzmich never attended church. Determined to have a firsthand look at the "saintly hermit" before leaving Siberia, he went to call on the old man. The rector of Tomsk Seminary, a man who shared Smirnov's suspicions, accompanied him. In their meeting with the starets "we pressed a number of questions related to the condition of the church and to the taking of Holy Sacraments." The rector urged the starets to attend church and partake of communion. Kuzmich responded in the negative, and when he did he spoke with strange intonations "that resembled a mix of Church Slavonic and Latin, with unrecognizable mystical, even apocalyptic phrases." The visitors came away disturbed and unimpressed. "We concluded that he was from western Russia, probably a Uniat preacher or a philosopher-mystic and Mason whose mind was touched." What is interesting, however, is Smirnov's notation, written in St. Petersburg, concerning certain of the old man's property. Kuzmich, "prior to his death, apparently requested that a certain icon and ring be delivered to the palace. These things were brought to St. Petersburg and delivered as directed. It turned out that these same items had apparently disappeared prior to the death of Alexander Pavlovich."

Who precisely Smirnov was we do not know. The language and content of his report, however, suggests that he was a churchman, perhaps a lawyer. That the two found Kuzmich's manner of speech strange is contradictory; all other reports we have of his speech comment on its clarity, albeit with a "Russian accent." Was Feodor Kuzmich simply upset by the irritating questions? Or was the fervor of his visitors' ultraconservative Orthodoxy too much to take? Perhaps the starets was merely toying with the two intruders.

4. The name Feodor Kuzmich

It is said that Alexander had in his service for many years a Cossack valet named Feodor Kuzmich Ovcharov. This man briefly served the emperor in the initial days of Taganrog. According to Bariatinsky, Ovcharov was given leave to visit his home on the Don and it was during his absence that the tsar died. On returning to Taganrog, the servant tried without success to pay his respects to the deceased, but Volkonsky and Wylie prevented him from approaching the coffin.

5. Issakov and the white stockings

In her memoirs, Princess Dolgoruky writes of a certain Issakov, "residing now in the U.S.," who told her of his grand-father. Issakov claimed that Nicholas I sent that gentleman to Siberia with two hundred pairs of white stockings for Feodor Kuzmich. Nothing seems to be known of this American Issakov, and it is impossible to authenticate the grandfather's story. But assuming such a delivery actually took place, is it likely that such a singular gift would have been carried halfway across Russia to an unknown Siberian starets at such effort and cost? It is a well-known fact, incidentally, that Alexander suffered from recurring athlete's foot, which necessitated frequent changes of stockings. Even during the 1812 war with Napoleon, the tsar received parcels of silk stockings from Paris.

6. Gagarina and cap

As noted earlier, it was Professor Nicholas Arseniev who in my youth sparked my interest in the Legend. I recall the venerable scholar telling me how his sister, Princess Vera Gagarina, shortly after the revolution was assigned the task of taking an inventory of items in the imperial palace at Gatchina. In her work, she came across a small casket belonging to Empress Alexandra Feodor-ovna, wife of Nicholas I. Inside, the princess uncovered a number of personal items of sentimental value, including Alexandra's first letter to her husband and, in separate envelopes, curls from her children. At the bottom of the container, wrapped in tissue paper, was a monk's velvet skullcap in which lay a piece of paper with the inscription, "The cap of the Blessed starets." It might well be asked why such an unlikely item would turn up among the most private imperial souvenirs. In her memoirs, Baluyeva writes of Gagarina's discovery, as does Princess Dolgoruky in her unpublished memoir, *Gone Forever: Some Pages from My Life in Russia, 1885–1919*. Both confirm what Professor Arseniev related to me in my childhood days. (In 1997, I examined this same cap, which now reposes in the State Archive of the Russian Federation in Moscow.)

7. The merchant Khromov visits with Alexander II

In his day, Victor Ivanovich Basilevsky was an extraordinary personality. Born of a noble family into one of Russia's greatest fortunes, he died in exile in 1929 on the Gulf of Finland at the age of ninety. He had outlived the reigns of four tsars. Before the revolution, Basilevsky owned some of the largest gold mines and estates in Siberia, and in his lifetime he gave away millions to charity.

In the late 1860s Basilevsky rented out one of his Siberian estates to the merchant Khromov and the two struck up a friendship. Sometime later, Khromov traveled to southern Russia to visit Basilevsky at his estate in Velikino. During that visit, in an outpouring of emotion, Khromov informed his host that he sensed his life was drawing to an end. He wished to confide to the nobleman a deep secret, one requiring Basilevsky's assistance. For years, he explained, he had farmed a parcel of land near Tomsk on which once lived a starets calling himself Feodor Kuzmich. On his deathbed the starets confessed to Khromov that in reality he was Alexander I. He asked Khromov to deliver certain papers and a picture to Alexander II, the reigning monarch. Khromov went on to confess that for whatever reason, he never executed the commission, although he preserved the small parcel of documents. He now wished to make good the promise he had made to the dying starets. He begged Basilevsky to assist in arranging an audience with the tsar. Basilevsky agreed and the emperor duly received Khromov. The two were closeted for a long time. Following the audience, Khromov failed to return to Basilevsky in Velikino, instead proceeding directly back to Siberia. Basilevsky, who never doubted that Feodor Kuzmich and Alexander I were one and the same, surmises that the tsar expressly commanded Khromov to hurry home. He wished no part of their conversation imparted to anyone.

Here the story is picked up by Natalia Baluyeva, Princess Gagarina's sister, granddaughter of Vassily Sergeyevich Arseniev, an official in the emperor's court. Arseniev chaired the commission that reviewed petitions to the tsar. She relates that the commission received a petition from the merchant Khromov for an audience with the emperor. Her grandfather took a special interest in this request, presumably because of Basilevsky's intervention. He agreed to receive the Siberian. "An elderly, presentable gentleman, dressed in the manner of a merchant, appeared in his study. He held himself with dignity and self-confidence. Arseniev asked Khromov why he was requesting an imperial audience. 'I've not come to petition His Majesty for anything,' Khromov said, 'but to inform him of the great and blessed person who had spent time in my family.'"

Khromov went on to explain that he had known Feodor Kuzmich well and offered many details of the starets's life. The merchant concluded by emphasizing his unshakable conviction that the person of whom he spoke was none other than Alexander I. He wished to present the emperor with a satchel he carried that contained a number of items left behind by the starets, including a Bible, a chaplet, a skullcap, and a few bits of paper with Kuzmich's notations. Arseniev agreed to arrange an audience and asked that in the interim the items be left with him. He particularly wished to have handwriting experts examine the papers for authenticity. Khromov agreed and surrendered the satchel.

Arseniev passed the papers over to experts at the Imperial Library but the scholars were unable conclusively to match Kuzmich's handwriting with that of Alexander I. The samples of comparison were at variance, yet there were certain unmistakable similarities. In time, Khromov was received by the emperor, and the audience, we are told, lasted over two hours. Upon its conclusion, the tsar ordered the visitor to maintain total silence about their discussions and to return immediately to Siberia.

An addendum to the Khromov records: one will recall an earlier incident, related by Anna Khromov, of her father's witnessing Kuzmich taking leave of a young woman and an officer in a hussar's uniform. There is strong possibility that the person in question was the tsarevich Alexander II, who from all the evidence at hand did visit Kuzmich. As a boy, Alexander was appointed colonel-in-chief of the Hussar Regiment and he rarely appeared anywhere out of its uniform, even as emperor.

A final word on Basilevsky's memoirs: he relates that Metropolitan Isidor informed him that the tomb of Alexander I had at one time been opened and that the embalmed body lying therein was exhumed and reinterred in a St. Petersburg cemetery.

8. Testimony of Grand Duchess Olga and others

In his researches on the Legend, Victor Basilevsky wrote Grand Duchess Olga Alexandrovna, then residing in Copenhagen, to ask if she felt that the meeting between Alexander II and Khromov had in any way shed light on the mystery. The grand duchess confessed quite openly that, although she was unable to comment on the meeting, she and the rest of her living family never doubted the connection between Feodor Kuzmich and Alexander I. This, of course, coincides with what the grand duchess told me personally in 1958. In the foolishness of youth, I neglected to ask her what she meant by "our family." Specifically, did she include her brother, Nicholas II? In reviewing the record, it would appear that the four tsars who followed Alexander I probably knew the truth, but members of their families did not.

It might be added that the Duke of Mecklenburg, nephew of Alexander I and Nicholas I, declared that in his opinion there was no doubt of the veracity of the Legend.

9. The three portraits

In 1874, State Secretary Mikhail Nikolayevich Galkin-Vraski, as director-general of prison administration, carried out a tour of inspection of prison facilities in Siberia. Upon his return to the capital, he reported in person to Alexander III. He met with the emperor in his private study and delivered his lengthy report. At the conclusion of the meeting, he related all that he had heard in Siberia of Feodor Kuzmich. In Tomsk and western Siberia, he said, the starets was widely revered as the Emperor Alexander I. The tsar received these remarks in silence, lapsed into deep thought, and then slowly motioned with his hand behind him. Suspended on the wall were two imposing golden frames, portraits of the full-length figures of Alexander I and Nicholas I. Hanging between them was a small portrait of Feodor Kuzmich.

Appendix A

Manifesto by Alexander I concerning the succession to the Throne

BY THE GRACE OF GOD, We, Alexander the First, Emperor and Autocrat of All Russia, etc., etc., etc., declare to all Our Faithful subjects that:

From Our very accession to the All-Russian Throne, We have ceaselessly felt Ourselves obligated before Almighty God not only to guard and increase the welfare of our beloved fatherland and people in Our own days, but also to prepare and secure their tranquillity and welfare after Us, through the clear and precise designation of Our successor, in keeping with the rules of Our Imperial House and for the good of the Empire. We could not, like our predecessors, designate him by name earlier, not knowing whether it would please God to grant us an heir to the Throne in the direct line. But as our days go by we feel we must place Our Throne in such a position that it would not for a moment remain vacant.

While we kept this sacred concern in Our heart, Our beloved Brother, Crown Prince and Grand Duke Constantine Pavlovich, of His own accord, submitted to Us his request that the right to the Throne, which he could claim by virtue of His birth, be transferred to the one to whom it otherwise belong after Him. He also expressed his intention to enforce in this manner the additional act concerning succession to the Throne that We had enacted in the year 1820 and that He freely and solemnly recognized inasmuch as it concerned Him.

We are profoundly touched by this sacrifice which Our beloved Brother decided to offer, with such disregard of His own person, in order to confirm the hereditary decrees of Our Imperial House and for the unshakable peace of the All-Russian Empire.

Having called upon God for help, and having deeply pondered upon this subject that is so dear to Our hearts and of such importance to the State, and finding that the existing provisions concerning the succession to the Throne by those who have the right to do it does not take away the freedom to abdicate this right when, in these circumstances, there would be no difficulties in the further inheritance of the Throne, with the consent of Our August Mother, by the supreme inherited right as Head of the Imperial family, and the autocratic power given to Us by God, We determined: First, that the voluntary abdication of Our first Brother, Crown Prince and Grand Duke Constantine Pavlovich, from the right to the All-Russian Throne should be firm and inalterable; that this act of abdication, for the sake of undisputability, should be kept in the Great Moscow Cathedral of the Assumption and in the three highest places of Government of Our Empire — in the Holy Synod, in the State Council, and in the Governing Senate. Second, as a consequence of the above, on the firm foundation of the act concerning succession to the Throne, that our successor is to be Our second Brother, Grand Duke Nikolai Pavlovich.

Thus, We remain in the serene hope that, on the day when the King of Kings, following the laws of those who are earth born, will call Us from this temporary kingdom to eternity, the Governing Ranks to whom this, Our present and inalterable will and this lawful decision, must be known in the appointed time, according to Our instructions, will immediately pledge their faith to the Emperor appointed by Us as successor to the one and indivisible Throne of the All-Russian Empire, of the Kingdom of Poland, and the Duchy of Finland: as to Ourselves, We ask all Our subjects that, with the same love that led us to consider the care of their unfailing welfare to be the greatest good on earth, they offer heartfelt prayer to Our Lord and Savior Jesus Christ that Our soul be accepted to His Eternal Kingdom according to His steadfast mercy.

Given in Tsarskoye Selo

On the 16th day of August, in the year 1823 after the Birth of Christ, in the twenty-third year of Our Reign.

ALEXANDR

The above was taken from one of the original copies of the manifesto, which reposes in the Archive of the Russian Federation, Moscow. (Ref: *Fond 679, opis I, dela 68, I, 2*). The author is grateful to Dr. C. Berdnikoff for the original translation and to Nicholas and Sophia Ozerov for the editing.

Appendix B

Protocol of the autopsy of Emperor Alexander, November 20, 1825

1. The body surface

The overall view of the body did not reveal any emaciation and little deviation from the normal. Neither the abdomen nor any of the exterior parts of the body reveal any swelling.

On the body's anterior surface, specifically on the hips, there were darkish and some dark red stains caused by the application of mustard plasters. On both the legs below the calf and extending to the malleoli, a dark brown and various other scars were observed especially on the right leg, remainders of healed wounds that the emperor had previously sustained.

On the posterior of the body between the shoulder blades, there is a fairly large area of deep red color extending to the neck, caused by the application of cantharide plasters [extracts of Spanish fly]. The shoulders, the entire back, the posterior, and all the soft parts that contain most of the fatty cellular coating were of dark olive color, caused by pooling of venous blood under the skin. On turning the body onto its prone position, some blood-colored liquid flowed from the nostrils and mouth.

2. The skull

On incising the flesh covering the head, from ear to ear, the skin was found to be very thick and fatty. Upon careful and meticulous separation of the top part of the skull by means of a saw, there flowed two ounces of venous blood from the occipital part of the skull. The skull had a normal thickness. Upon removing the dura mater — which in some areas adhered solidly to the skull, particularly under the occipital bone — the blood vessels throughout the entire surface of the brain were found distended by dark and, in some places, reddish blood caused by the rush of blood to this organ. On the frontal lobes of the brain, at the base of the skull, as well as the ventricles of the brain, there was found up to two ounces of serous fluid. The choroid plexus of the brain's left ventricle was found solidly adhering to its base.

3. The pectoral regions

When a straight incision was made from the larynx through the center of the sternum to the junction of the pubic bones, and two additional cuts from the navel to the upper edges of the iliac bones, the cellular cover was everywhere filled with a great amount of fat.

At the junction of the ribs with the edges, the cartilage was completely ossified. The thoracic cavity contained no liquid exidate. The heart was of normal size and in all its parts it did not deviate in shape or consistency. The same applies to all the major vessels proceeding from the heart. In the pericardium there was found about an ounce of serous fluid.

4. The abdominal cavity

The stomach, which contained some mucous mixture, was found in a completely healthy condition. The liver was large in size and its color was darker than normal. The gallbladder was stretched by a large quantity of deteriorated bile of dark color. The colon was swollen with gas. All other organs — pancreas, spleen, kidneys, and bladder — did not deviate from the normal.

The anatomical investigation apparently proves that the august monarch was struck by an acute illness, which first affected the liver and other organs serving the secretion of bile. The illness is its progression developed into a fierce fever coupled with the rush of blood through vessels of the brain, and secretion and accumulation of serus exidate in the cavities of the brain was finally the cause of the death of His Imperial Majesty.

1. Junior Surgeon Yakolev, Dimitryev State Hospital
2. Staff Surgeon Vassiliev, Cossack Life Guard Regiment
3. Doctor Laquier, Chief Medical Director of the Taganrog Quarantine Station
4. Court Physician Dobbert
5. Court Medical Surgeon Tarasov
6. Staff Physician Alexandrovich, Court Adviser
7. Medical Doctor Rheingold, Court Staff Surgeon
8. Staff Physician Stoffregen, Senior Staff Adviser
9. Baronet Yakov Wylie, Privy Councillor and Staff Physician

I have witnessed the physicians' description of the finding and I attended the autopsy of His Imperial Majesty the Emperor Alexander Pavlovich.

Adjutant-General Chernichev
Taganrog, Ekaterinoslavsky Province

This report was written in Russian and deposited in the Imperial Archives. It appears as an appendix in Shilder's *Imperator Alexandr pervy,* vol. IV, pp. 573–74. The author is grateful to Nicholas and Sophia Ozerov for the English translation and to Dr. C. Berdnikoff for the editing.

Reference Notes

Full details of the books and journals cited in this reference section will be found in the bibliography. I have used the following abbreviations:

GDNM: Grand Duke Nikolai Mikhailovich. *Legenda o konchine imperatora Alexandra I.* St. Petersburg: S. A. Suvorin, 1907.

IAP: Shilder, N. K. *Imperator Alexandr pervy.* St. Petersburg: S. A. Suvorin, 1898. Volume IV, unless otherwise noted.

1. Paris, 1814–Tomsk, Siberia, 1864

2   "It is enough that it be known": quoted by C. H. Choiseul-Gouffier, 175.

3   "Your nation has every right to my esteem": ibid., 183.

6   "Father, at least tell us the names": Grand Duke Nikolai Pavlovich, 457.

7   "The end is near ... having prayed to God": ibid., 459.

10   "Feodor Kuzmich captivates me more and more": L. D. Lubimov, "Tania startsa Feodora Kuzmicha," 211.

10   "whatever was hidden behind the name": S. A. Berezhanskiy, 1251.

10   "Let us hope ... that someday": GDNM, 48.

2. Conspiracy at Mikhailovsky Castle

14   "Rappelez-vous, messieurs": N. A. Sablukov, 86.

23   "His conversation, and everything": Shilder, 343.

23   "Why do children so often resemble": Robert Coughlan, 343.

28   "One was struck by the great vivacity": quoted by G. P. Gooch, 33.

28 "He combined plenty of intelligence": ibid., 34.
29 "I see into what hands the empire": ibid., 35.
30 "Catherine, who, judged from a distance": Adam Czartoryski, 65.

3. Tsar Paul's Revenge

34 "So enamored had he become": Shilder, *Imperator Pavel*, 161.
35 "You're conniving with the empress": quoted in Leonid Strakhovsky, 18.
36 "I never felt happier or more at ease": Czartoryski, 235.
37 "The fear in which we are living": Constantine de Grunwald, *Alexandre Ier, le tsar mystique*, 173.
38 "Under that attractive exterior": K. Waliszewski, *Le Fils de la Grande Catherine, Paul Ier*, 416.
40 "My father ... has declared war": Shilder, *Imperator Pavel*, 463.
41 "Great gloom permeated the capital's society": Sablukov, 70.
42 "Yes, Your Majesty ... a conspiracy": Shilder, *Imperator Pavel*, 473.
42 "the grand duke, employing the same": Choiseul-Gouffier, 37.
44 "Please don't go ... for I must immediately": Sablukov, 77.
45 "That evening ... we dined with the emperor": Field Marshal Kutuzov, 77.

4. Courage from the Cognac Bottle

47 "Vous êtes des Jacobins": Sablukov, 79.
48 "That night ... more than one of them": ibid., 86.
49 "The old linden trees of the garden": D. K. Miliukov, 53.
49 "Twelve of us entered the room": ibid., 55.
50 "Your Majesty, you have ceased to reign": ibid., 56.
50 "What have I done to you?": L. Lowerson, 226.
50 "Everyone in the room took flight": T. Shiman, in Sablukov, 147.
51 "struck the emperor on the hand": Sablukov, 88.
51 "revenged themselves of personal insults": ibid., 89.
52 "I cannot ... I cannot go on": D. H. Lieven, "Konchina Imperatora Pavala," 430.
53 "We, by the grace of God": Ivan Golovin, 67.
54 "1. All prisoners of state are set": ibid., 69.
55 "clothed in his uniform, booted and spurred": Sablukov, 96.
55 "Approaching the corpse, the empress": ibid., 97.
56 "a superb sun broke": D. H. Lieven, "Konchina Imperatora Pavala," 428.

56 "His sensitive soul will be": Grand Duke Nikolai Mikhailovich, *L'Impératrice Elisabeth*, 268.
56 "The grief and remorse which he": Czartoryski, 253.
58 "Until the end of his life . . . there would come": Alan Palmer, 46.

5. The Crowned Hamlet

64 "Alexander never was trained": Victor O. Kluchevsky, 136.
65 "Like a rudderless ship": M. Jenkins, 98.
65 "A cunning Byzantine": ibid., 100.
65 "had a strong soul and a weak character": quoted in Henri Troyat, 297.
65 "Alexander's character represents": quoted in Strakhovsky, 62.
66 "If Alexander were to be dressed in female clothes": ibid., 62.
66 "I spent . . . evenings in the same room": ibid., 172.
68 "My faith is fervent and sincere": Alexander I, Correspondence, 153.
70 "from the rising sun would soon arise": Troyat, 225.
70 "You have not yet approached God": ibid., 225.
71 "After the regicide . . . Alexander had felt": ibid., 241.
72 "The thought that one day": Golovin, 54.
72 "I repeat, my dear friend": V. I. Karazin, 79.
74 "When Providence shall bless me with bringing": Frédéric La Harpe, 215.
74 "When anyone has the honor to be": quoted in Strakhovsky, 205.
74 "I have decided to free myself": IAP, vol. 1, 276.
74 "I must tell you, brother, that I want": quoted in Strakhovsky, 107.
75 "As we appeared before the people": ibid.
75 "I have great confidence": Royal Dutch Archives.
76 "The prince was horrified" IAP, 350.

6. A Riddle Wrapped in a Mystery

80 "The apparition of such a man on a throne": H. Hans, 215.
83 "the almighty Speransky, secretary-general": Comte Philippe-Paul Ségur, 287.
83 "It is the personal relationship between": Grand Duke Nikolai Mikhailovich, *Imperator Alexandr pervy*, vol. 2, 321.
85 "Russia really does not need": de Grunwald, *Alexandre Ier, le tsar mystique*, 136.
85 "Guilty or not, Speransky must be": IAP, vol. 3, 60.

87   "If you had your arm cut off": ibid.
88   "What a glorious day . . . God has shown": A. S. Rappoport, 316.

7. The Defeat of the *Grande Armée*

91   "The evening was beautiful": Choiseul-Gouffier, 92.
93   "The interests of our two empires": K. Waliszewski, *Le Règne d'Alexandre Ier*, 225.
93   "In a mixture of bravado, idealism, vanity": Janet Hartley, 76.
93   "Inform [Napoleon] that this union between": Sergei S. Tatischev, 148.
93   "If only I had seen him earlier": quoted by M. A. Almedingen, 101.
93   "I have just seen Emperor Alexander": quoted by Palmer, 137.
94   "How can I help it if a great power": quoted in Emil Ludwig, 278.
95   "The emperor left the ball at the end of supper": Choiseul-Gouffier, 93.
95   "I will not lay down": IAP, vol. 3, 374.
96   "Which is the road to Moscow?": quoted by Choiseul-Gouffier, 102.
96   "I have no illusions": quoted in Strakhovsky, 119.
97   "There were no inhabitants to be found": Armand de Caulaincourt, 62.
98   "Your role is not merely that of captain": R. Edling, 221.
99   "old general Kutuzov, bloated and one-eyed", Troyat, 86.
99   "The public wanted him": quoted by Troyat, 149.
100 "These spontaneous impulses": Choiseul-Gouffier, 113.
101 "When it was all over and mist": Palmer, 244.
101 "I consider this retreat providential": Daria Olivier, 76.
103 "trails of fire follow their dreadful course": ibid., 60.
103 "Soldiers, convicts, and prostitutes ran": quoted by Troyat, 159.
104 "The taking of Moscow has brought the feelings": Edling, 256.
105 "I simply devoured the Bible": quoted in Strakhovsky, 131.
105 "Alexander spent his days plunging": ibid., 133.
106 "My people and I stand united": ibid., 136.
106 "Peace? . . . We have not yet made war": E. Tarle, 189.
107 "They were not regiments on the march": quoted in Troyat, 162.

8. The Crown: An Increasing Burden

110 "The armies of the allied powers": Choiseul-Gouffier, 168.
111 "My happiness and one desire is to be": ibid., 175.
111 "Europe has gained a peace which I hope": ibid., 183.

112 "Save us . . . save our religion": Patricia Grimstead, 259.
113 "Russia is enjoying the glory": quoted in Strakhovsky, 170.
114 "One cannot do all things": quoted in Strakhovsky, 171.
114 "his soul was troubled": ibid., 172.
115 "Soon also this great moment": quoted in Hartley, 168.
116 "Alexander knew that . . . he had a servant": Troyat, 244.
116 "Nothing could be more degrading": quoted in Hartley, 45.
118 "I understand entirely what your sensitive soul": Jenkins, 195.

9. God Is Punishing Us for Our Sins

119 "Alexander, discouraged and unhappy": quoted in V. Bariatinsky, *Le Mystère d'Alexandre Ier*, 171.
120 "People were surprised in the midst": Choiseul-Gouffier, 299.
121 "We're terribly concerned about the health": quoted by P. Rossiev, "Zhivuchaya legenda," 687.
122 "Although there is some amelioration": ibid., 687.
123 "Representatives of the Kingdom of Poland!": quoted by Troyat, 284.
125 "You know that I have shared and encouraged": Hugh Seaton-Watson, 185.
126 "I can't believe it . . . How could the doctors": quoted by P. Rossiev, "Zhivuchaya legenda," 687.
127 "The sea is not navigable": Robert Lee, 51.
127 "The idea of founding a capital in such a place": Nikolai Danilovsky, 55.
129 "Let's rely on the Almighty": quoted in IAP, 350.
130 "Pray, Tsar!": ibid., 353.
130 "Emperor . . . I am an old man and have seen much": ibid., 354.

10. Retreat to Taganrog

134 "Here ends the first part of our journey": I. V. (James) Wylie, 71.
135 "It is extraordinary . . . that the empress": IAP, 356.
135 "It was no more elaborate": ibid., 356.
135 "Thank the Lord: I arrived at my destination": ibid., 358.
136 "her head was only hanging on by the skin": Jenkins, 242.
136 "My little father, Your Majesty!": quoted in IAP, 359.
137 "the emperor supposed that Arakcheyev's mistress": ibid., 360.
138 "You're right. And I believe this too": ibid., 368.

139 "I'll soon move to the Crimea": ibid., 370.
140 "It might be noted, however": ibid., 371.
140 "appeared entirely healthy": D. K. Tarasov, 115.
140 "It's hard to understand": ibid., 116.
141 "Some of the wives . . . were beautiful": ibid., 116.
141 "Since the time His Majesty ordered": ibid., 118.
142 "What a tragedy!": ibid., 119.
143 "Wylie was highly disturbed": ibid., 120.

11. The Fatal Illness

145 "I dared to suggest to His Majesty": quoted in IAP, 374.
145 "My dear friend . . . I understand what you": ibid., 374.
145 "I'm very sick": ibid., 374.
148 "Refuses medication. He brings me": Wylie, 75.
148 "But . . . it seemed to me that His Majesty": quoted in IAP, 563.
149 "passed a restless night and had a fever": ibid., 564.
149 "This fever appears to be": Wylie, 76.
149 "finding the emperor in satisfactory condition": Tarasov, 121.
149 "He was in good humor": quoted in Bariatinsky, 46.
149 "The emperor is a bit better today": Wylie, 76.
150 "The fever persisted all day": quoted in IAP, 565.
150 "Since the eighth I've noticed that he is preoccupied": Wylie, 76.
150 "grief and remorse, which he was continually": Czartoryski, 254.
151 "I try each day to be upbeat but at night": IAP, 378.
151 "Farewell, my father . . . be assured": quoted in IAP, 378.
153 "At about five o'clock . . . I sent for Wylie": quoted by Francis H. Gribble, 261.
154 "important secret orders and ordered that": Tarasov, 122.
154 "Where does one find peace in life?": quoted in GDNM, 460.
155 "If I recall correctly": Wylie, 76.
155 "In the morning the fever continues": quoted in IAP, 565.
155 "All is going badly because he does not": Wylie, 76.
155 "I know exactly what's good for me": ibid., 76.
156 "Things can only become worse": ibid., 77.
157 "I know more than anyone else": IAP, 380.
157 "I immediately carried the news": Tarasov, 126.
158 "Very well, gentlemen, now it's up to you": ibid., 126.
158 "It all seems too late": Wylie, 77.
158 "we applied mustard plasters": quoted in Bariatinsky, 62.
159 "The emperor passed a restless night": Tarasov, 126.

159 "Dearest Mother": quoted in IAP, 383.
159 "But death already hovered over the poor sufferer": IAP, 383.
160 "From bad to worse": Wylie, 76.
160 "There is no hope to save my beloved lord": ibid., 77.
160 "The emperor passed the night": Tarasov, 127.

12. A Time for Mourning

163 "O Mother! I am the most miserable being": quoted in IAP, 385.
163 "Our angel is in the heavens, and I remain on earth": quoted in IAP, 386.
164 "Behold that splendid genius who was": ibid., 387.
164 "Deep down inside there was great idealistic beauty": IAP, 387.
165 "In fact . . . in his last days, the emperor": IAP, 388.
165 "Is he so ill that there isn't further hope?": ibid., 389.
166 "Prince Volkonsky and I supposed that the deceased": ibid., 578.
167 "I shall forsake the throne when I reach fifty": quoted in IAP, 350.
167 "With sadness in my soul . . . I have the sacred duty": ibid., 578.
168 "I now await with impatience orders": IAP, 389.
168 "filial feelings and respect for the emperor": Tarasov, 129.
169 "At nine in the morning, on orders": N. I. Schoenig, 280.
170 "The pungent odor of spirit, together with": ibid., 281.
171 "I went to see His Imperial Majesty lying": Lee, 40.
171 "On the second day, as I raised the muslin": Schoenig, 281.

13. From Taganrog to St. Petersburg

173 "My resolve is as strong as it ever": D. K. Miliukov, 299.
175 "What was in that head of yours": quoted by Anatole G. Mazour, 164.
175 "We are destined to die!": ibid., 164.
176 "We shall die. O, how gloriously": ibid.
176 "this is a hopeless undertaking": *Vostanie dekabristov: materialy.*
176 "I am certain that we shall all": *Vospominanya Bestuzhevykh,* 83.
177 "The ceremonial began at nine o'clock": Th. R. Martos, 491.
177 "The streets were lined with troops": Lee, 64.
178 "at ten o'clock, following the Liturgy": quoted in IAP, 434.
178 "All earthly ties are severed between ourselves!": ibid., 134.
180 "In addition to the personal instructions of the empress": Tarasov, 134.
180 "As the horses were being changed, the court coachman": ibid., 135.
182 "with his crying and tears expressed the full": ibid., 136.

182 "the muscles were strong and hard and substantially": IAP, 381.
183 "I replied in the affirmative": Tarasov, 138.
184 "Yes, this is my son, my dear Alexander": quoted in IAP, 381.
184 "body stinketh, for he hath been dead": John 11:39.
185 "At twelve o'clock midnight": Tarasov, 139.
186 "the face of the deceased emperor had become": ibid., 140.

14. The Life and Death of Feodor Kuzmich

192 "If only you knew who I am": M. F. Melnitzky, 222.
194 "Little father, is it true that you are the Grand Duke": K. N. Mikhailov, 241.
197 "they were leaving . . . it appeared to me that the hussar": ibid., 238.
197 "I never said that!": N. Balouyeva, 60.
198 "Wait . . . there's plenty of time to marry": G. Vasilich, *Imperator Alexandr I y starets Feodor Kuzmich*, 130.
199 "You really want to see the tsar?": Melnitzky, 99.
200 "Well . . . you've certainly got a daring young girl": Mikhailov, 245.

15. The Core of the Mystery

208 "After the coffin was uncovered, the remains": Alexandra Dubasova, 11.
208 "lay a long-bearded starets": A. N. Saharov, "Smerts ili uhod," 277.
214 "because the account is far from": Bariatinsky, 97.
215 "Wylie was consulted and pronounced": IAP, 190.
218 "although the body was embalmed, the face": Olivier, 44.
218 "The chemicals used for the preservation": Bariatinsky, 119.
218 "I could not bring myself to unveil": quoted in Bariatinsky, 174.
218 "I am under the same roof with the dear mortal remains": Olivier, 48.
219 "He covered 30 versts on horseback": M. Sokolovsky, 167.
219 "only twice daily, at noon and at nine": ibid., 171.
220 "On the 10th . . . called me out": ibid., 173.
225 "We've arrived in Taganrog and here ends": Wylie, 71.

16. Elizaveta and Alexander

228 "The entire suite rejoices at the state of affairs": quoted in IAP, 356.
228 "It gives me such pleasure . . . to have him": ibid., 358.

228 "In the solitude of Taganrog, the bond": Bariatinsky, 29.
232 "so long as he is here": Grand Duke Nikolai Mikhailovich, "Nekotorya sobrazhenie po povodu pisma 31ovo dekabrya, 1825," 738.
233 "She suffers from a tightening in the chest": ibid., 736.
235 "I suffer and am broken physically": quoted in IAP, 444.
235 "was in such bad shape that Your Majesty": Grand Duke Nikolai Mikhailovich, "Nekotorya sobrazhenie," 745.
235 "In each town I proposed a rest of a day": ibid., 740.
235 "We have been witness to the suffering of our angel": ibid., 751.
236 "a result of prolonged illness": quoted by Henri Pirenne, 314.

17. The Mystery That Will Not Die

238 "On July 18, 1901, one of my highly placed": Mikhailov, 21.
238 "During one of my visits . . . Pobedonostsev": ibid., 22.
242 "If at confession I did not declare": Leo N. Tolstoy, 403.
242 "is of neither school": ibid., 865.
243 "I had the impression that his words": Maurice Paleologue, 316.
243 "on the basis of certain detailed evidence": Lubimov, "Tayna startsa Feodora Kuzmicha," 211.
243 "he had changed his mind and now accepts": V. G., 865.
247 "Probably this was a rich aristocrat": Melnitzky, 104.

18. The Unknown Yacht

251 "This vessel was a private yacht": Strakhovsky, 237.
252 "He made an inquiry at Lloyd's and discovered": A. Dubasova, 11.
254 "By order of our Envoy of the Russian Court": Lubimov, *Tayna Imperatora Alexandra I*, 159.
254 "This Lord . . . is not unknown, and he comes from": Paleologue, 302.
255 "The testimony I have gathered concerning": Bariatinsky, 160.

19. The Final Testimony

260 "prior to his death, apparently requested": Smirnov, 530.
263 "An elderly, presentable gentleman": Balouyeva, 60.

Bibliography

Readers wishing to explore more fully the life and reign of Tsar Alexander are referred to the following popular authors: Edith Almedingen, Allen McConnell, Alan Palmer, Maurice Paleologue, and Henri Troyat (the last two also in French). A concise and factual retrospective is offered by Janet Huntley. The three prerevolutionary Russian works — standard reading all — are by N. K. Shilder, Grand Duke Nikolai Mikhailovich, and M. Bogdanovich.

*   *   *

Alexander I, Emperor. "Imperator Alexandr Pavlovich y Knaz Adam Chartorsky." *Russky arkhiv*, vol. 9 (1871), pp. 911–914.

———. Correspondence, taken from "Imperator Alexandr Pavlovich y Alexei Arakcheyev," *Russky arkhiv*, vol. 9 (1871), pp. 149–154.

Almedingen, E. M. *The Emperor Alexander I*. New York: Vanguard Press, 1954.

A. N. *Imperator Alexandr Blagoslavny y yevo vremya*. St. Petersburg: Government Printer, 1912.

Anonymous. *L'Histoire de la maladie et des derniers moments de l'empereur Alexandré Ier, fondée sur les informations les plus authentique*. Archive of the Russian Federation. Section 3; no. 163. Reproduced in Shilder, *Imperator Alexandr pervy*, vol. 4, pp. 568–572.

Anonymous. *Unpublished Details Relative to the Death of Emperor Alexander*. Bodleian Library (Duke Humphrey Room), Ms.Eng.Hist.d.263.

Anonymous. "Kratkoye opisanya goroda Taganroga." *Posledni dny imperatora Alexandra I*. Moscow, 1827.

Baluyeva, N. "Starets Feodor Kuzmich." *Sapisnoy knezhki Moskovskovo starozhila*, p. 60.

Bariatinsky, V. *Le Mystère d'Alexandre I*. Paris: Payot, 1929.

———. "Esche o 'Tsarstvenom Mystike.' " *Istorichesky vestnik*, vol. 136 (1914), pp. 579–584.

Belyanchikov, N. N. "Sushchestvuyet-ly 'taiyna Fedora Kuzmicha'?" *Voprosy istorii*, vol. 1 (1967), pp. 191–201.

Berezhanskiy, S. A. From "Perezvoniy." Riga: Salamander, 1927. pp. 1250–1251.

Bogdanovich, M. I. *Istoria tsarstvaniya imperatora Alexandra I y Russya v yevo vremya*. St. Petersburg, 1869–71.

Bourdykov, The Rev. "Novoye o startse Feodora Kuzmicha," *Russko-Amerikanski pravoslavnyii vestnik* (May 1956), pp. 103–104.

Bryanchaninov, N. V. *Alexandre I*. Paris: Bernard Grasset, 1934.

Caulaincourt, Armand de. *With Napoleon in Russia*. New York: William Morrow & Co., 1935.

Coughlan, Robert. *Elizabeth and Catherine*. New York: Putnam, 1974.

Choiseul-Gouffier, C. H. *Historical Memoirs of the Emperor Alexander I*. Chicago: A. C. McClurg & Co., 1901.

Chuloshnikov, A. "L. H. Tolstoy and N. M. Romanov." *Krasny arkhiv*, vol. 21 (1927).

Cronin, Vincent. *Catherine, Empress of the Russians*. New York: William Morrow & Co., 1978.

Czartoryski, A. *Memoirs of Prince Adam Czartoryski and his Correspondence with Alexander I*. Edited by Adam Gielgud. London, 1888.

Danilovsky, Nikolai. *Toganrog yly podrobnoye opisanye bolezni I konchini Imperatora Alexandra I-ovo*. Moscow, 1828.

Dolgoruky, Varvara A. *Gone Forever: Some Pages from My Life in Russia, 1885–1919* (undated typescript), pp. 21–23.

Dolgoruky, V. "Otshelnik Alexandr (Feodor) v Sibiry." *Russkaya starina*, vol. 56 (Oct. 1887), pp. 217–220.

Dubasova, Alexandra. "Noviya daniya o smerte Alexandra I," *Vozvrozhdenye*, 11 April, 1926.

Edling, R. *Mémoires*. Moscow, 1888.

Florinsky, V. M. "Zametki y vospominaniye V. M. Florinskavo." *Russkaya starina*, May 1906, pp. 296–301.

Gendrikov, V., and S. Sen'ko. *The Cathedral of St. Peter and St. Paul: The Burial Place of the Russian Imperial Family*. St. Petersburg: Liki Rossii, 1998.

Golitsin, N. S. "Naropdnya legenda ob Alexandre-otshelnike." *Russkaya starina*, vol. 29 (1880), pp. 742–744.

Golombiyevski, A. A. "Legenda y istoriya." *Russky arkhiv*, vol. 48 (1908), pp. 448–462.

Golovin, Ivan. *History of Alexander I, Emperor of Russia*. London: Thomas Cantley Newby, 1858.

Golovkine, Feodor. *La Cour et le Règne de Paul I*. Paris: Librairie Plon, 1905.

Gooch, G. P. *Catherine the Great and Other Studies*. London: Longmans, Green & Co., 1954.

Gribble, Francis, H. *Emperor and Mystic: The Life of Emperor Alexander of Russia*. New York: Eveleigh Nash & Grayson Ltd., 1931.

Grimstead, Patricia. *The Foreign Ministers of Alexander*. Berkeley: University of California Press, 1969.

Grunwald, Constantine de. *Alexandre Ier, le tsar mystique*. Paris: Amiot-Dumont, 1955.

———. *L'Assassinat de Paul Ier tsar de Russie*. Paris: Amiot-Dumont, 1960.

Bibliography

Gyrs, K. K. "Imperator Alexandr I na yuge rossii." *Russkaya starina*, 1888, pp. 387–392.

Hans, H. "Tsar Alexander I and Jefferson: Unpublished Correspondence." *Slavonic Review*, vol. 32, no. 78 (1953), pp. 213–225.

Hartley, Janet M. *Alexander I*. London: Addison Wesley Longman Ltd., 1994.

Haslip, Joan. *Catherine the Great*. New York: Putnam, 1977.

Jenkins, M. *Arakcheev: Grand Vizier of the Russian Empire*. New York: Dial Press, 1969.

Joyneville, C. *Life and Times of Alexander I*. London, 1875.

Karazin, V. I. *Istoricheskiye dokumenti iz vremen Alexandra I*. Edited by Kasprovich. 1880. pp. 73–93.

Kasropovich, E. L. *Istoricheskiye dokumenti ys vremen tsarstvo Alexandra I*. Berlin, 1880.

Kenney, James J. Jr. "Lord Whitworth and the Conspiracy against Tsar Paul I: The New Evidence of the Kent Archive." *Slavic Review*, vol. 36 (1997), pp. 205–219.

Kizevetter, A. A. "Imperator Alexandr I y staretz Feodor Kuzmich." *Russiya viedomostiy*, no. 299 (29 Dec. 1912), pp. 2–3.

Kluchevsky, Victor O. *A History of Russia*, vol. 5. New York: Russell & Russell, 1960.

Krylov, Alexander. "Smerts v Taganroge," *V novom svete*, 26 January 1996.

Krupensky, P. N. *Tayna Imperatora*. Berlin, 1927.

Kudryashov, K. "Yz istoricheskikh legendy: dokymenti o smerte Alexandra I." *Russkoye proshloye*, vol. 3 (1923), pp. 70–86.

Kulomzin, Anatol A. "The Siberian Hermit Theodore Kuzmich." *Slavonic Review* (1923), pp. 381–387.

Kutuzov, Field Marshal. *Kolektsiya dokument y materiali*. Moscow, 1947–1950.

Kuznetsvov-Krasnoyarsky, I. P. "Starets Feodor Kuzmich." *Istorichesky vestnik* (May 1895), pp. 550–554.

Kuzovnikov, P. "Kto byl starets Feodor Kuzmich." *Istorichesky vestnik* (July 1895), pp. 245–246.

La Harpe, Frédéric. *Correspondance de Frédéric-César de la Harpe*. Paris, 1864.

Lee, Robert. *The Last Days of Alexander I and the First Days of Nicholas I*. London, 1854.

Leonard, Carol S. *Reform and Regicide: The Reign of Peter III of Russia*. Indianapolis: Indiana University Press, 1993.

Lieven, D. H. "Kharakter Konstantina Pavlovicha." *Krasny arkhiv*, vol. 10 (1929), p. 20.

———. "Konchina Imperatora Pavala." *Istorichesky vestnik*, vol. 106 (1906), pp. 414–432.

Lincoln, W. Bruce. *Nicholas I: Emperor and Autocrat of All the Russias*. Dekalb, Illinois: Northern Illinois University Press, 1989.

Lisitsyna, L. "Versiya taina Alexandra I." *Mir Novostye*, no. 50 (15 Dec. 1997), p. 5.

Londonderry, the Marchioness of. *The Russian Journals of Martha and Catherine Wilmot*. London: John Murray Publishers, Ltd., 1934.

Lowerson, L. "The Death of Paul I and the Memoirs of Count Benningsen." *Slavonic and Eastern European Review,* vol. 20 (December 1950), pp. 222–231.

Lubimov, L. D. *Tayna Imperatora Alexandra I.* Paris: La Renaissance, 1938.

———. "Tayna startsa Feodora Kuzmicha," *Voprosy istorii,* vol. 1 (1966), pp. 209–215.

Ludwig, Emil. *Napoleon.* New York: Modern Library, 1952.

Lukash, Ivan. "Razgadana-ly tayna Feodora Kuzmicha?" *Vozvrojedenye,* 8 August, 1927.

Maria Feodorovna, Empress. *Pismo Marii Feodoroni k velikomu knyzu Konstantinu Pavolovichu,* pp. 156–180.

Martos, Th. R. "Posledni dni zhyzni Imperatora Alexandra I." *Istorichesky vestnik,* vol. 63 (1869), pp. 471–499.

Mazour, Anatole G. *The First Russian Revolution, 1825.* Stanford: Stanford University Press, 1937.

McConnell, Allen. *Tsar Alexander I: Paternalistic Reformer.* New York: Crowell, 1970.

Melnitzky, M. F. "Starets Feodor Kuzmich," *Russkaya starina,* vol. 73 (1892), pp. 81–108.

Mikhailov, K. N. *Imperator Alexandr I; starets Feodor Kuzmich.* Moscow, 1914.

Miliukov, D. K. *Alexandr I y evo vremya.* St. Petersburg, 1909.

Nikolai Mikhailovich, Grand Duke. *Imperator Alexandr pervy.* St. Petersburg: S. A. Suvorin, vol. 2 (1912).

———. *Legenda o konchine imperatora Alexandra I v Sibiri v obraze startsa Feodora Kuzmicha.* St. Petersburg: S. A. Suvorin, 1907.

———. "Nekotorye novoye materialy k voproso o konchine Imperatora Alexandra I." *Istorichesky vestnik,* no. 9 (1914), pp. 738–748.

———. "Nekotorya sobrazhenie po povodu pisma ot 31ovo dekabrya, 1825 . . ." *Istorichesky vestnik,* vol. 136 (1914).

———. *Znamenitye Russiane, 18–19 Vekov.* St. Petersburg: Lenizdat, 1996.

———. *L'Impératrice Elisabeth.* St. Petersburg: S. A. Suvorin, 1909.

Nikolai Nikolaevich, Grand Duke. "Nekotory novy materiala k voproso o konchin imperatora Alexandra I." *Istorichesky vestnik,* March/April 1914, pp. 738–748.

Nikolai Pavlovich, Grand Duke. "Harakteristiki knyagini D. H. Lieven." *Krasny arkhiv,* vol. 10 (1925).

Nikolaev, V. V. *Alexandr I — starets Feodor Kuzmich.* San Francisco: Globus Editions, 1984.

Obolensky, G. L. *Imperator Pavel I.* Smolensk: Tirania Publishers, 1993.

Olivier, Daria. *Alexandre Ier, prince des illusions.* Paris: Fayard, 1973.

Paleologue, Maurice. *Alexandre I, un tsar énigmatique.* Paris: Librarie Plon, 1937.

Palmer, Alan. *Alexander I: Tsar of War and Peace.* London: Weidenfeld and Nicholson, 1974.

Pirenne, Henri. *Alexandre I: Autocrat de bonne volonté.* Brussels: Les éditeurs d'art associé, 1988.

P. P. "Byl-ly siberskii starets Feodor Kuzmich imperatorom Alexandrom I?" *Pravoslavnaya Gyzen,* vol. 3 (March 1982).

Bibliography

Pyotr, Bishop. "Sibirskiy starets Feodor Kuzmich." *Russkaya starina,* vol. 72 (October 1891), pp. 233–240.

Raeff, Marc. *Comprendre l'ancien régime russe.* Paris: Seuil, 1982.

Rappoport, A. S. *The Curse of the Romanovs: A Study of the Life and Reign of Paul I and Alexander I.* London: Chatto & Windus, 1907.

Riasanovsky, N. *A History of Russia.* Oxford: Oxford University Press, 1963.

Rossiev, P. "Zhivuchaya legenda." *Istorichesky vestnik,* vol. 109 (1907), pp. 687–688.

———. "Starets Feodor Kuzmich." *Istorichesky vestnik,* vol. 109 (1907), pp. 1048–1050.

Royal Dutch Archives. Inv. A41-IIIB-2.

Russkii Biographichesky Slovar. "Feodor Kuzmich." Vol. 25. St. Petersburg, 1900. pp. 301–304.

Sablukov, N. A. "Vospomenaneye o dvortsa y vremenach imperatora Russiskavo Pavela I do yepohe evo smerty." *Tsarubistvo, 11 marta 1801 goda.* Edited by S. A. Suvorin, St. Petersburg, 1908. pp. 3–105.

Saharov, A. N. *Alexander I.* Moscow: Kiston, 1998.

———. "Smerts ili uhod." *Nauka.* Moscow, 1998.

Schiemann, T. *Alexandr pervy* (from the German). Moscow, 1909.

Schoenig, N. I. "Vospominanie Nikolaiya Ignatevicha Shnigna." *Russky arkhiv,* vol. 18 (1880), pp. 267–294.

Schuster, Norah H. "English Doctors in Early 19th Century Russia." *Proceedings of the Royal Society of Medicine,* vol. 61 (February 1968), pp. 185–190.

Seaton-Watson, Hugh. *The Russian Empire, 1801–1917.* Oxford: Oxford University Press, 1967.

Ségur, Comte Philippe-Paul. *Histoire et Mémoires.* Paris: Firmin–Didot, 1873.

Serebrenkoba, A. N. *Velikaya legenda, Imperator Alexandr I y starets Feodor Kuzmich.* San Francisco, 1967.

Shilder, N. K. *Imperator Alexandr pervy.* St. Petersburg: S. A. Suvorin, 1898.

———. *Imperator Pavel.* St. Petersburg: S. A. Suvorin, 1901.

———. "Alexandr I." *Russkii biograficheski slovar,* vol. 2. St. Petersburg, 1900. pp. 380–384.

———. "Taganrog v 1825 godou." *Russkaya starina* (1897), pp. 5–48.

Shiman, T. In *Tsarubistov, 11 marta 1801 goda.* Moscow: S. A. Suvorin, 1909.

Shoumigorsky, E. "Yz zapistnoy knezhky istorika: dve legendi ob impratora Alexandra I." *Istorichesky vestnik,* vol. 136 (May 1914), pp. 677–689.

Smirnov, I. "Otshelnik Feodor." *Russkaya starina,* vol. 56 (1887), pp. 529–530.

Sokolovsky, M. "Poslednie dni imperatora Alexandra I." *Istorichesky vestnik,* vol. 109 (1907), pp. 165–171.

Strakhovsky, Leonid I. *Alexander I of Russia: The Man Who Defeated Napoleon.* New York: W. W. Norton & Co., 1947.

Syroyechkovsky, B. "Ys zapistnoy knyzhkii arkhivista." *Krasny arkhiv,* vol. 21 (1927).

Tarle, E. *Nashestvie Napoleona na rossiyu, 1812 god.* Moscow: Volnnoes izd-vo, 1992.

Tarasov, D. K. "Vospominanie moye zhyzny." *Russkaya starina,* vol. 6 (1872), pp. 100–142.

Tatischev, Sergei S. *Alexandre Ier et Napoléon d'après leur correspondance inédite, 1801–1812.* Paris: Perrin et cie., 1891.

Tolstoy, Leo N. "Posmertniya zapiski startsa Feodora Kuzmitcha." *Sobranye sochineniy,* vol. 14 (1903–1910). Moscow, 1964. pp. 393–413.

Tomsk Circle of Followers of Starets Feodor Kuzmich. *Tainstveniy starets Feodor Kuzmich v sibiri.* Edited by D. G. Romanov. Kharkov, 1912.

Troyat, Henri. *Alexander of Russia: Napoleon's Conqueror.* New York: E. P. Dutton, 1982.

Uhtomsky, E. E. *Puteshestvye na vostok Evo Imperatorskovo Vysotchestva Gusudara Naslednika Tsesarevicha.* St. Petersburg, 1897.

Vasilich, G. *Imperator Alexandr I y starets Feodor Kuzmich.* Moscow: Obrozovanye, 1910.

———. *Voshestvye na prestol imperatora Nikolaya I.* Moscow: Obrozovanye, 1909.

V. G. "Po povodou legendy ob imperatora Alexandra I." *Istorichesky vestnik,* vol. 139 (1914).

Volkonskaya, Z. A. "Konchina Alexandra I." *Russkaya starina,* vol. 21, p. 139.

Von Bedel, Major. "Iz zapisok maiyora fon Bedelya."*Tsarubistvo, 11 marta 1801 goda.* Edited by S. A. Suvorin. St. Petersburg, 1908. pp. 137–155.

Vospominanya Bestuzhevykh. Edited by M. K. Azadovsky and I. M. Trotsky. Moscow, 1931.

Vostanie dekabristov: materialy. "Delo o polkovnike Leib Gvardi Prebrazhenskavo polka Kniaz Trubetskom." Moscow, 1925. Vol. 1, p. 19.

Waliszewski, K. *Le Règne d'Alexandre Ier.* Paris: Librairie Plon, 1925.

———. *Le Fils de la Grande Catherine, Paul Ier.* Paris: Librairie Plon, 1912.

———. *The Romance of an Empress: Catherine II of Russia.* New York: D. Appleton & Co., 1894.

Ward, John L. "Tsar or Hermit? The Mystery of Alexander I." *Chamber's Journal,* vol. 20, pp. 760–763.

Wieczynski, J. L., ed. *Modern Encyclopedia of Russian and Soviet History.* Gulf Breeze, Florida: Academic International Press, 1979.

Wylie, I. V. (James). "Dnevnik leb-medica baroneta Y.V. Villi, 1825" (from the French), *Russkaya starina,* vol. 73 (1892), pp. 69–78.

Zyzykin, M. V. *Tayna imperatora Alexandra.* Buenos Aires: Nasha Starina, 1852.

Index

Index

Index

maritime trade, 250–51
Russia's relations with, 37–38, 40,
    92, 95, 109, 251
Greece and the Greek Question,
    112–13, 153
Grenadier Life Guards, 176
Grey, Duncan, 228
Groudzinska, Jeanne, 166
Gruzino estate, 116, 124
Gustavus IV, king of Sweden, cancelled
    marriage of, 30–31
gypsies, 140

Hartley, Janet (historian), 93
Helene, Grand Duchess, 74
Hellenes, revolt of, 112–13, 153
Hesse-Darmstadt, Princess Wilhelmina
    of. *See* Natalia Alexeyevna
*L'Histoire de la maladie et des derniers
    moments de l'empereur Alexandre,*
    146–47
Holstein-Gottorp, Duchy of, 15, 19
Holstein troops, 17
Holy Alliance, 71, 112, 113
Holy Synod, 115
Horse Guard, 43
Hubbenet, Dr., 214

Imperial Guard (French), 96
Imperial Historical Society, 10, 243
Imperial Legend, 4
    author's learning of, ix–x
    believers in, 10, 240–42, 255–56
    continuing interest and research into,
        237–47
    cover-up efforts, and reason for,
        244–45
    impediments to research on, 205–6
    various testimonies to truth of,
        257–65
India, proposed invasion of, by French
    and Russians, 40
intelligentsia, 21
Issakov (man sent by tsar to Kuzmich),
    261

Jacobins, 47, 79, 85

Jefferson, Thomas, 80
Jews, 115, 140–41
Josephine, Empress, 93

Kaluga, 235
Karaites, 140–41
Karamzin, Nikolai, 85, 122
Kazan Cathedral, 186
Khans, 139
Kharkov, 152
Khromov, Anna, 195, 197, 264
Khromov, Simeon, 6, 194, 202,
    262–64
    widow of, 258
Kiev, 199, 253
Kievo-Pechersky Monastery, 199
Kleinmikel, Count General Pyotr, 151,
    193
Kluchevsky, V. O. (historian), 64
Kochubey, Count Victor, 37, 68,
    71–73, 74, 79
Komarovsky, General, 99
Korobeinikov, 191
Koshelev, Rodion, 67
Kourbatov, Apollon, 222
Koushelva-Bezborodka, Count, 139
Kovalevsky, Pyotr, 243
Krasnaya Rechka, 191, 192
Krasnoufimsk, 189
Kremenchuk, 199
Krüdener, Baroness Julie von, 69–71,
    111–12
Kulikovsky, Colonel Nikolai, 11
Kulomzin, Anatol, 201, 257–59
Kurakin, Prince, 82, 185
Kursk, 178
Kutuzov, Mikhail Ilarionovich, 45,
    98–104, 106
Kuzmich, Feodor, 189–203
    anecdotes about, 192–94, 196–98,
        261, 265
    arrest, beating of, and exile to
        Tomsk, 190
    burial place, 7–9, 210, 259
    cabin of, in Tomsk, 257–58
    corpse of, disinterment of, 210
    death, news of, 224

Index

Index